VOICE OF THE HUNTING GODS
By
Roy Rivett

Edited by; Susan Stewart
Archery chapter edited by; Susan Gray

**Published
By
Gr8 Hunter Products, LLC
1519 Pinehurst
Darien, Il. 60561**

**630-921-1519
www.Gr8hunter.com**

HUNTING WHITETAILED DEER, THE SEVEN RULES".

The first book, published in 2002 with the above cover photo and title, has sold out of print and is no longer available. The new book, "Voice of The Hunting Gods", was intended to be an updated and 2nd edition of "Seven Rules". However, during the process, it turned into a different and much better book, deserving of its own cover photo and its own title. "Voice" contains everything that was in "Seven Rules" with the addition of over fifty new pages of writing, more detailed advice, new illustrations, photographs and a couple whole new sections that were not in the first book.

Good hunting.

Table of Contents

Ranting and Raving

This is a no bull book about hunting Midwest White-tailed deer with archery and with firearms. It's written for regular guys who love deer hunting and who want to be more successful. You should know up front, that in several areas of hunting importance, my advice is different or perhaps exactly opposite of what you would read in popular hunting publications. For that, I expect to catch a hailstorm of grief. Let it come.

I don't make my living as an outdoor writer or am in any way connected with the hunting industry. I have no sponsors, no endorsements and no affiliations of any kind that would bias my writing.

The first book (*Seven Rules*) started in the winter of 1995 while I was visiting Mom and Dad, at the little yellow house where I grew up, on Sheridan road in Bridgeport Michigan. I was sitting at the kitchen table, reading an article in a magazine about the *"secrets for deer-hunting success"*. Parts of the article seemed so ridiculous that I read them aloud to Dad and my brother Jimmy to get their reactions. These articles usually tell you that the deer are so damn smart, that you have no chance in hell of ever getting one, unless of course, you're willing to try some top-secret new technique which will fool the genius deer. This garbage is hauled out, warmed over, and shoveled at deer hunters year after year. Somehow my ranting turned into a five dollar bet with Jimmy, that I could put the keys for success in deer hunting on a single sheet of notebook paper. Well, I can. It just took another hundred and some pages to explain the details. After eight years of part time writing it was a book "Seven Rules", published in 2002. I still believe I could get it all down to a single sheet of paper, but technically, I lost the bet.

Not much has changed in the twelve years since I first sat down at the kitchen table with a sheet of notebook paper and started writing. I can still go to the magazine section at the book store, pull out six hunting magazines, and read basically all the same sorts of stuff that ticked me off twelve years ago. It's more sophisticated, but it's basically the same. There's usually a photo of a happy hunter with his um-teenth trophy deer and an article telling the secrets of how, you too, can get one if you have the "super secret special stuff".

<u>All you need is:</u> A lifelike deer decoy sprayed with a bottle of estrus doe urine, a spray-bottle of scent eliminator, non-estrus doe urine, fox or skunk covering scent, knee high rubber boots and rubber gloves. You'll need a special pattern of camouflage and scent blocking clothes from head to toe. These must be kept in super-special scent blocking containers. You'll also need a range finder, binoculars, a remote infrared activated trail-camera, a global positioning unit, and an ATV to haul all this stuff out to the woods. You'll need a grunt call, a doe bleat call, a snort-wheeze call and a set of antlers for rattling. Also you'll need a moon-phase-chart and notepad to keep track of which scent or call to use, or not use, in pre-rut, early rut, peak of rut, or post rut. (Please excuse the sarcasm.)

I've been there too brother: I remember the days when I wanted a deer so bad, that I would have bought almost anything if I had the money. After forty-some seasons it begins to pile up. A section of my basement is dedicated to a halfway effort at organizing my hunting, fishing and camping gear. Salvaged shelves hold a mixture of small and large boxes and duffle bags full of stuff. A closet pole suspended from the floor joists holds a sleeping bag, blaze orange vest and most of my heavy hunting clothes. Two of the boxes contain pieces and parts of odd, old, broken things that might come in handy some day, or oddball stuff that doesn't seem to have a category. Once in a while I'm looking for something in one of these boxes and I end up finding some other thing from twenty years ago. I hold the item for a moment and say *"what the hell did I ever buy this piece of junk for"*. I toss it back in the box and try not to feel too bad about all the money I've pissed away over the years. On the other hand there's a whole different feeling about the knife I see dangling upside down off the belt in my hunting pants. One of my closest friends, Paul Buckner, gave it to me as a gift. It was a better and more expensive knife than I ever would have bought for myself at the time. Aside from its sentimental value which has grown over a few decades, it's a basic good solid piece of hunting gear. It would have been worth every nickel if I had bought it for myself.

A new generation of hunters, including my young nephews, is entering the woods these days. They've been heavily sold on the need for a truckload of fairly pricy items such as those listed above. I'm not saying that all this stuff is no good, or that it doesn't at least help a little. Maybe it does, especially if it goes toward helping you to follow the seven rules. If your finances allow you to spend money without much concern, it doesn't actually concern me in the least. It's none of my business anyway. I'm happy for ya, go ahead, God bless ya! But there's still something that's deeply, fundamentally, wrong with all this marketing-bull which pisses me off just based on principle alone. It's this. All the "super secret special stuff", is made to look very important for success in hunting, while the authors and editors carefully ignore the three real big gorillas in their success equation. Those big gorillas are; plenty of time, plenty of money and access to excellent hunting land. These articles are written by guys whose livelihood is in some way connected with the hunting business. They're basically semi-professional hunters. When you read major outdoor publications, remember that even the peddlers of junk have a huge advertising budget to spend. That money is worth a hell-of-a-lot more clout than the few dollars you spend for the magazine. So, an author who writes anything contrary to the advertiser's interest is never going to get published. With their livelihoods at stake and with hundreds of millions of dollars associated with the industries, authors and editors are forced to carefully omit some things and include others. Good hunting advice suffers as a result. The bull just gets deeper.

The semi-professional hunters may be able to spend over two hundred days per year in the deer woods. They often have sponsors or endorsements that take care of their expenses. They may have access to prime private hunting land managed for trophy deer. But that ain't us. Most of us, avid recreational deer hunters, envy them. Wow, what a great way to earn a living! But we have jobs, spouses, children, a house to take care of, and other interests and priorities outside of deer hunting. We beg borrow and steal whatever time we can find for hunting a few precious days each year.

So ask yourself what happens if we take the big three gorillas out of the equation and make the playing field equal for every hunter in the woods? I mean, what if we're just talking about the vast majority of regular average hunters who don't have an extraordinary budget and unlimited time and hundreds of acres of private property located in trophy deer country. What if the articles in the magazines were written by regular deer hunters who have no hidden agenda, no bias and aren't trying to sell you something else on the side?

What if, from among these hunters, we found the long time veterans who've been highly successful for the past three or five decades in the woods? What "*super secret special stuff*" would these guys tell you is important versus not important? I guarantee you that if it's not among the seven rules, its one of the closest cousins.

As you can probably tell, I find a few things extremely irritating about most professional outdoor writers, and the major hunting magazines. **So, I'll try not to do this to you.**

➢ Most writers come off like the world's greatest expert, who was born knowing it all and never goofed-it-up in his entire life. We learn the most from goofing-up and I've done plenty of that.

➢ Often they write as if you need to be a strategic genius and have a Ph.D. in deer biology in order to go hunting. You don't.

➢ Usually they write as if the deer are so damn smart, they could file your federal income taxes for you. They're not.

➢ Many seem to forget that not everybody can go out and blow hundreds or thousands of dollars on hunting trips and equipment. I can't, and probably you can't either.

➢ They seem to nearly scoff at a hunter who shoots anything less than trophy buck or maybe takes a doe for meat. That's bullshit.

➢ But, it's the well camouflaged marketing bull that's often buried in these articles, that I find the most irritating. As hunters, I guess it's our own fault because the marketers wouldn't do it, if it didn't work. We fear that without the "stuff" we can't be successful.

After all the dust settles from my ranting and raving, I can finally get to the point. You and I are stuck hunting with whatever budget and land and time we have available. That's just the way the deal turned out. Fine. Live with it. But suppose for a moment, that you could hunt with the same amount of time, on the same land, with the same budget as the pros, or on the other hand, suppose that the pros had to hunt where you hunt, for the same few days and on your small budget. This means that the big three gorillas are all exactly the same. What then, would make the true difference in their success rate versus yours? A keystone point of this book is that the true difference has very little to do with any of the super secret special stuff. It almost always depends on how good you are with the seven rules. **The only thing that supersedes over all the rules is…..the voice of the hunting gods.**

I come from a regular blue collar, meat and potatoes, Michigan, deer hunting family. With my father and brothers and a couple good friends I've hunted white tailed deer for nearly forty years. In the first dozen years we didn't have a lot of success, but some of our best hunting memories come from those days. In the most recent twenty years I have had a high success rate. But still, as recently as the past weekend of this archery deer season, I've personally discovered the fifty-first way to goof it up. So, I don't claim to know it all and I don't claim to execute it all perfectly.

As far as the deer biology goes, in my opinion these issues have been beaten to death. You already know the basics about the deer's sense of smell, hearing and vision. These highly developed senses are what make them challenging to hunt. You also know about feeding and mating habits and that the pointy end of the tracks is the direction the deer is traveling. Beyond that, increased success doesn't require you to know all that stuff about the digestive system, the gestation period, or the pre-orbital scent gland. It may be interesting in answer to our curiosity about deer biology, but it's not critical to success in hunting. **Most hunters would do better to learn more about their own biology and their abilities as a predator and hunting species. So, my advice focuses more on sharpening these abilities rather than on deer biology.**

I guess I'm sensitive about the high cost of hunting, because in our early years, the family could barely scrape together enough money for gas, ammo and license fees. We simply couldn't afford to have all the greatest gear in the world. I remember sometimes having a sense of despair from the idea that I didn't have as good a chance for success because I didn't have the best gear. So, I write with a warm place in my heart for young hunters who somehow find a way to get out in the deer woods on a tight budget. Hopefully this "no bull" writing might save you from unnecessary feelings of despair and from wasting money on expensive stuff that's really nearly useless. Now, I make a good living and can afford to buy good stuff. But, I know this as truth…deer hunting isn't only about "getting one" and it's not at all about having the greatest stuff. Not even close.

Prelude to A Kill

Many years ago some friends and I were cross-country skiing in northern Michigan when we came on a doe killed by wild dogs. We must have been a boisterous group laughing and talking and the sound of our approach must have scared the dogs away from their kill. The tracks in the snow and her wounds told the whole story. The dogs had chased her and several other deer in the deep snow nipping at her hindquarters until she was too tired to run any more. She was separated from the group. She stood her ground surrounded. The dog tracks had packed the snow in a roughly circular area about fifteen feet in diameter. In the middle she lay dead.

There wasn't a lot of blood in the snow and she had no major wounds that would have been fatal. She was a large healthy looking doe probably carrying a pair of half developed fawns by this late in the winter. She was still warm. Steam was venting into the cold air from a set of clean canine puncture wounds in her throat. The lead dog must have been an experienced hunter. Its jaws apparently clamped down on her windpipe in a single expert lunge and then never let it go. The exhausted deer, unable to breathe, finally came to the ground. The only other wounds were a few nips and a small hole in the soft part of her underbelly where another dog had pulled out a few inches of gut. Hopefully she was losing consciousness by that time. But, certainly in her last moments she knew that she was losing this fight for her life.

I back-tracked their trail to the point about forty yards away where the other deer had stood in their tracks. They shifted nervously leaving wide shafts, dark at the bottom, with a slight glaze in the snow. They stood for at least several minutes, perhaps even while the attack proceeded, trying not to look at what was happening to one of their group. I remember the odd questions that occurred to me. Why didn't they help her? How could they all just stand there?" For a moment I regarded them with contempt as cowards. Just as quickly, I realized that judging them by human attributes was entirely wrong. All of these deer had run for their lives to the very brink of exhaustion as they've been required to do routinely from time to time for countless generations. This one perhaps did not have the stamina or the speed or made some small slip that cost its life.

14

The other deer stood for a while breathing heavily, perhaps with some uneasy sense of relief. My friends and I stood quietly for a few minutes. The small clearing had a special stillness about it, like a church just after everyone has left the service. We had all seen mangled deer that died in agony on the side of the highway. It was a lousy way to die. But, this scene in the woods of a dramatic, savage struggle in the snow had a more powerful effect on all of us. It was a very odd mixture of feelings. We couldn't hate the dogs for being *"un-sportsman-like"*, or for doing what is in their nature to do in order to survive. They had no choice. It wasn't a matter of good guys versus bad guys. We couldn't say that the deer was valiant or courageous even though it did put up a hell of a fight. It had no choice either. As hunters, maybe there was an odd combination of a little species rivalry, in that *"they killed our deer"*. This was coupled with a touch of horror at the brutality of it.

But the feeling was larger than all that. It was the realization that struggles like this happen every day, everywhere in tens of thousands of square miles of the great outdoors. It was the striking reality and firsthand witness to a small part of an enormous brutal struggle involving life and death. The scale of magnitude of that struggle was awesome to consider for a moment.

Thirty-plus hunting seasons have passed since we found the doe killed by the dogs. During those years I regret to say that I have wounded two deer while bow hunting. One was due to an honest mistake. I kick myself for it and go on with my life. But the other was due to a lust for venison and a temporary loss of respect for the target. I needed to let down on my bow in order to make a small adjustment. A curly strand of loose thread was hanging down from my facemask in front of my eye. But this deer was so close, how could I miss? Besides, if I did let down, the deer would probably get away. So, I decided to release the shot. It was a stupid decision. The deer ran away wounded. I spent the rest of the day trying to track it down without success. I cursed myself for having lower moral status than a wild dog. I didn't need this venison for survival. I had other choices.

The really stupid part of this, is that if I had chosen to let down on my bow, and if the deer did run away unharmed......... so what! It might have bugged me just a little for a few days. I would then most likely have gotten another shot at another deer on another day. I probably wouldn't even remember this particular deer. But instead, I chose to take the shot, and wounding this deer for such a stupid reason has bothered me for years.

Every deer in the woods dies sooner or later in ways that are unpleasant if not quit brutal and horrific. The deer and every other wild thing that lives outdoors are in an almost constant state of paranoia if not downright terror about the fact that something else out there is going to kill it. To the deer, I suspect that hunters in the woods are no big deal. We're just one more thing, on a long list of things that might kill them. We've all decided long ago that we have no moral problem with hunting. Otherwise we wouldn't be out there. But every single one of us who has any moral conscience above that of a wild dog, believes in the importance of making a good shot and a quick kill. It doesn't always happen, but it is what we try for.

Good Hunting.

THE SEVEN RULES
Part - 1

This section, Part-1, is the bare bones, heart and soul of what I started out trying to do. It lists the few simple things that a deer hunter must do for the best chance of success. **These rules are deceptively simple!** If you do nothing more than faithfully and completely obey these seven rules, you will greatly multiply your chances for success. But if you violate any one of them, it will greatly multiply your chances for failure.

You probably already know every one of the seven rules. But what you might be missing are five thousand details needed to obey them all simultaneously. Each rule is like an ingredient in an old family recipe. If one of the ingredients is measured wrong or forgotten, it doesn't turn out as good. The seven rules are simple as dirt. The trick is that they work together in combination, but not singularly. So, the only thing that's complicated is obeying them all at the same time. Beyond the seven rules you get very little additional "bang for your buck." *Excuse the pun.*

The Measure of Success: I've cooked the numbers on a ton of deer hunting statistics covering the past five years in the top thirteen deer hunting states. The lowest statistic I've seen claims an overall hunter success rate of about 12% per season. That's only about one out of every eight hunters. A few states have much higher success rates. This got my curiosity up, so I started digging deeper into the numbers. It got to the point where I was looking at all kinds of ratios of hunters per square mile and deer populations and a dozen other variables. Finally, I realized that the statistics would need to go to the local township level to be of any real value. Deer populations can double in three years with mild winters and with a good food supply. But a poor food supply and a late winter snow / ice storm coupled with predation can cause it to drop drastically in a small region in a single year. The success rate is a local thing. Statewide statistics are of little value.

For the purpose of discussion in this book let's assume you have a local success rate averaging from one out of five hunters 20% to one out of three hunters 33%. This may serve as an <u>extremely crude measure</u>, of success and probably is not far out of the ballpark for most deer hunting regions. This would mean that if you've been successful on average one out of three years, or one out of five years, you're probably doing O.K. But think about what this crude average might mean. If you mess-up with just one deer, it could potentially be six to ten years before you're successful.

But here is another key question. Think about the past five or ten seasons and remember the deer you failed to get. What would your success rate be if you had killed those deer? What exactly happened that caused you not to get that deer? How many did you scare away without ever knowing they were there? Obviously the success rate may be higher or lower in certain counties during certain years as deer populations change. It may also be higher for hunters with access to private land for a number of reasons. Managed deer habitat, food supply, limited hunting pressure and self-imposed minimum antler restrictions may all go toward favoring both larger racks and higher numbers of deer. So you would simply expect these guys to have a higher success rate. **The point remains the same; improve your own individual rate of success**. What the statistics don't tell you though, is why, even if all the key hunting variables are made the same, certain individual hunters are consistently more or less successful than others. What causes this difference?

If you could take a large enough statistical sampling of hunters and make allowances for all of the key variables, you would probably see that the success rate follows what statisticians call a bell shaped, random distribution curve. In the tall fat center of the bell curve are the majority of hunters who have an average rate of success. On the left side are the hunters with lower than average, and on the right are the hunters with a higher than average rates of success. You might know of hunters who are successful on average one out of two years or possibly even nine out of ten years. Some may get several deer in a single season. But, it's also not uncommon to know a hunter who has never killed a deer in ten or fifteen years. I believe that there are two different forces at work that can explain this situation. To some degree these forces can be either with you or against you.

The first is something you have little control over. You may hunt flawlessly from a technical standpoint and still go for years without success. You also could be a complete hunting goof-up and be successful sometimes. This is entirely at the discretion of the hunting gods. If they're in your favor, you could probably walk through the woods playing a banjo and still get a deer. But, if the hunting gods are pissed off at you, there's nearly nothing that I can write that will help you. It's something that you'll have to get straightened out with them. However, the other force that is at work has everything to do with the seven rules. Obeying these rules is what will push your success rate from wherever it is now, toward the right side of the bell curve. These are the parts of deer hunting that you do have control over.

Brain Twist - The Problem of Proof: How-do-ya know if a hunting technique works or doesn't work? How-do-ya know if a special piece of gear is worth buying or not? If I show you pictures or video of a successful hunt using a technique or a piece of gear, it seems like powerful proof. The problem with proof of this type is that almost anything works some of the time and almost nothing works all of the time. It can twist your brain around backwards.

Last year, I listened to an archery hunter tell his story as he showed a photograph of himself with a huge buck. I enjoy hearing a guy tell a good hunting story and this one had plenty of color and great detail. At one point though, he mentioned that this hunt made him a believer in the use of scent block clothing. His photograph seemed to be powerful proof. So I started thinking about maybe getting a set of this expensive clothing before the next hunting season. But as I recalled the details of his story I couldn't see how the scent block clothing should deserve so much of the credit. He is in fact a good and dedicated hunter. He is good with his bow. He was up in a tree stand and the wind was right so scent should not have been a big issue. He had done all of the seven rules extremely well. He also had paid a lot of money to hunt on private land in an area known nation-wide for huge bucks. Scent block clothing certainly didn't hurt his chances for success, but nothing in his story suggested that he wouldn't have gotten this deer regardless. The flip side of this is that I could easily find dozens of photographs of hunters with big bucks killed buy guys who smelled like an ashtray in a smoky roadhouse bar with a gas station attached. These guys never even heard of scent blocking fabrics until just a few years ago. They've been very successful hunting without it for many years. This would seem like powerful proof of the opposite point. This kind of thing can get a guys brain twisted into a knot. So, what's the truth?

19

The "Big Rocks" Theorem: (*I'm unable to properly give credit to the original author of the "Big Rock" theorem. I read it somewhere long ago and the concept stuck with me. Here it is, as best I can recall and reproduce the idea.*)

Suppose that you could win a thousand dollars in a contest by being the first person to fill a large box with a certain amount of sand, stones and big rocks. It all has to go inside the box and you have to be able to get the lid closed on top. If you start by putting the sand or stones in first, it will be impossible to force the big rocks down into the box. But if the big rocks go in first, the stones can be added and shaken down to fill in the odd spaces. The sand can be added last and will shake down to fill in the smallest cracks between the stones. In this way it all fits in the box and you can get the lid on top. In deer hunting, the seven rules are the large rocks that you must get into the box first. It doesn't work backwards. The "big rock theorem" and its close cousin the "keep it simple principle", show up again and again throughout this book.

The problem for a guy who's totally new to hunting is that in their ears, all advice from advanced hunters sounds like it might be equally important. A new guy can't tell if success might be more dependent on a comfortable seat cushion costing twenty dollars, or on a bottle of doe estrus, or on a grunt call, or a new scope or a range finder or on four hundred dollars worth of scent blocking clothes. It's natural to think that the most costly items might yield the greatest success. But that's not true.

I don't mean to imply that the expert hunters are lying. They're not. They mean well and they're trying to share. The fact that they're willing to spend extra money on special gear only gives further testament to the fact that they are very highly dedicated to hunting success. It's the proportion of the credit deserved that seems to get confusing. The experts already have the seven big rocks in the box. A new guy probably doesn't. The experts may truly find some added benefit from spending extra money on more costly stuff which goes to finer levels of detail. A new guy probably doesn't. The expert may have been hunting for many years, and so purchasing one more item doesn't break their budget. But the new guy walking into a sporting-goods store quickly finds out that he won't be able to make his house payment if he buys all the stuff.

So, for a whole bunch of reasons, **the new guy needs to focus his attention on the items, skills and techniques that go toward helping him with the seven big rock issues first**. In the "tips" section of this book a dozen important "*stones*" are added. In other sections detailed "*sand*" is added to fill in the cracks. By the time you finish reading this book, your box will be very tightly packed.

Stop now! No trespassing! Do these paper exercises <u>before</u> you read The Seven Rules. Tell the story of at least five and hopefully seven to ten of your recent deer hunting outings. Start with the most recent and work backwards. Try not to skip any. Include outings when you didn't see any deer.
Try to include the following notes:
- Which stand were you at, for how long, AM or PM?
- How many deer did you see?
- Did you have a chance for a shot?
- Now, tell your story, "Why did you not get a shot? Why did you not get this deer?"

This can be as brief as five to seven words.
> *Glimpsed deer tail only*
> *Surprised by deer, didn't hear it, or see it.*
> *No clear shot*
> *Deer spooked by me- sound*
> *Deer spooked by me- movement*
> *Deer spooked by something else.*
> *Deer winded me*
> *O.T.H. (Odd Thing Happened) etc.*

How did you first become aware of the deer?
   "*Heard it, saw it*"
- How did the deer first become aware of you?
"S*aw you, heard you, smelled you*"
- What happened next?

The point of this paper exercise is twofold. First it's to get you to identify and eventually correct these mistakes. Secondly it gives you some idea in rough numbers as to the potential that might exist to increase your rate of success.

THE SEVEN RULES

Taken one at a time, the rules are flat rock simple. However, these rules do not work singularly. They work as a package deal. It does no good to become an excellent marksman if you cannot sit still and be quiet. It does no good to sit still and be quiet if you don't know how to use your ears or eyes. It does no good to use your ears and eyes if you rush for the shot or are a poor marksman.

1. Be still, or conceal any movement. This is the most important rule. Once you've settled at your deer stand, sit absolutely totally still. Don't stand. Sit down. By "sit still" I don't mean just in the same place or just for a few minutes. I mean sit **absolutely totally dead dog still….forever!** No scratching your forehead. No wiping your nose. No binoculars. No gadgets. Still! More than self-discipline, this simply involves being prepared and knowing how to stay comfortable in the woods. *Head, hands and feet are the problem.*

2. Be silent. This is the other most important rule. It means make no sound. Especially make no metallic or high frequency sound. No zippers, cigarette lighters, coins or extra cartridges in your pockets. No sniffling, no coughing, no pagers, no wristwatch alarm, no walkie-talkie radio, no cell phone. **Nothing that squeaks or rattles on your gun or bow or tree stand.** Muffle the metallic sound of your rifle safety. Be sure your rifle-sling swivels don't squeak. Be sure the arrow does not squeak or rattle against the launcher when you draw the bow. **Be absolutely totally dead dog silent….forever!**

3. Listen. Except for special hunting conditions (*wind & damp*) and for the necessity of making the shot, **your ears are far more important than your eyes as a hunting tool.** Your brain automatically evaluates every sound you hear for distance, direction, and speed. Once you've heard different animals moving in the woods under different conditions you'll be able to identify the sound as "*deer*" or "*not deer*" with a good deal of accuracy. This in turn can help you to keep "still" and helps with "make the move." Although your brain will evaluate, categorize and memorize these sounds naturally, most hunters can sharpen this ability by consciously focusing on what they are hearing. I will explain a great deal more about this in the "tips section."

4. Use your eyes. In damp or windy conditions and in some types of low ground vegetation, deer seem to move silently. So your eyes have to do the whole job. Keep your gaze mostly relaxed to the distant front. This helps prevent eye fatigue. It's amazing that your eyes will automatically pick up even a small bird or ground squirrel if it moves anywhere in your main field of view. You'll notice that this happens very naturally. Divide your frontal view into several smaller sections that you can easily see with head movement only. This will cover about 220-degrees. At intervals of about every fifteen minutes, begin a scan from the far right or left section, holding your gaze at each section for at least thirty seconds to a full minute. Allow your eyes to be drawn toward any movement. Be sure to include the region I call the "*transparent wall*" of cover. This is explained in the "tips section." Look for "*parts of deer*" such as a leg, ear or rump. Look for a broken horizontal line of the deer's back among the mostly vertical lines of the trees. Look for a slightly different patch of color. After the scan you might choose to risk moving your upper body enough to check the far right and left rear flanks. Go ahead and close your eyes for brief rest periods or short naps. I know this sounds nuts. I'll explain later. (*Much more on this in the tips section*)

5. Make the move. Resist the urge to quickly move into shooting position. The first four rules get you to this point. But this is when many hunters are most likely to screw-it-up. **I can not overstress the importance of this rule!** In the first moment that you see or hear a deer approaching there is a tremendous urge to get into shooting position immediately. Unless you're sure that the deer can't see you, it's almost always to your advantage to remain perfectly still. Keep your eyes or ears on it while anticipating its general direction and wait as it continues to move into better fields of fire. Also check to see if a second or third deer might see you make your move. It may be necessary to make your move in two or three stages as the opportunities present themselves. If so, try not to get caught in such an awkward position that you will have a hard time holding it for several minutes. (*The exception to this rule is when a deer has already been spooked by another hunter and is running straight toward you or across your shooting lanes. In that case your best and perhaps only chance is to move quickly into position*). There are other tough calls on this rule. (*Read: Tips, Scent cone, Deer eyes*)

6. Make a good shot. Do yourself a big favor by trying hard to make a shot into the vital "kill Zone" area. A double lung or heart shot will cause death in about six seconds. In that six seconds a deer could run eighty yards. Even if there is no blood trail, this is an easy area to search and recover the dead deer. But a fatally wounded deer shot in a single lung or in the liver can run much farther and might be much more difficult to recover. (*Be sure to read "After the Shot"*)

You don't necessarily have to be a superb marksman in order to be a highly successful deer hunter. (Read "Cornerstone Point"). But you do have to be good enough. Most hunters will experience an increased heart rate and breathing due to adrenaline at this time. This can be hell on marksmanship and therefore must be suppressed and controlled. Almost all of making a good shot comes from things you've done long before you went hunting. Now everything comes down to your performance under actual field conditions. But during practice you didn't have an uncertain time limit for making the shot. You didn't have low light conditions and the target wasn't moving at varying speed and changing direction through cover at uncertain distances. The target also didn't blend in almost perfectly with everything else around it and your heart wasn't pounding like a drum. Get in the habit while you are practicing, of going through a short **mental ritual checklist**. It may be "*safety off, gun up, kill zone, gentle squeeze.*" A mental ritual acts both mechanically and psychologically to help you make the good shot. (*Much more on this later for gun & archery*)

7. Find a good stand. Preferably, a few days or weeks prior to opening morning, spend a reasonable amount of time scouting to familiarize yourself with the general terrain. In good deer country you should be able to find a couple of decent spots within half a day. A full day is better. Two days is great. But I don't think you learn a whole lot more on a third day. (*Much more later on scouting*)
<u>Look for five things:</u>
➤ Two or more parallel or intersecting trails through good cover showing signs of recent use. (*tracks, droppings, browse damage*).
➤ A position overlooking but not directly on top of the trails, that is within range of your capability of making a very high percentage of kill shots.

➢ A stand that allows you to put all of its weaknesses to one side, your backside. This is a side where the cover and terrain somehow either gives the deer an advantage, or it limits your ability to hear, see or make a shot. It is also the side from which your scouting indicates it is least likely that deer will approach. As a bonus, if in addition the wind happens to be moving toward the weak side, this should be an excellent stand.

➢ A second stand meeting these same criteria, *(most likely adjacent to and covering these same trails),* as a backup in case the wind direction becomes a problem with the first position.

➢ A position that feels right to you. If it doesn't feel right don't sit there. Trust your instinct on this.

> Note: I have not insisted that you look for rubs or scrapes. The only thing that a *rub tells you is that there is at least one buck in the area. It's a good sign. Scrapes tell you that the rut may be starting soon. It's a better sign especially if they are large and smell nasty. But, with or without rubs or scrapes, look for the five criteria listed above for a good stand.*

Final ingredient: There's one more important skill you'll learn by the time you become a "*seasoned*" hunter. It's a skill that comes from seeing and hearing many dozens of deer moving in the woods under different types of conditions. Based on their direction, their pace, their body language and the terrain in the immediate area, hunters begin to develop a **skill for predicting what the deer is most likely going to do next.** Is it coming fast, or slow? Is it undisturbed or in a state of caution? Where's it coming from? Where's it headed? Will the deer keep moving, or turn, or stop, or slowdown. Is it about to reach for food, or look in your direction, or look away, or is it about to run off? Hunters can't usually explain exactly how they're able to do this. In their stories it often comes out in a phrase such as, "*I could tell the deer was about to _____ so I decided to _____.* This ability can be sharpened more quickly if you pay attention to detail as you watch deer. Notice how they react to other movements, sounds or scent. Pay attention to their posture, stance, head, nose, ears, and especially their tail movements. **The reason this skill is important is because it provides the final ingredient that goes into your decision about making the move.**

The *"move equation"*: The decision about *"making the move"* is the trickiest and most important part of deer hunting. **It can quickly tilt the odds either very much toward success or toward failure.** You'll need to read the advice in half a dozen other sections of this book in order to pull it all together and fully understand the paragraph below. Return to this page and read it again later.

The *"move equation"* has many factors. It includes all the lessons about the *"scent cone"* from the diagram of the "Happy-hunter". It includes the *"deer's eyes"* and peripheral vision. It includes the trails and the position of shooting lanes. It includes the topography, trees, mounds, bushes, and logs, providing cover for both the deer and the hunter. It might include important sign such as a hot scrape, a food sources or safe cover in the immediate area which could affect what the deer will do. <u>All of these factors are known to you in advance from scouting and selecting the stand. But the final ingredient is provided only in those few seconds when you first become aware of an approaching deer.</u> At that point, you need to make a judgment about what this <u>deer</u> is most likely going to do next. This gets plugged into the *"move equation"* to decide what <u>you</u> will do next. Sometimes the decision is complicated or needs to be made quickly. <u>It helps a lot if you've already mentally run the scenarios in advance.</u> You might decide to make the move now, or remain still in anticipation of a better opportunity. The wrong move is bad, but freezing up is bad too. Seasoned hunters get better at this. But even old pros sometimes get caught. There is no algebraic equation. It's hunting. You'll win some and lose some. Good luck pilgrim.

Do not wear white! In the original book I failed to mention that it's a very bad idea to wear white while deer hunting. This is so fundamental that it simply never occurred to me that anyone would need to be told. It's a bad idea for two reasons. First is because deer eyes are well attuned to white. It's the *"warning-danger"* sign given by their big white flagging tail. Secondly, there are nine-hundred-thousand deer hunters in the woods. If only one percent of them are idiots, it means that there are nine-thousand idiots in the woods. You do not want one of those guys to think you're a deer! So, no white! **Avoid yellow too.** Also, hunters orange clothing is required in most States for rifle, shotgun or muzzle loading season. It is not required during archery season when camouflage is normally worn.

Do not become fanatical about scouting. On opening morning nine-hundred-thousand other smelly guys will be entering the woods. Weeks of scouting are made instantly irrelevant because the other guy either spooked the deer out of its normal pattern or shot it himself. So, you might as well just pick a place, sit down, shut up and take your chances like the rest of us.

Get thy butt into the woods and stay there! This is a rule that did not make the final list of seven, only because, by definition, if you're not out there, you're not hunting! However this does require mentioning. If you hunt for only a few hours it drastically reduces your odds. If you spend the rest of the day back in town at the restaurant getting pie and coffee, then enjoy the pie and coffee. Just don't bitch to anyone about not getting a deer. Deal?

No....., your stand is not ruined for the day just because another hunter walks through the area. *In fact, he might be moving deer that will double back. Stay still, stay silent and stay especially alert in the next fifteen or twenty minutes after someone walks through. I'm not saying you should be real happy about it, but it's not the end of your day either.*

When to abandon your stand and take a hike: Stand hunting is by far the most likely to yield success. But I'm not so stuck on it that I can't sometimes see the advantage of abandoning your stand in favor of actively trying to go find deer. There are some conditions where this might make sense and there are ways to do it that work in your favor. The conditions that favor taking a hike are:
- When the deer aren't moving much on their own.
- When you have a good covering of quiet-type snow.
- When hunting with a longer range weapon. (Rifle)
- When you have plenty of acreage to wander.
- When there are few other hunters in the woods.

I accidentally stumbled upon an approach I call "ridge-popping", while I was on missions to get pictures for this book. It worked well for pictures so I tried it while rifle hunting and it almost yielded a shot opportunity. It works best in the above conditions and in hilly country. I don't favor trying to find and identify an individual set of buck tracks and then following them everywhere they might lead.

27

Instead, **use the terrain** to guide your movement in an almost random way probing into likely cover. **Move into or across wind,** on the backside of a ridge, or heavy cover. Use stealth and stay crouched low, or crawl as you approach near the crest of the ridge. This acts to shield you from being seen or heard. When you reach a good vantage point, rise to see over the crest into the valley and opposite hillside. Stay still for several minutes as you scan the area. Even with the advantage of snow, deer can be there that you don't see at first. You might decide to move into the valley to probe into likely heavy cover, or drop back behind the ridge and move along to repeat the process. Be ready as you approach snow covered brush or fallen trees. **Try to pick your path so you have an open shooting lane toward the likely escape routes.** Be prepared for the fact that shots are more likely to be at a moving target and at longer range. Since you've been walking, your breathing and heart rate might become a problem for making the shot. A kneeling position is often the best choice. Practice a few times at dropping down quickly into a solid kneeling position. Another option is to carry a bi-folding shooting stick which folds out very quickly to steady the front of your weapon.

This approach works because of a five point combination of conditions. You can **move very quietly** because of the snow, while partially **controlling your scent** direction moving into or across the wind, exploring **plenty of good deer cover**, and because the snow gives you **great visibility** in order to see antlers much more easily and because your **weapon has enough range**. However, on small acreage or when there are a lot of hunters in the woods or without any snow, or with a shorter range weapon, this approach doesn't make much sense to me. You'll just end up pushing deer off the land without seeing them well enough to get a shot.

Follow-up on your paper exercise.

I know you never did the paper exercise. But, let's pretend you did anyway. Write down the rule numbers that apply, next to each of the outings that you listed on the paper. Make any additions or corrections to each story. The tendency toward problems with certain rules is somewhat dependent upon which of the five stages of a hunter's life you are in. The list might show a recurring problem with one or two of the rules. It also might show that you randomly break different rules.

- If all you ever see are deer-tails bounding away through the woods, you're probably breaking rules one and two at least. (*still and silent*).
- If you're usually surprised to discover the presence of deer nearby, you may be O.K. with rule one and two, but need to do better with rules three and four (*listen and use your eyes*).
- If you get all the way to number five, "*making the move*" then you're probably doing well with rules one through four. But, if you mess-up at this point, it most often means a tough running shots, or no shot at all. I have several pages of good advice for this in the tips section. Even so, rule five is often a tough call.
- The good news is that if you get past "making the move" your chances for success are great. You can almost take a sigh of relief. Now you simply need to make the shot. If you have scouted and located your stand in the way I have described the shots should be well within your capabilities. You've done it a hundred times in practice. Take it.

Notice that there is additional information in the paper exercise. A particular stand might have a high number of deer sightings in the AM versus none in the PM or vice versa. This information can save you from wasting your time at a low percentage stand. Instead, you may end up with one stand for the morning and a different one for the afternoon. This increases your odds of seeing deer on each outing.

It can happen on occasion that I don't see any deer, even in stands that I know to be a normally good productive location. I generally stick with them. If this happens on more than three consecutive outings I begin to suspect that something has happened to change the deer movement pattern. So, it's time to try an alternative stand. For example, in the 1994 deer season I was at my favorite stand known as "the end of the earth" deep in the Huron National Forrest. After two and a half days I had only seen two deer. In the previous ten years this stand had rarely failed to show me at least half a dozen deer each day. I had heard some shooting in the surrounding area, so at midday I took a hike. I discovered that two new groups of hunters totaling nine guys had set up blinds in locations that affected my spot. So, I abandoned my old favorite stand for another called "heart attack hill." This new favorite spot has been very productive and almost never fails to show me deer.

Check your Data:

If the deer detected your presence at all, it was due to movement (*or sound caused by movement*), rather than due to your scent, by a huge factor, perhaps more than 8 to 1.

Once a deer has detected your presence or is suspicious, the probability of getting a decent shot opportunity drops dramatically, perhaps as low as 1 in 10.

If you are the first to detect the presence of the deer, your chance for getting a good shot opportunity improves dramatically. Perhaps as high as 8 out of 10. (*Provided that you have chosen your stand as I describe and that you know when to make your move*)

Once you succeed in making the move without being detected, you should have a very high chance for success, perhaps 8 out of 10. If not, you may have a marksmanship problem or "buck fever".

In good hunting conditions your ears, not your eyes, alerted you first to the deer or to anything else that is approaching by a huge factor, perhaps more than 10 to 1. In poor damp hunting conditions this is reversed, your eyes have to do all the work.

If you're not seeing any deer on numerous outings, you're probably breaking at least five out of the seven rules. After you've had time to reflect on your hunting skills, you will know that your wife and children went without venison, starved and died last winter, almost assuredly because you broke one of the seven rules. Mother Nature does not mess around. Learn from your mistakes, pilgrim.

Good hunting.

The Five Stages
Part - 2

Over their lifetime, I believe most deer-hunters typically go through a progression of five stages. I have named them (Bambi, Yearling, Rabid, Seasoned and Ol-Buck.) Boundaries of stages aren't so much in years as they are in experience and attitudes. Within several of these stages there are tendencies toward particular problems with one or another of the seven rules. There are suggestions throughout this writing to help you compensate or adapt to overcome these tendencies.

BAMBIES are usually first, second or third-year deer hunters who don't know how much they don't know. (No insult intended). I was a Bambi myself once, and so was everyone else. They're eager to go on their first hunts and may have learned a lot already from small game hunting or from listening to stories from Dad or Grandpa. The seven rules will, in theory, put them in a good starting position.

But, they will tend to underestimate the exact meaning and the importance of the rules. In addition they may not know the five thousand important details that can help them obey the rules. All of these pages of writing and theory are a poor teacher compared to one real world, cold and miserable weekend in the woods seeing nothing but tail-hairs of a deer.

Bambies may not have yet developed an eye for a good stand location. They might get into cover that's way too heavy and lacks shooting lanes or cover that's way too open. They usually don't run the mental scenarios of what to do if deer approach from different directions. Even if they happen to be good with rules one through four, this can lead to trouble with rule five "making the move." This in turn might lead to a difficult shot, which usually means a missed deer.

It's usually rule one (be still) that causes them the most trouble. This might be because they're bored and don't have the discipline, but it's more often due to the cold. No other experience in their life before this has required them to sit dead dog still in the freezing cold for hours at a time.

It's a real-life lesson in thermodynamics. If they don't dress right and experience bitter cold their first year, they usually show up dressed like the abominable snowman the second year. Neither one is good.

The second most frequent problem is with rule two (be silent). In both cases the source of the trouble can usually be traced back to a sporting goods store and the selection of the right gear. The sections "tips on still & silent" and "tips on cold" are important for them to read.

It's also important for them to have the company of an experienced hunter when they go shopping for gear. This is not just to save them money. It's to help them evaluate the important gear that might add or detract from their ability to be still and silent. Gear that looks good in the store often shows its drawbacks only after you get it out in the woods. An experienced outdoorsman can often look at a piece of gear and say: *"This material will crackle or crunch when it gets cold, this won't shed water, this is too heavy, this will be a pain to get on and off, this will rattle or squeak, this will make your feet cold or this will make your ass sore, or this is just a gadget."*

Bambies often have great eyes and ears, but need to learn how to use them. They simply need to be left alone in the woods long enough to begin cataloging sights and sounds in the mental register. Bambies also tend to have physical energy to spare coupled with more curiosity and less patience. This may cause them to want to walk all over the deer woods exploring. It's best to let them get this out of their system at some time other than the opening three days of deer season. Make sure they have a good lighter and/or dry matches. Make sure they carry a good compass and know how to use it.

A quick side-note on this. Although I once loved the U.S. Army metal encased folding style compass. The heavy metal gets very cold and opening it often while scouting can get to be a pain. In addition you usually don't need to be shooting azimuths. So, I would recommend a lightweight, clear, plastic-encased open face compass. Put it on a cord and tie it through a belt loop or button-hole. Check to be sure that the needle will get stable quickly without wobbling or sticking. Only one time in all my years of hunting have I thought that a GPS unit might be worth having. This was in heavy fog in the pre-dawn dark. Got lost as hell. No big deal, home for dinner.

YEARLINGS are those who somehow enjoyed the experience their first few years, regardless of success, and who come back for reasons they often find hard to explain: " *It's just something about being out there.*" The yearling stage can last several years for someone who is rather laid back about hunting. They may get a deer, and that's OK or they may not get a deer, and that's OK too. They're usually easy to be around in deer camp and can be surprisingly successful deer hunters. This drives a "Rabid" hunter completely over the edge.

The relaxed attitude of yearlings can work both for them and against them. While awake on their stand they may not take any of the seven rules very seriously. However they do tend to fall asleep a lot. Oddly this may turn out to be more beneficial than harmful. It helps them stay still and silent longer. Many hunters have an ability to sleep at a level that allows them to awaken at a specific type of sound and at a surprisingly low threshold.

Yearlings may have learned to be better at "still & silent" but continue to have trouble with "the move." If making the move seems to be a big problem and has cost you a chance for a good shot at a buck, you might consider trying your move on the next one or two doe you see. Even if you have no intention of shooting the doe, it offers you a chance to practice the move. I wouldn't recommend doing this all the time. Just until you gain a little confidence. Try to be reasonably sure that a buck isn't accompanying this doe.

It's possible to skip the yearling stage and go straight to Rabid. People who've hunted small game may spend only a very short time in the Bambi or Yearling stages and quickly go to the next stage, Rabid.

RABID deer-hunters come in two flavors. First is the amiable "*I know everything there is about deer-hunting*", sort. They'll talk to you about deer-hunting until you fall off your chair. The second flavor is the very intense hardcore "*It's opening morning so get out of my way or I'll kill you*" sort.

The first sort can be good with teaching Bambies and Yearlings. Rabid hunters have a wealth of knowledge about deer and can show a young hunter how to "read sign." Odd as it may seem a hunter who has never gotten a deer in years of trying can still be a completely obsessed, fanatic, and raving lunatic about deer hunting.

Its importance has somehow gone far beyond a normal healthy desire to go out and kill something to eat. He reads all kinds of articles and buys all kinds of equipment, and endures all kinds of hardships in order to be ready for opening day. He may talk hunting at dinner parties and business lunches to anyone who will listen. He may call in sick at work, or tell his boss to go to hell and drive all night long to be in the woods at sunrise opening day. This doesn't necessarily mean that they are better hunters. They still may make several of the common mistakes and are susceptible to the hunting bull, fad techniques, and buying all the "stuff". The problem is that this all can end up distracting them from a good solid hunting style.

If they have a higher success rate it may be in part because of tenacity. Even in the most miserable hunting conditions they are in the woods longer than anyone else. In addition these guys are ready to hunt. They have selected their stand, packed a flashlight, knife, compass, toilet paper, and extra socks, sighted their weapon, practiced their marksmanship, and packed a lunch for opening day.

Rabid hunters anticipate each deer season like a child waiting for Christmas. They can be quite disappointed if they don't "get one". They tend to keep score of how many deer they've gotten over the years. It's probably a habit that a lot of guys picked up from playing competitive sports. Unfortunately this can partially blind them to the camaraderie and the joy of *"just being out there"*.

One caution is that, in the rabid stage an otherwise good guy may be most susceptible to the temptations of crossing over legal and ethical hunting boundaries. Hunters can stay in the rabid stage for over a decade as I did. Around deer season Rabids can be hell on their friends and family.

SEASONED: Once a hunter enters this stage he will start to have the highest rate of success. Seasoned hunters are probably good at most of the seven rules. Selecting a good stand is almost instinctive by this point. Be still, be silent, listen, use your eyes and make the shot are all second nature. In my opinion, it is rule five, "Making the Move" that still might remain the most challenging. These guys will usually do the best that can be done with all the variables that go into the decision about when and how to make the move.

They've sharpened a skill that allows them to be fairly accurate at predicting the next likely movements of an approaching deer. This is the final factor that gets plugged into the "move" equation. It's very important. But even seasoned hunters still get caught once in a while. That's why it's called "deer hunting" not "deer slaughtering."

Seasoned hunters are usually mature yet enter this stage while still in fairly good physical shape. Following the rabid stage these hunters tend to come back to reality and get back to the basics of good solid hunting. It's not that the love for hunting has diminished in any way. It's just that the super-hype of opening day and big bucks gets put back into the proper perspective. They start to relax a little. If you ask them how many deer they've gotten, they might have to take a few minutes to go back through the years. It's not that they forgot. It's just that they don't bother to keep score any more. They aren't out there to compete with anyone. They make the best teachers for young Bambies and Yearlings. These guys will often tell stories about things they did back when they were still rabid that end with a chuckle and the phrase "we must have been crazy."

OL-BUCKs: A little old gray haired guy was driving a white Jeep pickup truck, fighting its way up the hill over the ruts and rocks and through the slush-filled puddles leading deeper into the national forest. At first, all we could see of him was some gray hair just above the steering wheel. We waved at him from the side of the trail. A rock or a rut would send his face with the thick round glasses bouncing up into view. He didn't, or couldn't wave back at us. He wouldn't release his death-grip from the steering wheel. Getting up this trail was serious business for this old-timer. I guess that was the first time my brothers and I saw him.

Over the years we had an occasional few passing words with this little old gray guy. The hearing loss caused him to talk loudly which made him seem even crankier than he actually was. We kinda got used to the fact that he simply did not begin or end any sentence without cussin. "Damn snowmobiles, damn four wheelers, damn government." These old guys know they can't go as deep into the woods as they used to. They *"don't hear so good"* or they don't *"see so good no more."* They get cold easy and have trouble sittin still. On nice days, mostly they fall asleep in the woods.

35

One Ol-Buck I know of through a good friend, has a superstition that you die in the year after you stop going up north for deer camp. He names half-a-dozen examples in his immediate family to support this theory. So every year, even though he doesn't actually hunt, he drives up to deer-camp and visits for part of a day. With diabetes, cancer and a bad heart, he figures the visit is enough to keep him alive one more season. Can't hurt.

Sometimes I wonder what it is that Ol-Bucks think about sittin on their stand. *"Maybe this'll be my last season"*. *I'm get'n too old for this. It ain't all that much fun anymore, alone."* Then perhaps something moves in the heavy cover and their heart is suddenly very young and very strong again. *"I'll be back next season."*

In ways they're like the yearlings again; they just *"like being out there"*. They've learned and partly forgotten everything that the hunting gods have been able to teach them in this life. Once in a while you run into one out in the deer woods, usually hunting alone. They watch the woods and they listen. They remember their brother who no longer walks these trails.

Kinda miss seein' the old guy with the white Jeep these past few years. He was walking real stiff, maybe a bad leg, the last time I saw him. Cussin loud about something too. Anyway, these guys do add character to the woods. Maybe help'em drag one out, if they'll let ya.

Good hunting.

Tips On Keeping The Seven Rules
Part - 3

Shut-up and hunt. In recent years I've taken joy in having my young nephews join in deer camp. But it started to change the tone of camp in a way that began to bug me after a while. I felt like I was talking way too much. The poor kids couldn't take six steps without Uncle Roy having to show or tell them something about some damn little detail. I'm sure they got sick of it. After a while I got sick of hearing myself too. I only wanted to help, but on the other hand, a little voice was telling me to just shut the hell up and enjoy the hunt. Let the boys make their own mistakes and figure it out as they go. Nobody wants to be pecked at all day even if it is well intentioned. The problem is that there really are a hundred "stone" sized nuggets that young hunters need to *"get in the box"*. **It's often one of those stupid little pesky details that nobody ever told them about that ends up causing them not to get a deer.** That's why this section of the book is important. It contains many of those details. These tips go directly toward improving your ability to obey the first five of the seven rules. (*I gave each of my nephews a copy of the first printing of this book. So, next year I ain't sayin nothin to nobody. I'm gonna just shut up and hunt)*

Tips on "listening": In my opinion your ears are your most important hunting aid. For that reason I'm going to use a lot of ink on this subject. Your ears can tell you approximately how far away, how fast, and in what direction something is moving. They can tell you that *"this sound is probably not a deer"* and therefore help you to obey rule number one by reducing unnecessary movement due to a noise made by a ground squirrel. They can also tell you that *"this sound probably is a deer"* and draw your eyes into the hunt. Chances are that your ears are already doing this, only you haven't been highly aware of it. Now spend some time thinking about what your ears are telling you.

Late fall hunting season in the north woods offers either wet, powder or crusted snow conditions, or dry leaves, frosty ground or damp hunting conditions. Each has an effect on the sound that critters make as they move through the woods. In damp conditions, a deer could nearly step on top of you before you would hear it moving.

In this case your eyes have to take over as the most important aid in hunting. This is extremely fatiguing, especially in low light conditions. It can also be frustrating as you discover that deer seem to be able to either appear or vanish before your eyes. In these conditions the deer has a great advantage. The only remaining hopes that you have lie in being absolutely still and silent. In wet snow or powder snow the deer also make essentially no sound. However, our eyes have a much easier job due to the visibility and contrast the snow provides. In hard crusted snow, frosty ground or dry leaves, deer make a fair amount of noise, as they move. These are the most favored conditions that bring your ears back into the hunt. The vast majority of Midwest hunters don't get the benefit of snow for early deer season. So, we hope for dry or frosty conditions. (*Oddly, a small squirrel can often make more noise than a deer, and a black bear can be much quieter.*)

What exactly do you hear? Suppose for now that the hunting conditions are moderately dry or frosty with little if any wind. Suppose also that you are seated at your chosen stand. What does a deer sound like as it moves into your area? What does a chipmunk or field mouse sound like? What about a fox, coyote, dog or wolf? How about a small bird? What about an opossum, raccoon, skunk or porcupine? How about a wild turkey? If you've spent some time in the woods you probably already find yourself reacting to sounds with a mental alert that says with a fair amount of certainty and accuracy "*now that sounds like a deer.*" Most likely you have not thought carefully about how it is that you are able to do this.

What follows is my theory: A number of qualities make up the sound that these various animals make. For my purposes I will call these qualities *heaviness, travel, sharpness* and *cadence*.

Heaviness is your ability to tell the difference between a raindrop striking dry leaves versus an acorn. It can also tell an acorn from a small stick, and a small stick from a heavy one. In the same way you can often hear the difference in heaviness between a deer versus a small bird or ground squirrel.

Travel has to do with lateral movement. Deer movement does not often include dancing around for a long time in one small area. (*The exceptions to this are in the acts of sparring, mating, rubbing or making a scrape. In those cases there's is not much doubt as to what is going on.*) For the vast majority of time the sound of deer movement involves travel over some lateral distance. I believe that your brain is also somehow doing a bit of instinctive geometry and math. (*No, you don't need a calculator and protractor. This happens subconsciously and by instinct*)

The geometry involves taking the point from where the sound was first heard to the point where it was last heard and calculating its distance speed and direction. The math involves taking the approximate distance traveled and dividing it roughly by the number of steps you heard. From having seen and heard deer move before, your brain knows that a walking, trotting or running deer covers a certain amount of distance in a certain amount of time with what sounds like a certain number of steps. A large dog or coyotee might take at least twice that many steps and a fox three or four time as many. So, even with your eyes closed your brain does a quick and dirty subconscious math problem that says "*too many steps for that amount of distance, not a deer*" or it causes your eyes to open with some certainty and your mind says "*that's a deer.*"

Sharpness is your ability to detect the difference between someone walking down a hallway in high heels versus boots versus house slippers. Hard ground with dry or frosty leaves under wide padded furry feet makes a slightly muffled sound compared to the sharp hoof of a deer. Even the sound of another hunter carefully approaching through the woods has a more muffled two-part sound. One is the heel sound followed by the shift to the ball. Sometimes when the conditions are perfect you may hear this sound and you will know that it is a human, not any other critter. This sound is not at all like the sharpness of a deer hoof.

Cadence has to do with the rate of repetition. The cadence sound that I try to keep in my mind is the same as a person picking wild berries. A berry picker is fairly quiet as he stops to get a few berries from the bush. However, he then periodically makes some noise as he takes a few steps looking for another bush.

An undisturbed deer foraging its way in the woods has a very similar cadence. Remember that the entire forest is one giant salad-bar for the deer. An undisturbed deer may have a hard time walking ten feet without finding something that it wants to taste. This makes for a periodic move-stop-move-stop kind of sound. In my experience these sounds rarely come as singles or doubles. They more often come as a set of five to seven followed by a pause and then another set of five to seven. Of course the cadence of a running or cantering deer is a whole lot different and you'll know this when you hear it too.

The Sound Fingerprint; All of the above qualities added together give the hunter what I call the "sound fingerprint" that our brains try to match up against a mental sound catalogue. I believe that this can be very accurate. Of course, if the deer is moving as a result of being spooked or with some serious intention of getting from one place to another, the sounds will be more constant and obvious as to the speed and direction. Several deer moving swiftly together in distant dry leaves may at first make a steady swooshing sound similar to wind in the trees. As you see various critters in the woods your mental register will begin to catalogue them. If you are an archery hunter up in a tree stand with full camo on, you'll have an opportunity to see and hear many things that few other people ever do. Sooner or later everything with fur or feathers, predator or prey will pass by. Small birds that peck and scratch or flitter from tree to tree will be automatically ruled out after a while. Field mice and chipmunks that skitter about nervously also are quickly recognized. An odd thing like a porcupine gnawing on a nearby tree may present a puzzle at first but at least you will be fairly sure it's not a deer.

For me, unless it makes one of the classic turkey vocal sounds, the ground movement of a wild turkey is the hardest sound-print to differentiate from a slow foraging deer. They are usually cautious in their movements. This drove me nuts one frosty morning as I thought deer were very close and sneaking through the heavy cover. I would get into position for a shot to one side and then hear a sound from another side. Finally I saw that I was surrounded by several turkeys. The good news is that if you are seeing many of these you are probably also hunting in good style for deer.

Caution: If the "sound fingerprint" tells you that *"this seems very much like a deer"* and the sound stops at some point nearby but out of sight, be especially careful. This deer has sensed something wrong and is waiting, listening, watching, and smelling. It is then especially important not to become doubtful of your own senses. Remain silent and still. Fifteen minutes may seem like eternity to you, but its nothing to a suspicious deer. The next one to move, or to make a sound, usually loses.

Tune your ear: The first time I heard the sound of a properly used deer grunt call I realized that I had heard that sound before while out in the woods. However, it had not registered with me on a highly conscious level. Now, my ear is tuned so that I consciously notice these sounds. It may be a good idea to watch a video and listen to the different types of vocalizations that deer make. This will tune your ear to pick up on these sounds. The most common grunt sound seems to me like a cross between a healthy burp, and a good old beer-belch. Another sound I have heard is like a cricket on steroids or an underpowered bullfrog. A good clue is that there are no crickets or bullfrogs around after the cold season sets in with snow, frost and ice.

What about the Deer-Ears: First of all, deer have about seven times more surface area than humans on their ear for capturing sound. Try this sometime just for fun. Take a couple of 5 x 7 inch cards and slightly curve them around your ears. Notice how much this improves your ability to capture sound. That will give you a small clue about what you're up against. Secondly, deer can rotate each ear independently 180 degrees. This can be fun to watch. It allows them to cover front and back at the same time and to locate the source of the sound more precisely. Sometimes though, a deer in a valley or hillside has a hard time figuring out where a rifle-shot came from due to the acoustics of the area. It might in fact run right toward you after the shot. Third, deer also can hear especially well in higher frequency ranges that humans can't hear at all. Humans hear at frequencies up to about sixteen thousand Hz. Deer can hear at frequencies up to almost twice that. That's why a high-pitched squeaky sound even at a very low volume could give your position away.

One season on opening morning a nice buck appeared to my right about a hundred yards away. It was a difficult "right on right" move for me, but the wind was perfect and its head went down behind a mound of earth so I knew he couldn't see me. As I carefully went for the first part of my move the tiniest squeak came from the point where my sling swivel attaches to the forearm of the rifle. This slight sound caused the deer to bolt and instantly vanish. I was astonished and disappointed. At the time, I didn't understand that in addition to the tiny squeak that I heard, the deer might have heard a lot more sound at frequencies that I am not capable of hearing at all. In this case, a single drop of oil might have made a huge difference in the outcome.

> *I have an aside point about this. It might explain something about deer jumping the string on archery hunters. Think in terms of the survival value for the deer. What does it cost the deer if he suddenly jumps and runs due to a sound that was caused by something harmless? Not much. But, what is the potential cost if it fails to respond to a sound that is a true threat? It's huge. So, evolution has favored those that do respond. The ones who don't respond have less chance of living long enough to reproduce.*

There's another thing about deer ears. I've watched deer take only a passing interest in the sound of various other critters as they come and go. But, one year I was watching a couple of doe work their way around the opposite hillside when I noticed a very cautious reaction to a sound they heard. They both turned their heads and ears to look and to better hear a sound that was coming from the logging road at the far end of the valley. In unison, they carefully moved around a hump on the hillside to a position where they could not to be seen from the logging road. They stopped again and kept listening. I wondered what it was that had alerted them a full minute before I was able to hear the sound. It was the classic heel-toe rhythmic sound of a single hunter walking on the squeaky-cold snow. The two deer stood still and listened along with me as the threat posed by the footsteps faded around a bend in the trail into the distance. It's only a theory, but I think deer can learn to recognize with fairly good accuracy the classic "sound fingerprint" of humans versus most other critters moving in the woods.

TIPS on "Still" & "Silent": The first five minutes getting settled in at your stand are important for how long, how quiet and how still you will hunt. While walking in to your stand, you have probably scared away any deer in the immediate area. Therefore, whatever noise and movement must be made is best to be made at this time. Brush away dry leaves or sticks that might make noise when you move. Prepare a comfortable seat. I stress the word "comfortable". That means dry, warm, soft. Place your lunch and anything else you may need within easy reach. Place your weapon so that it can be brought into firing position with the absolute minimum of motion. *(See the section "tips on making the move".)* Keep junk that you drag into the woods to an absolute minimum so it doesn't provide a temptation to fool around with. This junk will distract you, cause movement and possibly noise. I don't recommend the use of binoculars on your stand. These cause you to move once in order to look at something, again to put them back down, and again to bring your weapon into position. A scope on a rifle eliminates two of these unnecessary movements. ***Do not use your rifle scope to scan the woods for deer or to check to see if some distant movement is a deer!*** This would be stupid for two reasons. First, the scopes narrow field of view would require a great deal of movement in order to scan the woods. Second, you should know damn well that it's at least some kind of animal movement and not another human being before you point your rifle at it. It's rare not to be able to tell the difference with the naked eye even at extremely long range. Binoculars are fine for scouting deer but they're actually not much use while hunting. Avoid the temptation of your wristwatch. Take it off and place it so you are able to see what time it is without having to move. Some guys take a book to read while on their stand. It's not something I would recommend. But if you have good hearing conditions, can be sure to conceal it and if it helps you stay still longer, I guess it's not the worst idea in the world. Be sure to have a place to quickly stash it if you hear a deer coming.

I've come to favor making as much use of natural existing cover as possible in the deer woods. Typically I use whatever dead branches or logs might be nearby to build a blind that breaks up my outline. I especially try to conceal the area below my waist where my feet hands and weapon may need to be able to move. Tent-style ground blinds are now popular. They are compact, light weight, go up very quickly and help keep wind and weather off.

However, I personally have some kind of mental problem with these blinds. It bugs me to sit inside looking at the tent walls. If you simply find it impossible to be still, a ground-blind is your next best option. The trade-off for concealing your movements is that portable tent-style ground-blinds may slightly reduce your vision, hearing and shooting radius. Be careful not to let the freedom of movement inside the blind cause you to lose your mental hunting focus. Careless movements can easily turn into sounds. Sometimes an otherwise good deer stands has poor cover or a weak side in the cover. A roll of camouflage material suspended to form a low-level curtain might solve the problem. Add a few sticks, branches or local ground foliage to the curtain. This prevents it from buffeting in the wind and it adds authenticity. I like this solution because it takes nothing away from my vision, hearing or shooting and it solves my mental problem with the tent style blind.

After getting settled on my stand I usually note the time and tell myself not to reasonably expect to see any deer until I've been silent and still for at least fifteen minutes. Only a very few times have I seen deer within five or ten minutes of getting seated. These deer may be moving at a good pace. I suspect it is because most hunters head out to their stands at about the same time of day. This might cause a flurry of random spooked deer movement. At intervals of about every fifteen minutes I allow myself to move my head for a visual scan of the area. This is a mental game that helps me to keep still by giving me a set time with permission to move. Only a sound that I reasonably think is a deer might cause me to move my head sooner in order to see it.

If you have excellent conditions for hearing, go ahead and take a nap if you feel like it. **I know this sounds crazy**, so it needs some explanation. It would be ideal to stay alert and yet remain totally still. But, some hunters have a hard time staying "dead dog still" for more than five or ten minutes. They tend to fidget. Others try to stay awake by drinking coffee. The movement of fidgeting and the movement of sipping coffee, followed by the movement needed to then relieve oneself of that coffee, all does more to hurt your chances than does simply taking a short nap. Secondly, many mothers with newborn infants will tell you that they have an ability to sleep at a certain level that allows them to wake up at a particular type of sound and at an astonishingly low threshold. This is a different kind of sleep because you generally still wake up feeling tired. Many hunters have this exact same capability. This is very helpful with "still" and "silent". When you do awake, be careful not to be startled and move suddenly. Chances are that a deer in the area has not yet seen you. Listen for a few minutes and then do a good visual scan.

Smoking is not actually so much a problem due to the smell as it is due to the various movements it requires. Basically, if the deer can smell your tobacco then it can probably also smell you anyways. So, for most cases it is actually the movement that gives you away. Smell is not that big a factor. If you have a smokers cough or need to clear your throat every five minutes, your odds of getting a deer will drop to one every thirty-five years. The biggest problem with "<u>still</u>" is usually the cold. It's much easier to remain still if you can stay warm.

Tips on Cold: *To help keep still. I apologize in advance to old time hunters for the fact that this section is the most boring thing ever written. But, young, new hunters might never before in their lives have had an experience that required them to sit still in the cold for a long period of time. If they're not prepared it will either shorten their hunt or become a memory of a truly miserable, even painful experience. So, I couldn't cut this section out. Try not to whack your head on the table when you fall asleep reading.*

There are three things that will make you very cold, very fast. The first is the movement of cold air across your skin. The second is moisture as it evaporates off your skin or clothes. The third is direct contact with a large cold mass. Most decent hunting clothes do a good job of blocking the wind and rain and retaining heat. However, I have been disappointed with the performance of the expensive synthetic fabrics with the thin insulation. The advertising claims for these clothes are hard to resist, but, in my experience, overall they simply don't keep me as warm as goose-down or wool.

Goose-down is warmest but is bulky and loses almost all of its insulation capabilities if it gets wet. Wool is a bit heavy but retains most of its insulation capability even when wet. In any case, the general rule is this. If it gets wet, get it off. Dry off mechanically with a towel, not by evaporation. Don't continue to wear wet clothes and allow them to air dry while in contact with your skin. Do not allow a young dumb hunter (*like I once was*) to sit with wet socks and pants on in the car even with the heater blowing. Evaporation is still a cooling process even if the air is warm. It's a law of physics. Get the damn wet clothes off! On some rainy camp outs it gets nearly impossible to have dry gear. It might be necessary to go into a nearby town and find a coin laundry in order to use the dryer.

Dress in several thin layers rather than one heavy layer. The layer closest to your skin should be good quality long underwear. It should be smooth so it doesn't cause any rubs or itching. A turtleneck top is a good idea. It adds warmth and prevents itching around your collar. Be sure it's not white. Get it in green, brown, or dark gray. Next can be one or two insulating layers. I especially like the thick wool army commando style sweater for this. You can get them at an army surplus store. Depending on the temperature, the outer layer can either be a heavy coat or a light top with an outer layer that is water / wind resistant. Layering allows you to add or subtract as needed and avoid overheating while hiking in and out of the woods. Avoid the single piece jumpsuit style of clothes for that reason. In addition, the one-piece will force you to go through a wrestling match just at the time when you need to get the suit off in a hurry and find your toilet paper. Nobody needs that. *Thermal underwear now marketed as being like "underwear armor" seems way overpriced to me. But the stuff really works great. So, I guess Ya gotta pay what it costs.*

Contact with large cold mass is a more difficult problem. The weapon you're holding, the tree stump you're seated on, and the ground or the metal tree-stand that your feet are on, are all large cold mass. They will steadily and quickly drain heat out of your body. It is critical to break direct contact of a cold mass by any part of your body. Even your watch might be a problem. If the temperature is in the teens or lower you will curse the day you bought that big heavy watch with the thick metal wrist band. Don't sit out there with half-a-pound of cold steel hugging your wrist.

The soft rubbery closed cell foam material used as bedrolls by backpackers is good for breaking contact with the ground. For my seat and back I cut a piece to fit up inside the back of my hunting jacket and one to fit down inside the back of my pants. Recently I have seen a commercial version of this idea. On especially cold days I do not sit with either the rifle or the bow in my hands or in my lap. They are a large cold mass. Instead I carefully position them so that with a single easy motion they are in my grasp and in shooting position.

Cold hands: Even the best gloves I've tried did not keep my hands warm while still allowing me to handle my weapon. For moderately cold general purposes I have gone back to wool glove / mittens with the flip open top half that allows for the use of my fingers. On extremely cold days I sometimes ditch the gloves, unbutton two buttons in the front of my coat and fold my arms across my chest tucking them deep inside my jacket next to my body where it's about ninety-eight degrees inside. This takes advantage of my own body core heat-mass and warms my hands and fingers much better than any gloves. For this reason I prefer a <u>button front</u> to the wool coat rather than a zipper. It's a small thing but it's important.

Cold feet: The one thing that becomes coldest fastest and that may shorten your hunt or cause you to be unable to remain still is painfully cold feet. In the quest to keep my feet from freezing I have found that even cheap footwear works O.K. as long as I remain active. However, while remaining dead dog still for a long period of time, <u>no boots</u>, (*not even expensive ones*) did a great job. This is because the boots themselves are essentially a large cold mass strapped to your feet. The problem is that boots rugged enough for hiking through rough terrain tend to have a lot of mass, while boots with enough insulation tend to be bulky and very clumsy for hiking in the woods.

Your selection of boots and socks is one area that I would urge you to be very particular about. I don't mean necessarily to spend a lot of money. I just mean, be careful about some details and the style and fit. Because of all the troubles I've hade over the years, I've become somewhat of a nutcase about boots and socks. Poorly designed or bad fitting footgear can cause more very serious problems while hunting than any other piece of gear you drag into the woods. It's more than just cold feet or blisters or a twisted ankle. It's the possibility of a slip and fall deep in the woods while carrying a deadly weapon. The standard issue U.S. army combat boot from the 1970's and 80's, is an example in almost every way of the worst possible boot ever designed by man. Don't even let someone <u>give</u> you a pair.

When I was a young man only a couple manufacturers made great hunting boots and they were very expensive. Now, there are several manufacturers who make perfectly good boots that are reasonably priced. Inside of the boots there is often a removable insole cushion. The ones made with medium density foam do a fair job of insulating.

More recently, manufacturers have switched from foam to gel inserts which are very poor insulators. These seem to act like cold-magnets inside the boots. Avoid the gel inserts or replace them in cold weather boots. My advice would be to look for the following:

- Lightweight and easy on / easy off.
- Insulated inner sole. Not the gel sole.
- Waterproof outer surface. An inner liner that is waterproof doesn't do a lot of good if the outer part allows moisture to remain. Evaporation will cause your feet to get cold.
- Aggressive tread. A deeper and more aggressive tread will dig in and hold in uneven terrain. It's especially important in hunting hill country with rain or snow and on slippery clay logging trails.
- Semi-soft sole. Avoid the very hard material used to make indestructible soles. It has a lot of mass and very poor insulation properties. The semi-soft or semi-hard rubbery soles are lighter and have plenty of service life. They're also much quieter when walking in the woods.

Beware the downhill stick: *I have a special warning that might sound really dumb to those who only hunt flat land. But if you ever hunt in hilly county, this will happen to you sooner or later.*

*You may often find that you are walking parallel to the slope of a wooded hillside. During one of your forward strides you may step on a strong yet fairly small diameter stick, which is pointing downhill, and is covered by wet leaves, frost or snow. This slippery stick can take you off you feet with surprising speed. Especially if your boots have hard soles or don't have an aggressive tread. If it's the downhill leg, you will fall toward your face. If it's the uphill leg you will fall toward your rear and side. I try to avoid stepping on these sticks and feel for them under my boot before shifting weight forward. But still, once in a while a downhill stick gets me. It makes a guy feel really stupid. **But more important is to remember that you have a deadly weapon in your hands. Take the fall as gracefully as possible without losing control of the weapon.** I have demonstrated this to my young nephews. They think I'm nuts.*

I also believe that the quality of your socks is often more important than the boots. It's well worth the price for good, soft, snug, socks which are at least 70% wool. These may become your favorite all-purpose winter socks. But, don't wear them around the house in place of slippers unless you plan to replace them every few years due to the gradual loss of fibers from the bottoms. Don't make the mistake of thinking you can keep your feet warm by packing in another tight layer of socks. The tight pack causes the material to lose insulation properties and reduces the circulation of warm blood to your toes. It's best to have a comfortable snug fit with hunting socks so there is no heel-slip. This will avoid blisters. Don't use new boots on an extended long distance wilderness hunting trip of a lifetime. Break-em in first to be sure they don't cause any problems.

A caution about moccasins: *For a while I carried a pair of wool-lined sheepskin moccasin in my daypack. I would remove my hunting boots once I got to my stand and put on the moccasins along with an extra pair of sox. I also used a chunk of foam insulation to keep my feet from direct contact with the frozen ground. This proved to be the best way to keep my feet comfortably warm all day. But there are a couple major drawbacks. Moccasins have basically no tread on the bottom. So it's very difficult to stand up and walk on snow or on frost covered leaves on uneven ground. Just getting up to walk three steps to pee, got to be a life threatening ordeal. The other problem is that at the end of the day you still need to put your boots back on to walk out of the woods. It's like sticking your boots in the freezer for eight hours and then trying to get your feet back into them. It's not pleasant.*

In snow, ice, and extremely cold weather, no matter what boots and socks you choose, they are in a battle against the laws of thermodynamics. They will lose that battle with time if nothing is done. There are two ways to prolong the time or temporarily reverse the process. First is to carry an extra piece of the insulation material in your daypack. Use this at your stand to break contact between your boots and the ground. Be sure to do the same on the base of your metal tree-stand. It will buy you a doubling or tripling of the time before your feet get cold.

The second solution is to add an external source of heat energy. Chemical heat insoles work moderately well, but still have some drawbacks. On extremely cold days I carry a small can of solid or gelled fuel. I light it in a depression in the ground and roast the bottoms of the boots over it. I also usually cover the boots and legs with some material forming a small canopy to hold in warm air. I do this only after my feet have become so cold that I am unable to sit still. Within about ten minutes my boots and feet are toasty warm. This is low cost, low weight and requires very little room in my daypack. The two or three minutes of movement required may be worth the trade off if it buys two or four additional hours of silent and still hunting.

Also, odd as it may seem, I must caution you about the possibility of setting yourself on fire at just about the time a nice buck shows up. But, that's another story. Don't even ask.

I've read that some old-timers light a small campfire at their deer-stand in order to keep warm. They claim that the smoke from the fire doesn't scare away deer. Instead they say the deer is a curious animal and will actually come to investigate. Their proof is that they have actually been successful. I still think it's not a good idea. Campfires tend to sizzle, hiss and crack which will interfere with hearing a deer approaching. A fire also requires enough tending that the movement is a problem. Do things that tilt the odds in your favor, not things that tilt the odds against you. So, - no fires.

Tips on Making the Move: If you've done everything right up to this point, you've just heard a sound or seen the movement of a deer approaching. Instantly your body systems are brought from near boredom to a state of high readiness. There are still two-dozen ways you can screw this up in just the next few seconds. Among the calls to action is a strong urge to grab your weapon and rush into position to shoot before it gets away. **This is almost always the wrong choice! This deer which you should have killed will have a good chance of getting away.**

The situation is similar to going fishing with a child who hooks into his very first big game fish. For some reason the kid thinks the best thing to do is grab the rod, jerk hard and crank like hell to get the fish landed before it gets away. The line snaps and all the waiting for a big fish is wasted. But watch that same kid fishing a few years later. He waits and watches the tugging at the rod-tip. He feels the fish take and then sets the hook with just a tug. He applies firm pressure, gives and retrieves as he plays the fish and then brings it in easily.

Back to the issue; First of all, if the deer catches your movement and especially if it's already suspicious, you are probably not nearly fast enough to win a game of "quick-draw" against the deer. *For example,* think back about a time when you've seen an idiot dog-owner try to swat at his pesky, obnoxious little rat-dog. Before the idiot's arm is even into the down stroke, the rat-dog is crouched and pushing off with all four. The idiot hits nothing but air. It's about the same if you get caught trying to play quick-draw with a deer. During the one point five seconds it takes to get your rifle to your shoulder and get your sights lined up, the deer booster rockets have kicked in. By the time you get fur in your sights the deer is doing thirty-five miles an hour horizontally, bounding vertically, making sharp turns and putting two-hundred feet more cover between you. **All you've done by rushing, is turn what might have been a fairly routine shot, into a very difficult shot!** Secondly, the deer was originally moving toward you or into your shooting lanes and had not detected you. Sudden movement can only hurt your chances. Stay still until you have the best chance to make the move without being seen. Remember that there may be more than one deer in the area. Check to see that these deer won't set off the alarm when you make your move. This gets tricky when a bunch of deer are present.

Be sure to read the part about the scent cone, deer's eyes and see the diagram of their field of vision. If you don't have an obvious opportunity to make your move when the deer is looking away or when something is interfering with the deer's line of sight, a good time to try is when a deer reaches for something to eat. At this point it is using front vision to look at what it's about to eat and not peripheral vision. If a deer seems suspicious of you by giving a foot stomp, stare, head bob or head weave, be ready also for a fake. They may pretend to reach down for something to eat and then quickly look up. Caught ya, – Ha!

Some guys believe that deer will flick the tail just before they raise their heads from eating. They use this to read as a warning signal to freeze their move if necessary. I don't think this is a highly reliable signal. I've also seen the tail flick just before lowering the head, just before making a step forward, and I've sometimes seen no tail flick at all associated with these moves.

The hardest move decision is on a deer that you've heard approaching from behind. Mentally consider its distance, speed, direction and the cover and terrain between it and you. It may be necessary to take a chance on moving just enough to be able to see it. You might try a partial "corkscrew" move. Also consider your scent cone. If the deer seems to be headed directly toward you or into your scent cone it may be best to make your move sooner than later. *(Detail about this in the section on wind & scent.)*

It's a good idea to keep your bow in a holder rather than across your lap. The holder will position the bow so it's already oriented in nearly a firing position. This reduces the major movement of lifting the bow from your lap and then rotating the whole thing into shooting position. Be sure the holder releases the bow <u>easily</u> and <u>silently.</u> Have your arrow already knocked. With the rifle I generally do keep it low and in my lap unless it gets too cold and I need to break contact with the mass. Then, I lay it carefully near my side in a nearly horizontal position. This makes for a single easy motion to bring the rifle into shooting position. Don't position the rifle so that it is pointing up or down. This requires that you rotate the entire weapon ninety degrees in order to get it into shooting position. This up or down swing of the barrel is much more movement and it's more noticeable than simply keeping the weapon horizontal.

The most cumbersome move to make is in the case of a right hand shooter having to turn all the way for a deer approaching on his right side (*or left-hand shooter on the left side*). Try this on your deer stand sometime. Take a seat facing forward with your weapon. Pretend that a deer is approaching on a line to your immediate side (*left on left or right on right*). Notice what happens as you try to bring the weapon into shooting position. This move requires that you turn your entire body 180 degrees. This means adjusting the feet, hips, arms and shoulders in order to get your weapon into proper shooting position. In contrast, notice how easy the opposite move is to make. If the wind is right it may be wiser to stay still and wait for the deer to pass completely to your opposite side. Then make the move for a quartering away shot. This takes nerves of steel.

Tree stand move; This is more important late in the season after the leaves are down. On your next outing, before you get to your tree-stand, relax your eye and take a look at the woods. Notice the gray-line along the horizon where the branches are dense enough that you can no longer see the sky behind. Every wooded lot or forested area has this gray-line at a different level depending on its age and density. To our eye the gray-line continually appears to change and move as the angle of our viewpoint changes when we move through the woods. From a good distance and from the direction you expect deer to approach take a look at the trees in which your stand is hung. If your tree-stand is above that gray-line, you are silhouetted by the sky. An approaching deer will have a good chance of seeing any move you make. As you approach, take special note of the point on the ground where your tree-stand appears to be above the gray-line. The decision about making your move may depend on the location of this spot. But, there is another important factor to think about. This has to do with the natural vertical angle of the deer's peripheral field of vision. This angle makes it more likely that the deer might detect your movement from farther out. It also works to the hunter's advantage, as the deer gets closer to the tree-stand. The upward angle becomes steep enough that movement overhead is not in the deer's natural field of view. At thirty yards the deer is much more likely to detect your move above than at ten yards.

So, what does all this mean to you? Be aware that it's the movement of your head, and feet that most often gives you away first. You may tend to move your head in response to a sound. You might get away with that. But then, you need to move your feet in preparation to shift your body into position for a shot. Be sure that the movement of your feet is either completely concealed or is timed so that the deer does not see it. Also be aware of a patch of forest floor that I call the *"double caution, don't even blink zone"*. When the deer enters this zone, the hunter is both in the deer's natural visual angle and silhouetted *above* the gray-line. It's extremely hard to get away with any kind of movement when the deer is in this double caution zone. Even if you are quite confident of making a forty-yard kill shot, it does you no good if you get caught trying to make the move. So, a better choice may be to remain dead dog still while the deer is in the double caution zone. At some point as the deer comes fifteen or twenty yards closer, you regain the advantage of the steep visual angle. Then, you'll have a better chance of making the move and the kill shot too. Late-season "wizened deer" do tend to look up in the trees. It might be better to just say "to hell with this tree-stand" and move to a ground blind.

Trick: I have not tried this. An archery hunter told me that when a deer is very close, he sometimes tosses a stick from out of his tree-stand into the brush in order to make sure that the deer's attention is directed away from him. He then makes his draw. This is interesting and seems feasible. But it also could completely backfire if the deer is more startled than curious and simply runs away. Also, if I can get away with the move to make the throw, why not use that time to make my move for the shot instead So, I would not recommend this trick.

The corkscrew move: My good friend Jim, told me that his grandfather taught him this move when he was a young man. Try this experiment with your eyes and head some time while you're seated. First turn your head to the left and to the right taking note of the location of some object that's at the edge of where you can see comfortably. This will probably cover about 220 to 240 degrees. If something is moving behind you and is beyond those angles, and if you absolutely can't resist trying to see it, try the corkscrew move. Lean your upper body just a bit forward and then twist to the side dropping one shoulder while pushing back and up with the other and rotating at your waist. Keep the elbows tucked in close to your body. Tilt your head to the side and down a bit. If you do this correctly your left and right eyes will no longer be horizontal to the ground on top of a neck that has simply rotated. Instead they will be nearly perpendicular to the ground looking back behind you on a neck and upper body that has corkscrewed and rotated slightly. If you do this smoothly, it takes two seconds and it's not nearly as much movement as trying to turn your whole body around. Notice that this enables you to see nearly all the real estate beyond those original angle limits to the left or right. I would only try this when I am reasonably sure that my movement is blocked from view. Otherwise, it's better to stay still.

Also remember, there are times when a deer just goes a different way simply because it decided to go a different way. It doesn't necessarily mean that you did anything wrong. You might have been there to see it, or you might have been home in bed. The deer just did what it did. Not everything that happens in the deer woods is always about you.

Tips on using your eyes: The picture below was taken at late afternoon in mid September.   Notice how important the lighting, color, contrasts and background is for your ability to see the deer.

Do you see antlers? Are you sure? Notice the horizontal lines made by the back and belly versus the vertical lines of the trees and bushes. Notice the dark brown and white at its tail. Sometimes in heavy cover this is about all you might see.   The white underbelly may not be visible. Sometimes it's the black nose outlined in white that is visible through the brush.   Look for the eyes too.   Notice how important background light might be as it helps to nicely outline the left ear. If that ear moves your eyes will definitely pick it up. **Even when a deer is standing still in heavy cover, the <u>ears, nose and tail</u> are the parts that are most likely to move and give away its position.** One side of this bucks rack does blend in fairly well with the brush. Heavy cover with no background light and no contrast can make it hard to see antlers.   But if it moves, the antlers move too and it's usually not so hard to see.   Sometimes you get lucky with a lighter color or even a shine off the antlers.

Another thing to think about with the antler picture is the shot placement and the kill zone. The small tree that lines up with the deer's front leg is exactly in the way of the perfect kill zone shot. With a rifle or shotgun I might take the front shoulder shot through the opening. This shot into the heavy mass of the front shoulder will transfer a lot of energy and, take the deer down on the spot, as my dad would say, "*ass over teakettle*". I'm not sure where this phrase comes from but it's exactly correct. With a bow, I would not take this shot. I also don't like the idea of trying to thread an arrow through the trees. It might be better to hold at full draw and wait for the deer to take one slow half-step forward, exposing the perfect kill zone shot in the opening.

The photo below was taken at dusk in late November. The deer is harder to see. Its color is greyer than the September deer and blends in better with the gray background. What you most often get while hunting is the grey color, low light, little contrast, poor background light and you can add in plenty of obstructions.

You might notice a slight shine depending on how light hits the fur. It's fairly easy to see the deer nosing the ground near the center of the picture. Notice the deer laying down to the right of the big tree. Look for the black nose, tiny black eyes and the tips of the ears.

Your eye is drawn toward the color, shape and outline of the deer tail. This first gives away the deer. Then you pick out the eye, ear and nose. Get used to this. Notice the other deer left and farther out.

Looking straight at you: This deer is less than twenty yards away. See the nose and eyes looking toward the camera from between the trees in the center.

Leaf Trail   **Grass Trail**   **Snow Trail**

Another way to use your eyes is to notice subtle changes in the ground cover. Notice the deer trails in each of these pictures. Many times you will not have clear tracks to follow. With leaves on the ground you need to see the trail of disturbance. Even with a little snow, you need to see the general pattern of a trail. Notice the path through the grass which is a little shorter, bent and more green than the rest of the grass. Sometimes these can't be seen unless you are at the correct angle. Learn to scan and occasionally crouch, kneel or sweep with you're vision to the sides as you walk.

The "transparent wall": For an example, take another look at the picture captioned "looking straight at you". The deer is actually standing broadside to the camera. Notice to the right of the trees where there is a slightly different patch of brown color. See the horizontal line of its back that break up some vertical lines of the trees. See the small tuft of white at its tail and parts of the rear leg.

My favorite deer-stands often overlook young growth forest with heavy cover. There are two tricks that this can play on your eyes late in the fall when most of the leaves are down and before there is snow on the ground. First is that the trees and cover can appear to blend into a solid wall of silver-gray and earth tones. Your eyes would lead you to believe that this wall is the limit of your visibility. However, when something moves through the area just beyond that wall, you begin to notice that you can in fact see farther out than your eyes would lead you to believe. This wall is actually transparent out to another (X) amount of distance. With snow on the ground you can see how much farther that distance actually is. But without snow, if a deer gets into this region undetected, and if it becomes wary, remaining motionless, it will be very hard to see. It will blend in nearly perfectly with the wall. If you move or make a sound at this point, you will probably be surprised to see only a quick flash of shadow-like movement as the deer leaves the area. So, be sure to include the transparent wall as you do your visual scans.

A second trick is that during certain periods of the day, the sun can cause a reflective glare on the wall that can in fact prevent you from seeing through it. At one of my stands this glare lasted for over an hour in the mid-morning. During that hour I was frustrated to be able to hear a deer moving slowly through the cover just beyond the glare. I never did see it, but I knew that if I moved it could see me. I abandoned this stand in part for that reason.

Vanishing deer: Part of the reason I am so picky about keeping my rifle in a good position has to do with a deer's ability to vanish. Let me explain.

The area that I hunt during rifle season is quite hilly. My favorite stands are often somewhere between one third and two thirds of the way down the side of a hill overlooking a valley with heavy cover on the opposite side. Good deer trails more often tend to run parallel to the slope rather than up and down the hills. It's these trails on the opposite side that I am most interested in covering. Since the ground on the opposite slope is basically tilted up toward me, it allows me to see these trails over the entire area up the slope nearly to the ridgeline and far to the left and right. This gives me a lot more visual field to cover. It's great if there's snow. It's still great without snow if the hearing conditions are good. But it's very tough on gray days when things are moist and quiet. It's a huge visual field to try and cover with eyes only. In these conditions it's always surprising when deer movement shows up in the middle of my visual field. I wonder how the hell this deer got in there without being noticed. How long has it been there? Where did it come from? Even more amazing is the vanishing trick. I spend half an hour wondering where the hell the deer went to. Are there such things as deer tunnels?

In these hunting conditions, if I take my eyes off the deer for just two seconds while looking to reach for my rifle it can be very hard to locate the deer again. Then I have to waste time trying to find the deer somewhere in the large visual field. That's why I'm careful to position the rifle so I can reach for it without looking and with one smooth motion. My advice is, <u>don't take your eyes off the deer.</u> If you use a scope, practices finding your aim point by first focusing on a particular target spot with both eyes open as you bring the weapon up into shooting position. Then look to see if the spot you wanted is in the scope. Practice this a few times. Also, if you have an adjustable scope, it might be better to use lower power magnification so as to have a wider view.

What about deer's-eyes: This section goes to one of the hardest and most important decisions for a rookie deer hunter to learn about without first messing up on half a dozen deer. So, I'm going to use a lot of ink and paper on this point. When a deer is known to be nearby, the problem isn't with "*staying still*", it's with "*make the move*" <u>when the deer can't see you.</u> It's a hard point to write about. <u>I want to stress its importance but at the same time I don't want to cause you to freeze-up on your deer-stand when you should be making the move.</u>

First I'd like you to do a couple short experiments with your own eyes. It works best if you can step outside and have plenty of objects in a larger area to view. Pick a fixed direction to point your nose and eyes straight ahead at a central object. Keep both eyes open and take a relaxed view of the image in your brain. Notice that your brain draws attention to anything that might be moving in the peripheral part of the view. Without moving your head, close one eye. Notice that objects disappear from view in about a third (just guessing) of the image from the outermost side of the closed eye. This is the peripheral part of the image from that eye. About two thirds of the original image toward the center remains in view. This means that approximately two thirds of the image you have in your brain is basically a duplicate of the cross-over region of the image from the other eye. This is your predominantly forward looking binocular vision, the vision of a predator. Now try another experiment to get an idea of what a deer is able to see. Close one eye, and while keeping your head still, move your open eyeballs to see more of the side view. (*Both eyes will move, but only one is open*) Notice how much more of the side view you are able to see. Hold the image a few seconds and then do the same thing with the opposite eye. Imagine what it would be like, if your eyeballs were mounted on your head in such a way that you could comfortably see both the far left and right images at the same time without going through all these gymnastics. But that's not even half of the story. It's only a poor sample based on what human eyes can do. Instead of having $2/3^{rd}$ frontal binocular with $1/3^{rd}$ peripheral, the deer has vision that is more like $1/3^{rd}$ frontal binocular and $2/3^{rd}$ peripheral. Human peripheral vision goes out to bout 170 degrees. In his book, Way of the Whitetail, Dr. Leonard Lee Rue III, says that a deer's eyes are mounted on its head so that a panoramic view of 310 degrees might be possible. Also, deer are not completely color blind as many hunters once believed. But they are a little limited in this regard. They see very well in the (UV) and yellow parts of the color light spectrum. Hunters are able to wear blaze orange because although it's highly visible to humans, it's not in the portion of the light spectrum that is highly visible to deer. Night vision is another issue. The deer's UV light sensitivity coupled with a much larger eye, more rods inside the eye, and a reflective layer called the tapetum (*which is what causes the deer's eyes to reflect a shine at night*) give the deer night vision that is thought to be 1000 times better than humans.

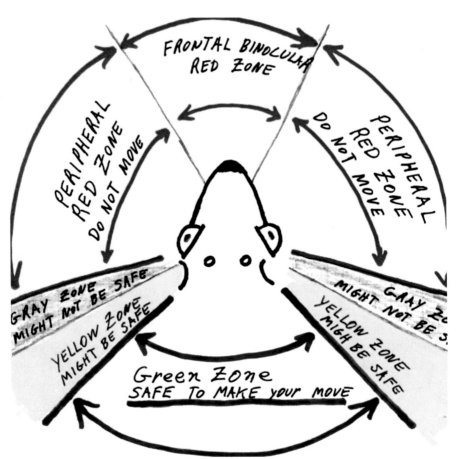

When the deer focuses forward using predominantly its binocular vision, the red zone collapses forward somewhat and the green zone expands. The yellow and grey zones are also pushed forward. This gives the hunter more safe zone for making the move.

My *"best guess"* advice about not getting caught by the deer's peripheral vision has to do with the above diagram. There are a whole bunch of disclaimers. <u>So be careful how you interpret this.</u> Also, my diagram assumes the worst case scenario in which you have no choice to wait for an obstruction and the deer doesn't reach for food to create an opportunity. I also assume that you are at ground level with the deer, not up in a tree stand. From up above in a tree stand you may be able to get away with making your move at angles that you would never try on the ground.

Let's suppose that the deer is standing still or moving slowly and looking around with a somewhat aroused sense of caution. Maybe it caught a bit of scent and is a little suspicious. You remain perfectly still, watching and hoping for a chance to make the move. When the deer turns its head (*Not necessarily its body*) so that you are in the green zone relative to the deer's head position, it is safe to make the move. When a deer is reaching for something to eat it is almost always focusing forward with frontal binocular vision which greatly reduces its peripheral vision. That too may be a good time to make your move even if you are in part of the red zone. (*Watch out for the fake*) If the deer's attention is drawn to some other sound or movement in the woods, it may look in that direction using frontal binocular vision which reduces its peripheral view. This might provide an opportunity to make the move even if you are in the yellow or gray zone. **But you've got to be silent too.** The ear is likely to be overlapping coverage of the yellow and grey region. If a deer is moving quickly, there is a good chance that it is using mostly frontal vision. The faster the deer is running and in wooded cover, the more likely it is that they are using forward vision. They can seem blinded to the sides. But this is tricky. I suspect they are sometimes alternating as they run. So you might have a 70/30 chance of getting away with the move if you are off to the sides. It's best to try and **wait for an obstruction if you can.** If the deer is standing still or at a walking gait it's best to assume that it's using wide view. In that case, **if you are anywhere in the red zone, do not move.** Let the deer pass until you have an obstruction or a better angle.

Jet fighter: *Take another look at the vision diagram and imagine that instead of a deer, it's actually the nose of a jet fighter aircraft. With no offensive weapons, the pilot knows that the best chance for survival is the fact that it's the fastest thing in the sky. The only way any predator could possibly have a chance to intercept this fast mover, would be to attack with pursuit angles greater than 45 degrees from the sides. That's why the pilot is always doubly concerned with any unseen threats coming from those angles. Once a threat is detected, all the pilot has to do is turn so the angle of pursuit drops to his favor and then kick on the speed. The predator is left behind just looking stupid. The way a deer's eyes are mounted on its head is not a coincidence. A deer is the fastest mover in the woods.*

For about the past thirty years it has been well known among hunters that clothes need to be made with fabrics that don't contain U.V. emitting dies. In addition they should **not be washed in the detergents that have fabric brighteners.** To the eyes of a deer, these dyes and detergents make you glow in the blue U.V. spectrum like a neon sign. As a young hunter I once experienced this myself. Tracks indicated that deer routinely entered an open field to get at abandoned apple trees. I stationed myself near their exit trail along a fencerow about a hundred yards away, confident that I was invisible because of my camo. The wind was in my favor and I made no sound. I watched three deer feed for a while on apples that had fallen into the tall grass. But before they started across the field one of the deer got a glimpse of me and then did a double-take. The deer stared straight at me and then so did the other two. At the time, I wasn't sure what had happened, but I knew without a doubt that they saw me. Back at camp I told the story to my good friend Paul. He told me that he read about the brighteners in laundry detergent. For the first time in my dullard brain, it occurred to me that reading was not simply a task of drudgery required for schoolwork. It could be an important hunting weapon. That's when I started reading everything I could get my hands on about hunting. In the event that someone has washed your camo in this type of detergent I would recommend that you put it through the washing machine a couple times without any detergent to try and rinse out the brighteners. In addition hang the clothes outside for a couple days. When you get to the woods you might also rub them around in fresh dirt or a mud hole. (*No, I'm not kidding.*)

So anyway, assuming that you're not glowing like a neon sign, all you need to do is avoid detection from the deer's wide-angle vision when you try to make your move.

Time versus coverage problem. Think about yourself as a very sophisticated high-tec sensor device. Your vision sensors best cover the front door and parts of the side. Your hearing sensors cover all 360-degrees and are most heavily relied on for covering the backdoor. Each sensor has its limitations of distance. In some directions you can see farther than you can hear, or you can hear beyond what you are able to see. The combination of these limits make up your effective coverage of the area. It changes with differing hunting conditions. Every stand will have at least one weak spot for coverage. But, if you are reasonably alert, your sensors will probably pick up a high percentage of deer that enter the area. Those deer are not the problem. It's the ones that slip in undetected, or the ones in the gray area behind the transparent wall, or the ones beyond your coverage, never detected until it's too late that are the problem. These deer might represent a possibility of increasing your success rate.

But now think of it from the deer's point of view. Suppose a deer is moving generally toward you by natural inclination from somewhere thirty to fifty yards beyond your coverage. Suppose that it is exercising a moderate level of caution as usual. Now remember, the deer has sophisticated sensors also, and they are all better than yours. In some ways the deer may have better coverage than you do. The time problem is this. How much time does it take for this deer to move the additional thirty to fifty yards before it gets into your coverage? **From the deer's advantage point, how much time are you inside its coverage, while the deer is still outside of yours?** Just guessing, let's say that on average it takes three to five minutes for the deer to close that gap. This is an absolutely critical window of time. Think about it. What happens to your odds of seeing this deer if you move or make a sound on average every six minutes? They drop by some very large factor. But, if you're still and silent for twice as long, your odds increase by a very large factor. The difference is huge! Don't blow it in the last few minutes.

The whole idea is this. It's a contest involving your sensors versus theirs. It's a time versus coverage problem. You need to reduce the effectiveness of their sensors by remaining still and silent for a long period of time, while at the same time using your own sensors to their best effect. I don't think it's practical to try and be on full alert with detailed sensor scans constantly all day. You'd be fatigued in an hour. So, all I'm saying is that it's reasonable to sit still and silent and do a careful scan once every fifteen or twenty minutes. This gives you decent coverage and a good possibility of detecting the deer. In addition it provides a short window of time with the least possibility that an undetected deer might be present. This is the best time to give yourself permission to move if you must. Otherwise, stay still, stay silent.

The last moment: It's a little maddening to have done absolutely everything right, and then fail due to something extremely small and picky that happens in the last moment. The last moment occurs at a time when the deer may be very close. You've defeated the deer's nose, and eyes up to this point. The final problem in the last moment is most often the deer's ears. At close range they're like precise radar with 360 degree detection which will nail you if you make a sound. This is especially important to archery hunters who must get close for the shot.

On a crisp October morning just before the sun peaked over the horizon I was up in the tree with my bow. Within half an hour I heard a deer approaching and then saw a patch of brown moving in my direction through the trees. I made the first part of my move for the shot and then waited. It was a nice buck heading for the exact spot I wanted, a shooting lane with a clear broadside shot at fifteen yards. This was one of those rare moments when everything had gone so perfectly that I began to think about the story I would tell and the venison steaks I would have in my freezer. I started to draw the bow. Oops! Suddenly I was reminded of a small detail that I had failed to correct. This bow had a habit of creaking on the first draw. Not on every draw, but just on the first draw after it sat for a while. The buck looked up at me in mid draw and then made a move that was truly breathtaking in terms of speed and athleticism. From a safe distance it turned back to stomp its hoof at me and to give me a little hell about being out in the woods with a creaky bow limb.

This past season I went to the woods with a new tree-stand that I had selected after a good bit of studying. It was expensive. But it too had a few unexpected problems. I immediately took it home to my garage and "doctored" it up a little. The built-in bow holder needed some stick-on neoprene to make it quiet. The stand also creaked when I stood up shifting my weight from the seat to the platform. This would be the ultimate no-no and would almost guarantee a lost opportunity at the last moment. I took the bolts apart at all the stress points and added a little silicone grease between the Teflon washers. Now the stand is perfectly silent.

These are only two of endless examples of the types of extremely small things that will certainly cost you a deer in the last moment if you don't fix them in advance. I can't list every possibility here for you, but you get the idea. **Find em and fix em.**

Other Handy stuff to keep in mind:

   Emergencies: I was an Army medic and also while in college, an Emergency Medical Technician. However, for some reason I never carried first-aid gear with me while hunting. One time I cut two of my fingers on my broadhead blades. These weren't life-threatening, but they were annoying and difficult to stop from bleeding. Later I gave this some thought. It's stupid of me to be walking around deep in the woods without even so much as a band-aid. What about a bad fall with a broken bone or getting seriously stuck with an arrow or a gun accident? These are remote but real possibilities. So, now I carry a small homemade medical first-aid kit in a plastic bag. Don't bother with the stupid little first aid kits in the plastic box that are available in the local drug store. They're mostly just nice packaging. They're expensive for what you get and they don't contain the key things you might really need if you have a serious accident. For the small stuff I have a few band aids, but I also carry some medic tape, gauze pads, and elastic bandage. You will of coarse have your knife, belt, boot laces and perhaps other sources of useful material. In a serious situation you should be able to seal a wound, stop almost any type of bleeding or make a good splint if needed. All this was inexpensive, light weight and takes up very little space in my daypack.

   Hollywood: It is only in the half-baked, numb-nuts, minds of some Hollywood movie writers that I have ever heard about any hunter having a tradition of eating the liver or any other uncooked part of a deer. (*as in "Red Dawn"*) Also, only in the movies does a supposedly experienced deer-hunter ever tie his deer to the <u>front hood</u> of the car for the long drive home. (*as in "The Deer Hunter"*) Everyone outside of Hollywood knows that the heat from the engine would not be good for the meat. Tie it to the roof or the trunk. Furthermore, only in the movies does a really serious hunter go out with a bunch of drunken idiots. And if one of those idiots were to take my rifle from the trunk and carelessly toss it on the pavement, (*as in "The Deer Hunter"*) a very intense, eyeball to eyeball, "R" rated adult language type of dialogue, would certainly have followed.

Save $ Ground-Blind: Go to your local fabric store when they're having a sale and buy a few yards of camouflage material. Stop at your local hardware store and get an inexpensive grommet kit. Fold the material so it's doubled near the edges where you put in the grommets. This will give it plenty of strength. Tie a couple lengths of cord (not white) to the material so that it can easily be suspended or draped over the existing cover at you blind. This will eliminate all the holes in your blind and leave the top open so you can see and hear. It's a good idea to lean some branches from nearby cover against the material. This gives it more authenticity and helps keep the wind from buffeting it.

Save $ Four-Wheel Drive: If you must use a family vehicle that doesn't have four wheel drive in order to go into remote areas where roads are not plowed and where ruts can quickly turn bottomless, I suggest that you carry a couple good long lengths of tow-straps and a device commonly called a *"come-along"*. Don't get a junky cheap one. When you need it, you really need it to work without trouble. This is a heavy duty ratchet device with a long handle and a cable or strap that will pull with a force of one or two tons. That's enough to pull a vehicle out of almost anything you could get stuck in. The trick is that your vehicle needs to be within reach of another vehicle or a good sized tree to act as an anchor point. That's what the two long lengths of tow straps are for.

Save $ Clothes: Wearing a garment made with hunter's fluorescent orange is required by law in most states while hunting deer with a gun and also while hunting upland game. These laws are very specific depending on what state you're in. It may require a hat and/or coat, or even specify a certain minimum number of square inches. This might force you into having to go out and buy additional clothes for hunting even though you may already own something that would be perfect except for the color requirement. Instead of doing that, I wear my hunters orange upland game vest over top of my wool outfit. This keeps me in compliance with the law, allows me to use any of my favorite cold weather garments, gives me double use of my upland game vest, saves me money and gives me a nice large additional pouch in the back for carrying my seat cushion and some extra socks.

Save $ Hardware / Home-garden stores: Some gear can be found in hardware stores at about half the price of specialty sporting shops.   (*Folding saw, pruning clippers, jelled fuel, strong cord.*) Strong cord is a handy thing to have. Often times its better to tie back a leafy branch at your stand rather than clip it off. Tied back, it will provide cover and helps break up your outline. Consider a cheap plastic toboggan style sled for use as a deer drag. This is much lees costly than a specialty deer drag and it works great. Also stop in and look around at your local Army / Navy store.

Flashlights: Do not use a flashlight that has a simple sliding or toggle (on-off) switch that can be accidentally turned on while inside your pocket or daypack. Its batteries may be dead when you need it most. It's also good to try and use the same size batteries in flash lights, radios, GPS, etc. In this way, chances are good that you'll have a back-up if you need one in case of an emergency.

Baiting: When you see a gas station parking lot stacked with piles of bait, it can suddenly seem like a good idea to buy a bag and toss it into the truck. In part, this urge is playing on your desire to have an added edge in attracting deer. Depending on your state game laws, baiting may or may not be legal and there might be a bunch of special restrictions about when, where and how much bait you can use. For some hunters it's also an ethics question regardless of the laws.   In years past, I've heard about guys dumping two ton truckloads of bait on their property. To me, that seemed excessive and unsportsmanlike. It's also thought to contribute to the spread of disease in the deer herd and is mostly illegal now.

One morning, while archery hunting, I found a few remains of an abandoned bait pile in the woods. I decided to hang my tree stand nearby. A nice big doe approached quickly until it got to within about thirty yards.   Then it became extremely wary.   Not just that it *happened* to be looking up in the trees, it was *purposely* looking up. Got me! The deer skulked off carefully. I've never had a deer act like that in all the years I've hunted in none-baited areas. Two of my nephews have had a very similar sort of thing happen. The deer simply became much more wary. In my opinion, if you scout and set-up as I describe in this book, your chances for success are actually better without the use of bait.

Conservation Officer: My Dad kind-a liked to bump into a C.O. once in a while back in the 1970's and 80's. They were friendly and had good information about where the fish were biting, where the partridge numbers seemed to be up, and reports about the deer population. They were often avid outdoorsmen themselves who shared in our values. Mostly, the C.O would just check to see that we were properly licensed. We figured it was part of their job, so we didn't mind. I was impressed by how polite and respectful they always seemed to be, especially toward my dad and toward other older hunters. It was as if they knew that their job required them to intrude on sacred time, so they approached with almost an *"I'm sorry to bother you"* type of attitude. I envied them for having jobs that allowed them to spend so much time in the woods, until one of them explained that since it's their busiest time of year, they almost never get time off themselves to enjoy the opening of hunting season.

Beginning around the 1990's, and for the past two decades, a lot of hunters detected a shift in the attitude of new young C.O.'s. From numerous stories I've collected, it seems like a trend with wide roots. I suspect that the ranks of the C.O.'s are being filled more with young men and women who are not necessarily hunters themselves, and who might not have be raised in the culture of a hunting family. So, they don't fully understand hunters or share in our values. They may have pursued their college degree in an atmosphere steeped with liberal environmentalism. Their attitude tends to treat hunters in general, more as bothersome pests that have to be controlled and tolerated. They tend to be overly intrusive and authoritative. They start from a more adversarial, suspicious presumption that the hunter is probably doing something wrong. They seem more interested in finding a way to issue a ticket. It's sad, but that's just the way it is.

Just For the record, hunters have been "green" since long before it became a popular fad. Hunters supported the passage of the Federal Aid in Wildlife Restoration Act., also known as the Pittman-Robertson act of 1937 which is still in affect today. This legislation placed a special tax on guns and ammunition to be used solely for conservation purposes. (*Archery equipment was added in 1970*) These funds created the U.S. Biological Survey, the U.S. Fish and Wildlife Service, and purchased the lands at a time when no-one else cared. It remains today as the primary source of funding for departments of natural resources and conservation in all fifty states.

The price tag paid directly by hunters due to this legislation is now over $5 billion. In addition this law prohibits the states from using license fees for any purpose other than for the fish and game departments. Hunters, do more to preserve habitat, land, water and wildlife than the entire list of "green" anti-hunting environmentalist groups combined.

Every year, the book of hunting regulations becomes thicker, more detailed and more complicated due to endless tinkering by bureaucrats. Depending on the state, and even the county within that state, certain things may or may not be legal. Some of these laws go to extremely fine detail. They may specify the exact legal hunting time down to the minute, the draw weight and type of bows, the size and type of arrow tips, the caliber and type of firearms, the number of rounds in the chamber, the use of radio communication, the use of bait, drives, lights, how much hunters orange is required down to the square inch, and tagging and transporting the deer carcass for meat processing or for taxidermy.

Don't let a great day in the woods be spoiled by an unnecessary problem with the Conservation Officer. <u>Your hunting time is far too precious!</u> By precious, I don't just mean due to the time, effort and expense. I mean the actual <u>rarity</u> of the mental and spiritual enrichment you get from these few hours, alone in the woods, free from any source of anxiety. Any gain that you thought you might have derived from *knowingly* violating the rules is simply not worth it. Even if you get away with it, the pride of acomplishment, joy, and tranquility within yourself is destroyed. This is the heart and sole of why you're out there. If you <u>do</u> get caught, it's also a good assumption that the C.O. has probably already heard any of the half-baked dipstick excuses that you might have cooked up in your teeny tiny hunters mind.

On the other hand, if you *un-knowingly* violate some obscure, dumb-ass game law, it's a good working assumption that the C.O. is <u>not</u> going to use discretionary judgment and give you a reasonable break. It's best to think of it as a game, in which the state is looking for some way to give you a ticket, and you are trying hard not to let them score. Get a copy of the hunting regulations which are usually in a booklet available where your buy your license. Read it carefully and <u>pay attention</u> to the <u>little asterisks and the fine print</u>. I know it's a pain, but it's your job, and it's your best defense.

Daypack Lists: (*I hate lists. Make your own list. But read this too.*) Small things that you might forget can do no harm, so long as you <u>don't</u> really need them. But it's odd how they can sometimes cause a minor problem to cascades into a serious situation, if you <u>do</u> need them. Suppose that it's raining and cloudy. You get a little lost and then discover that you forgot your compass. You wander around until dark. Or perhaps you've fallen and broke an ankle. Not a big deal, you make a splint, you'll survive. These situations might cause you to spend an uncomfortable few hours or even a whole night in the woods. Still you should survive. But then you find out that the matches in the plastic baggie you've been carrying in your hunting jacket for the past three years are all wet from the rain. The rain starts to freeze or turns to snow. This night is going to be miserable at least, and could end up costing your life, simply because you can't make a fire. You'll be O.K. without food and water for the night or even for a few days. Water is important but it's easy to find in deer country. But if you're lost or injured and need to get warm, you really need fire and you need it right now. The irony is that this kind-a-shit usually happens to guys who are experienced woodsmen and who should know better. They get too comfortable with being in the wilderness. They lose fear and therefore lose caution. A guy with a little fear will have a knife, compass, and a way to make fire every time. I'm not shit'n about this! If you forget your compass then you better damn well <u>not</u> forget your lighter! Not matches, a lighter! Not a little dumb-ass safety lighter either! A flame thrower! You can get good ones at cigar shops. Forget about carrying a flint or rubbing sticks. The wood is wet and snow covered and this situation is no time to screw around trying to prove you're an Eagle Scout. If you <u>do</u> carry matches, make sure to put them in something positively water tight. I don't care what else you put on your survival list, but mine starts with the big four; compass, lighter and knife. Toilet paper is fourth, but that's just me.

Good hunting.

The "Big Deal" About Scouting
Part - 4

I expect to catch the most grief because of my caution in the seventh rule against over-scouting. Most outdoor writers would be inclined toward the idea that scouting is of the utmost importance. It's a little more important for archery hunters than gun hunters. But it's not nearly as important as magazines would lead you to believe. My problem is with the fanatics. Volumes are written about scouting every year and if you believe it all, you need to be a genius to figure out where to sit your butt in the woods. Authors focus on the layout of terrain and signs of deer movement including runs, droppings, tracks, scrapes, rubs, food, water, and bedding areas. Some authors have recommended spending weeks in the woods "patterning" deer movements. Hunters in the rabid stage (*and this includes me*) are most susceptible to believing a lot of this bull and overbuying, over-reading and over-scouting. The truth is that within a single day of scouting in deer country you can find several good stands and have a general idea of the terrain and trails in the immediate area. At that point, your odds are nearly as good as anyone else's. It's a giant deer-scramble in the first two or three days of gun deer season. Tilting the odds in your favor simply means finding a good stand, and then obeying the other six rules. The primary reasons why spending weeks "*patterning a deer*" can be instantly made irrelevant on opening day is that; *"There are nine-hundred-thousand other smelly goofballs tromping around in the woods". They will either have spooked the deer out of its pattern or shot it themselves!"*

If time was not a big issue I would probably like to have about two full days to scout my hunting area, especially for archery hunting. The additional information that I might get on a third day isn't all that valuable. But, even one day of scouting is usually enough to find out what you need to know. Half a day can be adequate. If you only have a few days to hunt, time is even more precious. Don't spend it looking at deer-shit through a microscope.

Finding a good stand: <u>Go back to part one and read the criterions in rule seven very carefully.</u> Ideally, you should spend some time scouting for locations that meet these criteria sometime prior to opening morning. **But, if for some reason you find that you must hunt in an unfamiliar area on opening morning, my advice would be to find a decent stand soon rather than a perfect stand later.** It's more important that you get your butt still and get silent. Take a compass reading and head into the woods.

- **Look for the edges** where one type of terrain changes into another; young growth versus mature trees, cattail lowlands versus upland, farm fields versus woods, hills and valleys versus a plateau. Game-trails often follow the edges.
- **Look for some young growth** a few years following a forest fire or an area that was logged.
- **Look for what a deer looks for when hunted.** A place with plenty of cover, plenty of quick and easy escape routes and a place where it's hard for anything to sneak up on them undetected.
- **Look for two or three, well-used, intersecting or parallel trails.** Then look for a stand within range of them. This gives you more real estate to cover and more possible shot opportunities with less concern about the wind direction. It also improves the chances for having a crossing broadside shot.
- **Look for the weaknesses in a potential stand.** Even a great stand has a weak side. This side has the most difficulty with your ability to make a shot, make the move, hear, see, or with wind direction. Try to put all the weaknesses on one side. If possible, make that your back side. It's good if the weak side also appears to be the least likely approach for deer. In addition, if the wind is also moving toward that direction, you have a great stand location.
- **Look for a backup stand.** In the event that the wind becomes a problem it makes good sense to simply find a second stand by scouting the opposite and adjacent sides of the same intersecting trails that your first stand is covering. That solves the wind-scent problem fairly easily.

Sometimes you may be deciding between stand locations that are only five or ten yards apart, but which might offer one advantage or disadvantage over the other. Have a seat for a few minutes at each spot and think through the scenarios. Trust your gut on this.

Trail types: It's probably a little <u>more important for early season archery hunters</u> to think about the types of trail patterns you're covering. Rifle hunters usually have enough range that these things are of less concern. In my experience, it seems better to cover a few well-used trails instead of a whole bunch of lesser-used spider trails. It makes it easier to predict the general approach and probable direction of deer moving in the area. In the past I have favored going deep in the woods to get away from the other hunters. But overlooked nooks-n-crannies that are not too deep can be just as good.

This paragraph is a very tricky point for me to write. It will seem like double-talk, but its not. Well used trail are sometimes referred to by trophy buck hunters as "doe trails". This is because they are predominantly used by doe. Doe are more plentiful than bucks and more often travel in groups along trails in a routine almost daily pattern. This leaves a very noticeable deer trail. But, just because these are called "doe trails" doesn't mean that you won't see a nice buck on or near them. It's not like there's a sign in the woods that says "*no bucks allowed*" on this deer trail. For most hunters these trails are good places to start looking for a stand. On the other hand, if you are an avid "buck only hunter", you need to use your eyes to see a different and much more subtle trail of disturbance passing through the foliage. These are used less regularly by a deer that is more likely traveling alone. You might suspect that this is a buck trail. That might be true. But without more evidence, it still could be a trail from a lone doe, perhaps along with a yearling. It's best if you can follow it enough to find another sign of a buck such as a scrape or rub or larger than average tracks. But still, <u>food </u>and <u>sex </u>are the keys. Stay close to major intersecting trails that lead to **food sources**. The doe will be going for the food and bucks will be going for the doe.

> *Trail patterns continually change from one type to another and to another and back again as they go from bed to food to safety to water to shade to scrapes and back to food or safety or beds.*

Spider Trails: Spider trails are usually found in feeding areas where the deer have a habit of meandering as they munch. In some cases you can find a stand that allows coverage of nearly the entire area. But it might be better to find a spot along one of the main entrance or exit trails and within range of another major crossing trail.

Single Trail: I usually try to avoid hunting on a single trail unless there is something special about the situation. In one case I was hunting on a small plot of woods on private property bordering some farmland. A single trail was the best I could do. But it was aided by a nice funnel of cover that encouraged a lot of deer traffic. It turned out to be a very good spot. When I'm hunting on larger acreage I often simply follow the main trail until I find another good crossing trail. This offers the potential for more deer traffic and more stand locations with less concern about the wind direction.

Crooked "Y" Trail: Often you'll find a main trail that splits off into two well used trails forming a crooked "Y" shape. These are about the same as a single trail as far as the likelihood of deer passing, however you have more options for a stand locations. Tracks might help you guess the direction of deer traffic either moving from the main and splitting, or coming from the split trails into the main. Your stand might be located on either side of the intersection or up inside the split trails. This allows you to take advantage of the best position for the wind direction and available cover.

Parallel Trails: If you find a good single trail that you think you want to cover, it's often easy to find another parallel trail that would double your coverage. I like these situations for archery hunting but not so much with a riffle. I usually take a short walk directly away from the first trail and count off 50 or 60 paces while looking and hoping for a parallel trail. If I find one, I start looking for a stand that splits the distance. This doubles the real estate I'm able to cover and shots on either trail are still well within my range.

Crossing Trails "X": Well used crossing trails offer a very good pattern. These allow four possible stand locations facing the intersection. I like to back away from the intersection placing greater importance on having shooting lanes to the sides covering both main trails. This stand might be good in several wind conditions but is most excellent if the wind is coming from the intersection. You gain the additional advantage, that even deer approaching on the trails from behind, might never be inside the width of your scent cone. But it also means that you must be doubly sure to be still, silent, and use your ears as deer may be approaching from behind.

Parallel Trails & One Crossing Trail: I call this the "**H**" pattern even though the crossing trail doesn't actually dead-end. This pattern of trails is not terribly hard to find if you scout for them. These are excellent because it increases the possibility of deer traffic by another third. The special note about these is that you need to have good cover for a stand location inside of either the top or bottom of the "H" in order to get the best coverage of all three trails.

Double Parallel Crossing Trails #: This means for example, you have parallel trails going east-west and another pair going north-south forming a box. These are harder to find. It's even more uncommon that good stand locations exists in the center of these trails with good cover and open shooting lanes within range of all four trails. If all of this came together at one place I suppose it would be the perfect stand. I happened to find a double parallel spot recently. It nearly drove me nuts trying to decide where the best location would be for my stand in order to take advantage. I ended up simply treating it the same as an "H" pattern favoring three good sides and giving up on one of the trails. I'd rather cover three trails from a great location than try to cover four trails from a poor location.

E-Scouting: I highly recommend that you visit the U.S. Geological Survey web site. This site makes it very easy to view and print USGS maps and aerial photographs of your hunting area. The aerial photos used in combination with TOPO maps are a powerful tool. The photos can show you details such as the type and density of the cover and where crop fields are bordered by forest, while the TOPO map of the same area gives you the ridgelines and contours. The first few times you look at a TOPO map might be a little confusing. It's best to start with an area that you already know from being there on the ground. It helps to scale the maps to the same size as the aerial photos. The photos go down to one or two meters resolution. E-scouting can quickly point you to several areas worth checking out before you even get there. The State Department of Natural Resources also has help on their web site. If you don't already have a hunting area selected, you might want to check into the statistics on deer harvest for the counties you are considering. It's also a good idea to look at the availability of State and National Forrest lands open to hunting.

Trail Camera: Remote trail cameras continue to become more sophisticated and the price-tag seems to be coming down too. The pictures of what goes on in the woods over time can be fun and interesting. A picture of a big buck might help to weld your butt to a tree-stand that you otherwise might have abandoned. You also find out the time of day (*or night*) when deer tend to move through the area. Trail cameras might also provide a good, fun excuse, for spending more time tromping around in the woods to hang cameras. I can understand why guides and game ranches use them. If I owned some wooded hunting acreage, I would probably place trail cameras more for the purpose of catching vandals or poachers, rather than for seeing deer. I'm not against the use of trail cameras, but I don't think they should be high on the list of things you must have to increase your chances for success. You'll do fine with good basic scouting. Besides, I kinda like the sense of not knowing everything that has gone on in the woods. It makes it more interesting.

Fast-Track Scouting: Most hunters already have a general idea of the area in which they will end up hunting. They return to the same general patch of woods each deer season. Some also use small game hunting as a good excuse to get familiar with these areas. But if for some reason, on the day before the season opens, you find that you are hunting in an unfamiliar patch of woods, there is no reason to panic. There are a couple quick things you can do.

Gets a map of the county roads showing public hunting lands. Take a drive into the woods looking for the kind of terrain and cover you like to hunt. Watch for deer tracks in the dirt crossing the road. Don't stop at the first good area you see. Instead, take note of three or four possible good locations. From among those, select the one that looked best. Grab your compass and start walking. I like to meander the area allowing interesting features of the terrain and cover to guide my directions. But a quick and methodical way is to take a compass reading and head out on that bearing for twenty or thirty minutes. Then switch direction ninety degrees for another twenty or thirty minute. Repeat this working your way back to the starting point within about two hours. In that time you will have covered a fair chunk of ground and most likely will have found at least one decent stand. If not, you still have time to repeat this at one of the other locations. Relax, you can find good stands in half-a-day.

But don't develop some kind of phobia about the idea of over-scouting either. Some authors are all concerned that over-scouting will give the deer a Ph.D. in evasion and craftiness. This is in fact already being done on most State and federal lands. These areas are also hunted for squirrel, rabbits, partridge, turkeys, fox, coyotes and bear. In addition hikers, bikers, snowmobilers, fishermen, photographers, loggers, poachers, rightwing militia, bird watchers and nature nuts are in these areas throughout the year. Certainly, one more goofball tromping through the woods isn't going to make much difference to the deer!

For example, one afternoon while in my tree-stand I saw several doe, a four point and later a trophy buck. All were apparently unaffected by the fact that five partridge hunters with a dog had walked through the area a few hours earlier! So, if you enjoy it, go ahead and scout all you want. My problem comes from the fanatics who write that in order to "bag that trophy buck," you need to seal yourself into a chemical warfare suit and then go plot out the location of every rub, scrape, poop pile and gopher hole within a five mile radius. Ya don't need to do that.

Let the deer teach you: This will help a novice hunter to develop an eye for a good stand. There are a few ways to do this. First is to watch the deer carefully as it moves through your area. Then go and trace its route. Another way is to simply take a day and go follow the largest most well used deer trails you can find. Explore some of the smaller trails that branch off from it. Notice the features of the cover and terrain that the trails pass through. Start to think like a deer as you walk the trail. Ask yourself why the deer take this path. Why don't they go another way? What are the features of the terrain and cover that cause this? Mentally mark the spots that might be good stands. Then run the scenarios. If you hunt this spot, how do you expect the deer to approach? What direction is least likely for them to approach?

Last year I heard and glimpsed a deer headed south, along the side of a ridge about 150 yards to my front left. It stopped for a few seconds in good cover and then turned heading west. I was hoping it would either continue south toward a shooting lane or turn east across my front shooting lanes. I was curious about why the deer changed direction at that point. Later in the day I walked its path. At the point where the deer had stopped in heavy cover was a small clearing on a saddle of a ridge between two valleys. Crossing that spot would have exposed the deer on both sides. In order to stay in cover, it had a choice between east and west. It happened to choose west. But, it seemed clear that on the third day of rifle season this deer was not going to expose itself by continuing south across that clearing.

Let a Big Buck Teach You: The next time you see a big buck, even if it's after hunting season is closed and you aren't actually hunting, or if someone in your hunting party has downed one, and especially if there is good snow, use this as a great learning exercise. Take some time to follow or back track this deer for as long as you can. A half mile or more would be good. See where it goes or where it came from. You know for sure that this is a big buck. But, this is an opportunity to look at the signs that would help build the case even if you didn't know already. Notice the kind of terrain it passes through versus the terrain it avoids. Notice where the tracks indicate that it slows down or stops or runs. What are the positive clues and indicators that this was a big buck? All along this route look for places where you would want to have your stand.

Backtracking a known big buck, is not something you will use as an active part of hunting. It's just that if the opportunity presents itself, it's a good way to help you quickly develop an eye for a good stand location based on reading the sign, terrain, food sources, cover and deer trails.

Run the scenarios: This is important! As you consider the final selection of your stand, give some thought to the likely approaches deer may be taking based on the trails, cover and terrain. Stand at the spot before you commit to it. Look for the weak side. Look at the wind direction. Look at other nearby spots that might solve a problem or give you a bit more of an advantage. Run some mental *"what if"* scenarios. *What if they approach from this direction? Will I see or hear them first? Will I have cover? Can I make my move? What if the wind shifts?* This might make the difference between selecting one stand versus another option that's only a few yards away.

Check your perimeter: It's a good idea to place your hunter-orange hat at your stand as you walk the perimeter just to the point where it's still visible. This way you learn what the terrain is like just out of view from your stand. Look back at your stand to see how visible it may be to approaching deer. **Make note of any topography that might allow deer to vanish or appear suddenly.** It's more important to know the immediate area around your stand and perhaps fifty yards beyond your visibility than it is to try and know everything in four square miles of forest.

Walk'n in: You have a choice to make on this. You can walk to your stand with extreme stealth, and get there later. Or you can walk more quickly so you can get still and silent sooner. The stealth approach might get you a shot opportunity as you sort-of hunt your way in. It's a low probability and it's of more value with gun hunting than with a bow. In my rabid years I was an absolute stealth fanatic. This made me a pain-in-the-ass for my younger brothers to hunt with. But, after the DNR decided to bull-doze the logging trails closed, my favorite stand (E*nd Of The Earth)* got to be a travel-time problem. It was a full hour of stealth walking and still impossible to approach without spooking deer once I got there. So, I used a garden rake to clear a narrow path the last hundred and fifty yards to my stand. I called it a "quiet trail". My brothers just kind-of looked at each other a little sideways and never actually said out loud that I must be nuts. Anyway it did work. I cut my travel time to about twenty minutes getting to the quiet trail. Then I switched to stealth and could move into my stand the last hundred and fifty yards without spooking deer. I admit, it was a little nuts. I would not do it at most stands unless I really had to. (*An odd thing happened with this quiet trail one season. A doe was crossing behind my stand when she came upon the trail. For some reason she felt the need to jump over it as if it were a three-foot high fence.*)

Yearling mistake: You may discover a really great deer trail crossing-point with tons of tracks while hiking into the woods on an old logging road or a four-wheeler track. Usually these crossing points happen near curves and dips in the trail since these expose the deer least. It's tempting to a young hunter to think this is a good spot to get a clear shot. Don't be fooled by this. Don't try to cover this spot by setting close to the open road. Deer approaching these crossings will most often stop first inside the cover and check carefully before crossing. Then, if they decide to cross, they usually move quickly. After crossing they often stop again in the heavy cover. It might look good in theory, but the actual possibility of getting your weapon on line in time for an open shot is very poor. In addition every other goofball entering the woods by this trail will come tromping past you. Be assured that if only one guy comes past this spot in the next seven hours of hunting, it will happen during just that three minute period when a deer was also coming. *It's the hunting gods. They think this is funny.* If you want to cover this deer-trail it's better to get off the open road into the woods by at least thirty yards. In this way you might take advantage of the deer's tendency to spend more time as it stops on either side. Still, I would probably look for another spot just to avoid the people traffic.

Water hole: In my experience hunting in Michigan, Illinois, and one season in Wisconsin, watering holes are not much of a factor for attracting deer and selecting a stand. Most holes will have some tracks around them, but not any more highly concentrated than can be found in a lot of other places in the woods. There are just too many places for deer to get water. In addition a great deal of water is contained in the seven pounds of green vegetation they eat every day. It might be a different story in Texas.

A bogged in lake, large silt filled beaver pond or a muddy river can be a terrain feature that might limit the possibility of deer approaching your stand. I'm not saying deer can't swim. They are good swimmers. I'm just saying that it's less likely they will cross the water and it is more likely that a deer trail skirts the edge of the water. So think about this if you have a choice to hunt near the edge of a lake or river. It's a judgment call. The water represents a patch of real estate with less likelihood of a deer passing through. However, it also is a terrain feature that may encourage a concentration of deer movement on the trail skirting the water. If there is good sign and good cover, I might look for a stand located within range of that trail, but also having a second parallel or intersecting trail a bit farther out. This way the water isn't steeling solid real estate from my coverage area.

Bedding area: Recently I read two different articles within the pages of the same issue of a magazine in which the authors had exactly opposite opinions about hunting in or near bedding areas. One guy says "*find-em and hunt-em, it's the best*", the other guy says "*stay out*". Many writers would advise you to never push the deer up off their beds while scouting, for fear of spooking the deer out of the area forever. I think this is based on models of deer behavior that are way too simplistic and don't take into account all kinds of other human and predator activities in the woods. Most authors would advise you to scout enough to know the bedding areas, feeding areas and the trails in between. That seems reasonable and probably doesn't hurt much. If you hunt in a region of mostly farmland with mixed patches of woods and limited cover, you're more likely to find concentrated bedding areas with more deer which return to the area more regularly. It probably doesn't hurt if you bump deer out of these areas once in a while, but I would avoid doing it repeatedly. Either change the entry route or change the time you head out to your stand. But it's different in the "big woods" where deer have unlimited cover to range. The beds are usually less concentrated and the deer don't return to the same area regularly. So, if on occasion while scouting, you bump some deer up from their beds, it's not that big of a deal.

On occasion, I've been at my stand and had deer come in and lay down for a few hours. It's not that I was purposely hunting in a bedding area. It's just that my stand locations are often where deer tend to feel safe. These incidentally, are areas where deer might bed down if the mood strikes them. I've also bumped deer out of beds, set up my stand, and had deer return in less than an hour. Again, it was not that I was purposely looking to hunt in a bedding area. It was just that the area happened to meet the criterion I look for in a good stand location. Deer don't return to the same bedding area with the same regularity as they often do for feeding areas. They might lie down for a little while at midday, mid afternoon, evening or midnight and at just about any place where they feel relatively safe.

Remember, you're probably not the only goofball who has tromped through a bedding area and seen the white tails running away. Also, even if you can get into a bedding area early enough to wait for deer, it's not a high probability that they will come back to this particular area. In my opinion, it's better to stay closer to trails leading to major food sources where deer return more regularly.

I think you put yourself at a disadvantage to try and purposely hunt in or close to the edge of a bedding area. During the pre-rut I might give some favor to hunting away from the downwind side along trails that lead between a food source and a bedding areas. Bucks sometimes prowl this region to catch the scent of a doe in estrus.

Reverse ambush: Try this sometime just for fun. Take a seat at a deer bed and start to notice the combination of things. Take some time and think about what it was, that made the deer feel safe at this particular spot. The deer basically want to be able to see, hear or smell any predator that might be approaching, and then be able to get away. Imagine if your sense of smell was as good as a deer. Think about which direction the wind might have been coming from and then find the area where this sense was the deer's advantage. Notice the directions of areas where vision and hearing were to the deer's advantage if something was approaching. It may be that a predator would have to approach from across an open hillside where they could be seen, and where sticks and leaves would make a lot of noise. Another side may be a safe region provided by a swamp, bog or beaver pond. There might be thick prickly low ground cover that makes noise and will impede a predator in pursuit. Imagine that you could run like a deer and then notice the escape routes. Notice how fast the deer could be out of sight, across a ditch, over a ravine, over a hill, over a fence, into heavy cover, or beyond some obstacle. In flatlands and farm country beds are often near the edges of fields, in patches of weeds and thick grassy areas or along creeks. In the big woods, they're often on hillsides or just inside the borders of dense new growth. There may be a small patch of thick cover, a large tree, or a deadfall to their backside. The most common features are surrounding cover or terrain that forces any approaching predator to cross a region where they can be seen heard or smelled, and a quick escape route. The deer chose the spot very much in a similar way as you would choose your stand location. This is kinda fun to look at, but it still doesn't do you a lot of good as a hunter. It just gives you a look at the world from the deer's perspective.

Many hunters have stories about how a deer waited on its bed until they had moved into the worst possible place to get off a shot. At just that moment, the deer jumps up and bounds away. I don't think this is because the deer are strategic geniuses. I think it's an extension of something they routinely do for survival. Deer don't want to spend all the energy it takes to get up off their bed and run away if there is no good reason. So, they wait on their bed to check out the source of the potential threat. It most often ends up being nothing more than a turkey or a squirrel or it might pass off on another direction. Survival is improved by simply waiting.

But survival is improved again, when necessary, by running at just the right moment. That moment often might be when there is plenty of thick cover or obstacles to prevent a predator from easily giving chase. For us human predators the deer has simply done what it usually does. It just so happens that the worst position to give chase is also most often a bad spot for a hunter to get a clear shot. This is not strategic genius by the deer, but it's not by accident either. It's the genius of natural selection. The deer waits and then pulls the trigger on its best survival skill, its ability to run. The deer has gotten you in a reverse ambush. Welcome to the big woods pilgrim.

Feeding areas: Deer will eat damn near anything that grows. Local deer may show a preference for certain foods that deer in other areas don't seem to eat. They often come to feeding areas on a more routine basis. Browse damage with lots of spider trails is a good sign. But in the fall, the feeding pattern can suddenly change. Browse areas seem to be abandoned. Deer that you might have seen in the open fields disappear for a few weeks. It's usually near the end of September when the acorns have fallen. Acorns are the best source of food for the fat the deer need to survive the winter. So, my advice is, go find the oak trees.

Super Secret Special Stuff: For the huge majority of recreational deer-hunters, and especially for new guys, my advice is to stay far away from these techniques unless you really know what the hell you're doing. *(Grunt calls, snort calls, wheeze calls, fawn bleat calls, estrus doe urine, covering scent-skunk or fox, rattling antlers, false scrapes, trail cameras, and lifelike deer decoys)*

Rattling antlers at the wrong time or in the wrong way, using the wrong type of scent or the wrong deer call at the wrong time, and thrashing around in the woods is not likely to help and is more likely to scare deer away. I'm not saying that some of these things don't work. I know they do sometimes. It may be worthwhile for a person who has the time to burn and who is willing to scare away some deer before having success. But, not for most guys who only have a few precious days to hunt each season. You are much better off to simply find a good spot and then just be still and silent.

The Fortunate Few: It's easy to get your brain all twisted around the idea that you need to be doing *"super secret special stuff"*. These techniques are heavily marketed by *"experts"* in magazines and video. It seems like powerful proof. But remember the "Big Rock" theorem and its close cousin the "Keep it Simple" principle. Also remember the real nine-hundred-pound gorilla's in their success equation. Yes, I'm a bit envious, but I've got no real bitch about the fact that their position in life allows them to do things that I can't do. In fact, I'm happy for these fortunate few. I get a vicarious fantasy about what it would be like to have special access to hundreds of acres of land in a region known for huge trophy bucks. In these fantasies, I imagine being able to write–off my trip as a business expense, or having enough vacation days to spend even a fifth of the time in the woods as they are able to spend. But that ain't me. It's probably not you either. It's the very fortunate few. Good for them and God bless-em. But the thing that actually pisses me off, is that the magazines try to sell hunters on the critical importance of these special techniques while ignoring the real big gorillas in the equation. It sells a lot of magazines, a ton of advertising, and a billion dollars worth of stuff. What I'm trying to do in this paragraph is help peal your brain back down from the ceiling and get you back to reality. In the vast majority of cases the special techniques don't deserve the large proportion of credit they receive.

We can all use, or not use, the special techniques which may or may not help. But none of us, not even the fortunate few, have a good chance of killing any kind of deer, much less a trophy buck, if we don't obey the seven big rock rules first. A fair amount of my own success in hunting comes from the fact that I remain still and silent while using the sounds and movements of other hunters to perhaps send deer my way. But sometimes it works backwards too. Recently during early archery season, I was hunting on crowded public land. Three doe were casually moving toward my stand from the west. I was thinking about maybe taking the largest one. But another hunter off in the wood line a hundred yards farther east decided to use his doe bleat call. He could not possibly have seen these three deer. I'm not sure why he decided to use the call, but all three deer immediately turned tail and moved off in the opposite direction. I've seen this type of thing happen when other hunters have used grunt calls, bleat calls and with rattling antlers. These have been misused and overused by hunters to the point that deer now more often just stay away.

My advice about avoiding special techniques is based on a theory that I have no way to prove. It's just my advice. Here's my thinking: Guys who <u>do</u> know what they're doing with this stuff and who have been successful, probably already are very good with the seven rules. Therefore, the deer they got was somewhere in the vicinity, and they found a good stand, and they had a very high probability of getting the deer anyway, even if they had not used the special technique. On the other hand, guys who've never practiced these techniques might be either <u>good</u> or <u>bad</u> with keeping the seven rules. The bad guys have little chance of success anyway. Deer may not be in the vicinity, they may not have a good stand location, and even if a deer is accidentally attracted by one of these techniques, it won't do them much good because they're not good with the other "big rock" rules. It's like saving pennies while wasting dollars. But, if you <u>are good</u> with the seven rules, you <u>do</u> have a good chance. So why screw around with something and mess it up? Techniques can end up becoming the focus of what you're doing and thereby distract you from good basic hunting style. Another part of this theory is that special techniques add a level of complexity to your hunting which, if correctly used can work. But, it's also *"some kind of law"* that the more complex a thing gets, the easier it is to screw-up and the less likely it will work in the hands of an idiot. The same is true here.

Quick Survey: On my return trip from hunting the Michigan gun-deer season, I stopped at a roadside rest area which served as a DNR deer check-in station.   The parking area had two lines of vehicles with dead deer.   A half dozen DNR officers were measuring and taking statistics.   It suddenly occurred to me that this was a unique opportunity to do a quick *"reality-check"* with a whole bunch of real live successful deer hunters.   So, I got a notepad and made up survey questions with columns for checking yes or no etc.   Every hunter I approached was more than happy to talk.   It was a nice mix of hunters from a few young guys who had killed their first deer, to a good number of guys with eight or twelve kills in about twenty-some seasons, and a few old timers who had killed over thirty-some deer in about fifty seasons.   Buy the time I had reached the 42nd contact, the survey was already clearly one sided.   Not a single hunter reported the use of rattling antlers, or deer calls of any kind.   None used attracting scent, covering scent or deer decoys.   Only two guys said they were wearing scent-block clothes, but they quickly added that they didn't think it had anything to do with getting the deer.   Only two used bait.

I wish I had the time and resources to get a thousand contacts from successful hunters.   But my quick survey did at least clearly support the idea that most of the *"super secret special stuff" is* not necessary for success in deer-hunting.   The highly successful older hunters were especially perplexed by some of my questions.   They looked at me like, *"what's the matter with this guy?"* and sometimes even scoffed at me, *"Hell no, I never use any of that stuff"*.

Rifle stand versus bow stand: Many times I've noticed that when deer are at a moderate level of caution, they tend to stop and use their eyes, ears and nose to scan ahead for danger.   They do a fairly good job of scanning out to the perimeter limits the terrain allows, before moving forward into what they believe is a safe region.   They usually stop again inside the new safe zone and scan forward again.   I picture this as a sort of traveling safe zone.   My theory is that the deer are mostly concerned with any threat that may be forward and at side angles, and especially within a certain distance of perhaps thirty to fifty yards along their intended direction of travel.   This may simply be because the deer are confident that with a thirty to fifty yard head start, nothing in the north woods is fast enough to catch them.

Oddly though, once the deer enter their new safe region they sometimes seem to let their caution down a little inside the immediate area. Especially once they pass the point of those important side angles. They may check their back-trail and then pause to eat. They generally seem more concerned with scanning farther ahead to the next perimeter rather than the immediate area which they mostly presume to be safe since it has already been scanned at least once. It seems ironic to me that deer are sometimes overly concerned with the perimeter, thirty yards away, while I'm undetected ten yards from them. The tricky part is getting inside that region.

For archery hunting, earlier in the season and at very close range, there are advantages and disadvantages for the hunter and for the deer which are created by all the foliage. For rifle hunting later in the season and at longer range, there are advantages and disadvantages due to the lack of foliage. Archery hunters have the added challenge required of getting well inside the deer's safety zone. Rifle hunters have the additional challenge created by the fact that the deer can scan out to perhaps five or ten times farther distance after the foliage is down.

With the rifle, it's to your advantage to locate your stand much farther away from the trails you're covering. The mistake is to set up too close to deer trails or too deep inside heavy cover. My advice would be to try and avoid setting up for any rifle shots that are closer than thirty or forty yards. With a bow, you are required to set up near trails and in somewhat heavier cover. The mistake is often in setting up too close to these trails. Try to avoid shots that are closer than ten yards. (*Read the archery section about close tree stand shots.*) **Even in this somewhat heavier cover, try to have a combination of hearing and visibility, far enough out so that deer don't just suddenly pop up out of the cover without any advance notice.**

Try this as an experiment sometime: Scout the edges of young cover versus older growth woods to find a well-used deer trail near the edge passing along through good heavy cover. Find a stand within fifteen or twenty yards of the deer trail. Then look for the shooting lanes. Notice that the best possibility for a lane is the shortest distance through the cover straight toward the trail. But, check for possible lanes angling to the right and left toward the trail.

If you're in dense cover, these angles won't be very wide and the shooting lanes won't be very long. **This stand might be borderline O.K. for archery hunting, but it's a very poor rifle stand.** You'll only be able to cover a very short part of the deer trail. It may be as little as twenty or thirty yards angling to the left and right. **This spot will handicap you in a number of ways and gives the deer several good advantages.** You have far fewer and much shorter shooting lanes. You have much less visibility of deer approaching that would otherwise be well within range. The deer will be very close when you do finally see or hear them. **This is not a good thing.** It means you will have much less reaction time for making the move and the shot. In a couple of bounds the deer can quickly put more heavy cover between you, and eliminate any shot even though the deer is still well within range. The stupid part is that you have a weapon with two-hundred yard shot capability and you are sitting in cover that reduces it to twenty or thirty yards.

Now continue the experiment by moving across the edge into the less dense cover of the mature trees. Find a stand overlooking the same deer-trail fifty to seventy-five yards away. Look again for shooting lanes. Notice, that by backing away into less dense cover, a number of shooting lanes are available toward the deer trail straight ahead and also at angles far to the right and left. You can effectively cover the deer trail as it meanders along the edge of the heavy cover a hundred yards to each side along with the addition of any incoming side trails. This is a much better rifle stand. It gives you a lot more time to detect the deer, make your move, choose the best shooting lane and take advantage of the weapons range.

I made this mistake as a young "Bambi-stage" deer hunter. I sat in heavy cover with my rifle across my lap and my back against a tree with a well used deer trail crossing immediately at my feet. Someone spooked two deer that came running fast from my right. I heard them and instinctively turned my head as they were about ten yards away. The lead deer saw my movement and simply jumped over me. The second deer did the same. I got a great look at their under-bellies but not much more. They appeared and disappeared before I could even get my rifle out of my lap. Lesson learned.

Hunting The Rut: Every fall there are two-dozen warmed over articles written to tell you the "*secrets of hunting the rut*".   It actually boils down to something very simple. The deer, especially the bucks, move around a lot more and are much less cautious. Doe may be a bit skittish for a week or so before the actual rut. Their cadence seems to switch from move-stop to a longer move at a slightly faster rate followed by fewer and shorter stops. So, the time-lapse between when you first hear them coming to the possibility of a shot gets much shorter.   You may need to get ready a little faster. They get agitated 12 to 24 hours before coming into estrus.   They move more, visit buck scrapes and dribble urine.   **Be aware of the doe body language.** It's different than how you normally see them move. If the doe seems like she's being pushed, it may be that she is not yet ready for the romantic interest of a buck that's following her. The buck may have its nose down on the trail following a scent laid by doe-urine and from the interdigital gland.   The urine has the scent that tells the buck if the doe is ready to breed.   If something seems odd about the way the doe is moving (a *little too fast, head out front or down instead of up, almost like skulking away with the tail cocked to the side, not very cautious, not stopping to munch on anything*), a buck is probably following. Stay ready.

      I was getting ready to climb up into my tree-stand when a big doe came very close, moving in just this way. The problem was that my bow was attached to the rope to be hoisted up the tree. I tried to get it unhooked for a shot but by the time I was able to draw the bow it was too late. As I let down on the bow, my peripheral vision caught a movement about forty yards off to my right. It was a buck that was following in the exact trail of the doe. I know damn-right-well that this deer saw me move and it knew that I was standing there. Yet, it did not alter its course. It kept following the path of the doe coming within fifteen yards of me, driven to commit suicide by its own hormones. It was a small buck, so I let him walk, but still it was a dumb-ass thing for this deer to do.

      The simple truth about hunting the rut is this.   Bucks in particular may do some incredibly stupid things! Just like human teenage boys at hormone time, bucks are out of their cotton-pickin-mind! They will virtually risk their stupid life in pursuit of some female attention. This makes it easier for them to get killed. So, it's a good time for a hunter to be in the woods.

Deer Biology: I promised in the beginning not to write a ton of deer biology that wasn't relevant to actual hunting. But I think one page about bucks, antlers and the rut isn't out of line.

> *This is extremely condensed and simplified. Credit for the majority of this page should go to the best book ever written about deer biology and behavior.* "**Way of the Whitetail, by Dr. Leonard Lee Rue III.**, Voyageur Press, Copyright 2000.

Mature bucks generally rub the velvet from their antlers in early September causing them to harden. (Also r*ead the sections about rubs and scrapes*) Mature bucks in an area know their relative social standing based on testing each others strength while sparing. The idea of sparing is to establish social dominance without a bloody war and without expending a huge amount of energy that could be better used for surviving the winter. The sound of sparing is part of the reason that some hunters use the technique of rattling antlers to attract other nearby challengers. *Rattling too hard and with too large of antlers can actually scare away a good buck.* Since dominance has already been established, the mature buck can fend off most challenges for breeding-rights in his territory with only a brief display of aggression without a serious fight.

In October, bucks will scent a doe they believe may be receptive to breeding and begin following / chasing. This is pre-rut. The doe will run and soon squat to urinate in the trail leaving a scent signal that tells the buck if she is in estrous or not. There doesn't seem to be such a thing as buck's breeding grounds. The choice of when and where seems to be more up to the doe. In November, the buck will pair up with a receptive estrous doe and breed with her several (4 to 6) times over about 24 hours. Meanwhile, other lesser bucks may be taking breeding-rights wherever their dominance might prevail. The buck will move on to find other receptive estrous doe and will bread with an average of four to six doe over the rut season. During the rut, if two equally matched bucks challenge for dominance in an area, the fight will not be simple sparing. It will be deadly serious. If a doe is not bread, or if she failed to conceive, she will go into a second estrus cycle about 28 days later. This is what some hunters call the second rut. About 95% of all doe conceive each year. It's normal to have a pair of fawns born in the end of May or June. Predators, primarily coyotes, black bear, bobcat and dogs, may kill in the range of 50% to 70% of the newborn fawns.

The Moon and the Rut-Hunting Recipe:

Ingredients; One tablespoon aged American Indian wisdom, two pounds deer biology, one cup moonbeams, sprinkle with sifted data, add a dash of facts, mix well, add two large crocks of fresh warm bull shit, and sell to hunters.

Recently some guys have updated an old Indian tradition that involves hunting based upon the phase of the moon. The theory tries to predict the timing of the rut and the best period for hunting by the use of a "moon chart." In short, the theory says that the best time to hunt whitetail deer is approximately from four days before, and until ten days after, the second full moon that follows the fall equinox. (*Ya got that?*) This has been commonly known as the hunter's moon for hundreds of years.

There is usually some element of truth in beloved legends. I think it's the same for the moon theory. There's probably something that's right about it. But, there's still a whole lot that's wrong, unknown or just plain bull. The main ingredients in the recipe are still missing. Until they are discovered, moon charts may not work any better than a coin toss. (*Just guessing, the Indians might have preferred to hunt deer at this time of year simply because; the corn had already been harvested, the deer were easier to kill, the deer put on a lot of fat for the winter, and also because refrigeration of meat would be much less of a problem.*)

If I was forced to just take a wild-ass-guess at the best time to be in the deer-woods with hopes of catching a lot of deer movement driven buy wild hormones, I would target Halloween plus or minus a few days. My advice is to make the moon chart fifth on your priority list. First, try to hunt opening weekend when the deer are not in a high state of caution. Second, try to get out after the first good frost or after a few days of cool dry weather. These conditions favor excellent hearing, your most important hunting asset. Third, try to get out after the first one or two light snowfalls that stick and cover. Sometimes it takes a few days for deer to figure out that the snow has them silhouetted. Fourth, hunt at every available convenient opportunity. Get your deer, and then go check the moon chart.

Genius-deer: As I mentioned in my ranting, some authors write as if the deer are capable of explaining your federal income-tax return. Therefore, you must have fourteen thousand dollars worth of product X in order to have any chance against these genius-deer. This is not entirely true and it is not entirely false. It depends on what the deer in the area have learned and what they have become accustomed to. Contrary to myth, doe can be geniuses too and some big bucks can be complete morons.

I have a theory about genius deer, but first I need to explain what I learned from genius bird-dogs. I had the privilege of hunting upland game with the good company of three generations of outstanding bird-dogs. The first two dogs were trained and exposed to a lot of bird hunting early in life. I witnessed a rookie pup grow into a decent pheasant dog after only a few weekends in the field. By her second season the pheasants had almost no chance against this dog. I then saw her quickly adapt her hunting style for the partridge in the north and for quail in the south and then back to pheasants. But, the third generation dog became my brother's family pet and was never exposed to hunting or guns until it was quite mature. This past fall it was the only dog available for a family outing to a game-hunting farm. This dog went from "not having the slightest clue", to finding birds, learning to work together with the guns, and finally knowing her business and making a rock steady point, all in one day.

As part of my theory I estimate that the deer's ability to learn is probably at about the same level as the best breeds of hunting dogs. Deer reactions to humans are based on what they've been exposed to and what they've learned is threatening versus non-threatening. That's why wilderness deer react differently from farmland deer, versus suburban lawn-eating deer and deer in areas with heavy poaching versus protected park area deer. They also act differently in areas frequented by fishermen, hikers, picnickers, photographers or nature nuts who pose no threat to the deer. It all has to do with what the deer have become accustomed to. It explains why in some areas deer will run from the sight of a car while in other areas they will stay and browse. Some will browse as long as you don't stop the car and open the door. My impression is that deer in general have become a bit more wary since the numbers of archery hunters grew so dramatically due to the popularity of the compound bow about twenty years ago. The deer have simply learned and adapted to the tactics and the additional hunters spending more time in the woods. It also may explain the small areas with populations of so called genius deer. These deer have simply had the good fortune to survive the hunting pressure long enough to get smart. Being shot at, and missed just one time, probably doubles the deer's I.Q. If an area has relatively high hunting pressure from people with mostly poor hunting skills, it's like providing a free education for these deer. They become harder to hunt. Some learn to try and fake you into making the move if they aren't sure what you are. They put their head down as if they are starting to eat, or they look away trying to act casual. Then, they quickly look back to catch you moving. In some areas deer learn not to flag their big white tails as they run away. Instead they tuck them under and move away with more stealth.

   After escaping two or three encounters with hunters the deer is a certified genius. If suspicious of you, it might "jump your arrow". It might jump up or it might dive for the dirt at the sound of your release. I've seen this twice in my years hunting. It might lay low in heavy cover and let you pass within fifteen yards. I've seen this twice too. The deer might go nocturnal; it might stay still during the day, it might move out of an area at the first sight, sound, or scent of a human. (***This can be to your advantage if it moves out of someone else's area and into your area where you are waiting still and silent***)

Examples: *My good friend Paul had been sitting in his spot early one morning for about twenty minutes when coffee demanded its release. He took four or five steps from his blind and unzipped. At that moment a trophy buck laying just another ten yards away stood up and made its escape.*

   On another occasion a large buck remained lying motionless on the opposite side of a fallen Oak-tree twenty five yards from my stand. It finally spooked and ran when I started to pack up my gear to leave almost three hours later. It's funny because I remember that I ignored the little voice telling me to knock an arrow and go check the fallen Oak-tree before I sat down that morning.

Although these examples show that this kind of thing does happen, don't let it get your brain in a twist. These are rare occurrences. These are the only two examples from among many close hunting companions on hundreds of outings over many years.

Even if it actually occurred at twice the rate we know of, it's still an extremely rare thing. So, I would not be inclined to change my hunting style or to get all paranoid nuts about it. **Genius deer are not as common as most of the magazine publications would lead you to believe. It's just that the myths about genius deer sell a lot of magazines and more importantly, they sell a ton of merchandise.** The truth is that genius deer are extremely rare. More often it's simply that they have gone nocturnal due to hunting pressure. But when they do exist, the average recreational deer hunter has about the same chance of fooling them as the pheasants had against my genius bird-dog. Almost none. But, here's the good news. There are plenty of dumb deer around and they taste just as good as the smart ones.

Counter-measures: If for some reason you are stuck hunting in an area where you believe the deer are mostly geniuses, there are a couple things you might do to improve your chances. First is to absolutely fanatically obey the seven rules! Next, realize that it means you will have to <u>spend a lot more time on your stand while making zero mistakes</u> and hoping that the deer does make a mistake. It might also be especially important for you to <u>try timing the rut.</u> This might give you a needed edge. Next, you might try going beyond the seven rules by borrowing tactics used by trophy deer hunters. But please remember that this book was written for regular guys who love deer hunting, who get out a few days each year and who simply want to increase their chances for success. **Trophy-class, semi professional hunters are an <u>entirely different bunch of guys.</u>** They've dedicated a huge amount of time to scouting, hunting and learning to correctly use special tactics. They may pass on a nice buck knowing that they have plenty of time and bigger deer to choose from. But, the realities of life force most deer hunters toward being a bit less picky. Before you get sucked down into this stuff, be sure to read the section "Fortunate Few".

If you insist on trying to hunt genius deer, a few tactics might include the following: Scouting earlier and much more carefully, choosing a completely different stand location, using attracting deer scents, deer decoys, rattling, and calling. Other options are to cover a completely different trail, hunt in deeper and heavier cover, wear scent blocking clothes including rubber boots and gloves, choose a different exit and entry route, enter or exit at a different time of day.

I still think most guys are better off avoiding this super secret special stuff. In my opinion, all of this begins to build up to the point where some guys can get way too serious and way too technical about deer hunting. It ends up taking most of the fun out of it. Why not just say *"to hell with it"*, and go hunt where there's dumber deer.

Desperate measures: If the deer have you completely frustrated, you might try to organize a "drive". Note that drives may be illegal in some states. Check the rules. Also pursuing deer with the use of dogs is illegal in most states. Drives can work especially well if you have control over a large tract of private land. However it's not practical on public lands in areas where there are a lot of hunters in the woods. Every two hundred yards might be another hunter sitting on his stand. You'll most likely hear the shot he makes at the deer you drove toward him. Thanks.

A drive takes a coordinated effort from a number of hunters. It also means that you need to have a good idea of the terrain and escape routes that the deer is most likely to take. In large areas of wooded cover a spooked deer will typically run only about a hundred and fifty yards. Often they turn left or right and then start to double back. This means that if the guys on the wings of the drive stay dead-dog-still for fifteen minutes after a deer is jumped, there might be a chance for a shot. If you are hunting at your stand, and see or hear some guys making a drive near you, my advice is to stay put for at least half an hour after they pass and stick to the rules. *(Note that in open fields and farmland areas a spooked deer will tend to run much farther and probably won't double back.)*

If you don't have enough guys for a drive and if the deer are simply not moving, it can be productive for rifle hunters to switch to something more like the tactics of a rabbit hunter for a portion of the day. This means going into the heaviest, thickets, god-awful cover you can find. You'll most likely have a running shot. So, be sure to have your scope adjusted to its lowest magnification. This gives the widest field of view for getting on target quickly. If you have the choice between focusing your attention on two or more jumped deer in order to try and see antlers, watch the one that's running without flagging its tail or with its head down.

Note that in mixed woods and farmlands there are often small island-like patches of thick cover out in an open field. It might be only twenty yards in diameter and would not normally be the kind of place you would look for deer. The deer know this, which is why they're out there. Take a walk.

Also, consider hunting the late season. This usually means much colder weather and a change in the pattern of deer movement which may favor mid-day rather than early morning. So don't go out to your stand at the crack of dawn and then be too cold to stay through mid-day and early afternoon. Sleep-in a little.

A stand that feels right: The 5th criterion in rule seven "*a stand that feels right*" is important because it means that you have a sense of confidence in seeing deer. Look for the features and signs that I have described, but also trust in your sixth sense instinct about this. This means you're more likely to resist the urge to get up and wander. Your odds then increase because you spend more time being still and silent on your stand. A spin-off advantage of building a ground blind or using a tree stand is that the work involved causes one to be more selective in the location. If you have a good feeling about the spot and you have invested some time and work in it, you're more likely to stay.

Knowing the terrain extremely well does have one practical advantage that indirectly may yield a slight increase in success. It enables you to get to your stand, or from one stand to another, across country by the shortest route. This translates into spending more time being still and silent on the stand. This falls into the category of, "Get thy butt into the woods and stay there". It's more helpful than knowing the location of all the rubs, scrapes, and poop piles in a four-square-mile area.

Good hunting.

The "Big Deal" About Wind & Scent
Part – 5

This is another subject that I expect to catch a lot of grief over. Hundreds of magazine articles and tons of product marketing are dedicated to the wind and scent issue every year. This has a lot of hunters all paranoid nuts about scent. Twenty years ago some guys (*including me*) were driven so far as to pissing into mayonnaise jars for fear that the scent of human urine would scare away the deer.

If you've scouted to find a stand location as I've described, it will provide good hunting with a simple fix or with little concern about the wind direction. You can't control the wind. It may change direction a dozen times on the day you hunt. But you can control the choice of a good stand location so that the wind direction has little effect on weather or not deer might approach. This is the first part of "*hunting around it*". Beyond that, give the scent and wind advantage to the deer and don't worry a whole lot more about it. Most of the time you're simply not going to fool the deer. You are a human and you smell like a human and that's that. I'm not convinced that covering scents or scent blocking fabric is much better than just taking a shower before you go hunting. Besides, remember, there are nine hundred thousand other smelly hunters in the wood as well. The wind and scent issue has been way oversold. It really doesn't have to be such a big deal. It might have some effect on where you locate your stand but **more importantly, it effects when you might decide to make your move.** This is the second part of what I mean by "*hunting around it*." This will make more sense after you finish this section and if you've read the section about scouting.

Your scent cone: In the early summer I sometimes watch the cottonwood trees release floating white puffs into the air currents. Sometimes they hang in the air and float a short time giving a 3-D view of what the air currents are doing. I think about how these air currents would disperse my scent if I were hunting. Some days the white parachutes switch direction ninety degrees on the compass every few minutes. But on many days, it's remarkable how far and how straight they go in one direction and on a relatively narrow path. The next time you have a chance to observe a smoky campfire or a lighted cigar, pay close attention to what happens as the smoke moves away in a crossing wind. It spreads out wider wafting in the air left and right, up and down, becoming less dense until it can no longer be seen. This is analogous to my drawing of the scent cone and the happy hunter. This simple drawing will be important to the entire discussion of how scent might play a role in some critical hunting decisions. Notice the wind direction and the major deer trails on the drawing. The blue shaded area and the spots behind the hunter are intended to represent the intensity of the scent as it's carried away on the air. Of course this doesn't happen in an exactly uniform pattern. Due to a natural process of diffusion into the air, the scent spreads out in a generally cone like pattern as it is carried away from the hunter. The intensity of the scent is highest at the closest and narrowest end of the cone near the hunter. It decreases in intensity at an exponential rate as it spreads wider and gets farther from its origin. At 80 yards the scent cone is much wider, but it is also much less intense than it is at 40yards or at 20 yards etc.

Lessons from Max & Brooke: Max was a beagle. He hunted by following almost totally ground scent. He was at his best with a little help from morning dew on the grass. His tail would stick up like a little white flag in the bean field as he bayed following a pheasant in a pretzel pattern. (*Yes, I know Beagles are rabbit dogs, but Max was a hell-of-a pheasant dog too.*) He was relentless on their trails until they came up to fly in splendid colorful glory against the blue autumn sky (*for a couple of seconds*). The thing with Max was simply to get him onto a hot ground scent.

Brooke was a Brittany. She hunted using much more air-born scent than ground scent. The best use of her amazing nose was to hunt heading across the wind. This way she would not only cover the immediate ground as she quartered ahead, but also pick up any scent on the crossing wind. Having complete faith in Brooke's nose, I learned two things about air-borne scent from watching her work. The first, was that if the breeze was in the wrong direction, she could sometimes fail to detect a bird that was very close-by. But the more astonishing thing, was to see her flag her nose into the crossing breeze and pick up a distant scent. She would change direction, quartering into the wind. Her quartering turns would become tighter as she worked back and forth inside the edges of the scent cone. Soon she would be on point of a partridge that she had first scented in the wind from perhaps fifty-yards away.

Lessons from a dead skunk: Suppose that a skunk perfumed itself in its last living moments. Suppose also that there are mild air currents moving generally from North to South. If you are crossing or approaching anywhere south of the stinky dead carcass and within the width of its scent cone, you will detect the skunk odor at a considerable distance. But, if you're approaching from any direction that doesn't include the scent cone, you might walk within a few feet of the skunk before you smell the plume of odor immediately around it. The same thing applies to deer hunters. If a hunter is dead-still and dead-silent, **a deer approaching from outside the scent cone might easily come within ten or fifteen feet before smelling the plume immediately around the hunter.**

The Scent Alert Threshold: At some distance there is a scent threshold of intensity that will alert a deer to your presence. I don't know of reliable information on how far out that threshold typically might be. Some outdoor writers have claimed that this distance is as far as a half mile. This I would believe possible only in perfect scenting conditions. Certainly the alert threshold distance must depend on a number of factors such as how fast and how steady the breeze is, turbulence caused by terrain and brush, updrafts, downdrafts and most importantly, how stinky the hunter is in the first place. The reason to be concerned with the direction of your scent cone and this alert threshold is that it may affect your decision on when to "make the move." I'll write more about that later.

Based on seeing deer react to airborne scent, I would estimate very crudely that in typical conditions the scent alert threshold is triggered downwind as follows: Always inside twenty-five yards. Very often out to fifty yards. Sometimes out to seventy-five yards. A few times out to one hundred yards. Beyond this point, it's just too unpredictable to even guess. Again, a lot depends on how stinky you are in the first place.

> *Skeptical readers might find it curious that my yardage estimates are in at twenty-five yard increments. Please loosen your grip and get the concept. It's not a formula. I readily admit that this is actually a dumb-ass guess based on what I've experienced. It's a general guideline. If you don't like my numbers, plug in your own. But the concept remains the same. O.K.?*

Here's the theory and the logic. In my opinion the ideal setup involves more or less giving up on shooting lanes directly to your rear in favor of good heavy cover and facing into the prevailing breeze. All you're losing is perhaps thirty or forty-five degrees of real estate directly behind you. This region has less likelihood of a deer approaching due to your scent. It's also the hardest for making the move, and is least likely to offer a clear shot. You are trying to put all of the weaknesses of this stand on one side. This leaves you to focus on the remaining three-hundred-thirty degrees of better possibilities to your front and sides. There's also some logic in setting with your back to the wind if you have shooting lanes and can make your move before the deer enters the scent cone. (*More on that later*)

But the ideal setup rarely actually happens. Often we hunt at our favorite stand while air currents might be moving in any direction. So, deal with what you've got. Do some mental exercise before a deer is approaching. **Check the direction of your scent cone and look at the terrain, cover and shooting lanes while asking yourself a series of questions about what you plan to do if a deer approaches.** (*You ain't do-in anything but sit-n there anyway. It won't kill ya to do a little thinking.*) This might allow you to hunt a favorite stand almost regardless of the wind direction. In the vast majority of cases it's simply a question of when to make the move and when to take the shot. In the few cases where the scent cone does play a part, you'll at least have some kind of plan thought out beforehand.

A deer can *hear you* from 360 degrees on the compass. It can also potentially *see you* from 360 degrees on the compass. But, it can only *smell you* from the 30 or 45 degrees that is covered by your scent cone *if it happens to be in the right location at the right time*. **This is why being "dead dog still" and "dead dog silent" is far more important than worrying about how you smell!**

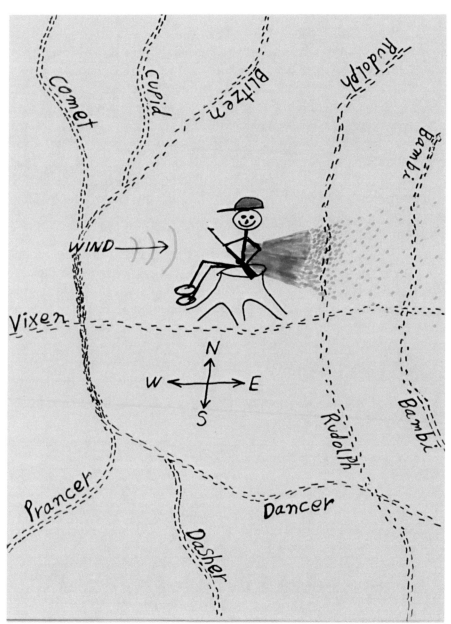

*This **happy hunter** is hoping that deer will cross in front of him on the generally northbound or southbound trails. The wind is coming from west to east. Assume that he has good cover. In the real world these trails are not flat and clear. They pass through an infinite variety of hills, valleys, brush, logs, mounds and trees that provide cover for both the deer and the hunter.*

What if the wind is blowing in the opposite direction? This is actually still not a bad setup for the happy hunter. Although the scent cone would then be toward his front over the main trail, this doesn't really change much about the probability of deer approaching. The happy hunter would then need to be aware that better possibilities exist for an approach somewhere from his rear. But, the major north and south trails still would have good possibilities of producing deer. By the time deer on these trails have entered his scent cone, they may be well within good shooting lanes. If they do detect his scent they will often stop and look for him. If he has already made his move this can offer an excellent shot opportunity. In that case he has used his scent cone to his own advantage.

Now take another look at the diagram and start thinking about what happens if the wind is in any one of eight different directions. What you'll begin to notice is that in each case, as it reduces the probability of deer approaching from certain trails it also leaves open other good possibilities. Many good deer stands are like this. This is part of the reason why I have advised against getting all fanatical about your scent and what happens with wind direction. If it's a favorite stand, and if the deer move through in different directions, stick with it, make some mental adjustments and hunt it regardless of the wind.

For the purpose of my happy hunter diagram I simply guessed that the scent cone might spread out at about 15 degrees. I then doubled it to account for normal, slight shifts in the wind so it effectively covers 30 degrees. On some days the angle might be 60 degrees or 90 degrees on the compass. But, the idea is still the same. O.K.?

This scent cone leads to a whole bunch of practical points for hunters in the field.

1st Your scent is only affecting a very small percentage of the possible shots at deer that you may get. Therefore, even if you could do something about your scent, it would only increase your chances for success by a small amount.

2nd If you insist on worrying about your scent, <u>take a shower with unscented soap.</u> This will reduce the intensity of your smell thereby decreasing the distance at which your scent reaches a threshold that will alert the deer. Your hunting companions won't mind it either.

3rd The shower may be more important for ground-stand archery hunters who must get close. Rifle hunters can often shoot at distances far beyond the scent alert threshold.

4th It may be more practical to simply concede this advantage to the deer. Either stop worrying too much about it, or if the wind is wrong, simply move to a different stand.

5th Hunters who are up in a tree-stand may have a slight advantage. Deer may actually walk in close enough to pass underneath the scent cone and never detect them.

6th Smoking tobacco may not hurt your chances <u>due to scent</u>, but it does cost you in the required movements. Movement, or sound caused by movement is the number one reason a deer will detect you. (Also, h*eavy smokers often have an unconscious cough or need to clear their throat. It's like hunting with a small alarm clock at your stand that goes off every five minutes. Your odds drop to near zero.*)

7th Mosquito repellent may not hurt your chances so much either due to scent. If it allows you to sit still longer without swatting or scratching, it's worth the trade off. (*In some states during early archery season there can be bugs and mosquitoes even into October*)

8th "Scent blocking clothing" is mostly a great marketing gimmick. At best, it might provide only a tiny possible increase in your chances for success at an enormous expense.

9th (**Very Important**) The scent cone can have a big effect on your decision about <u>when to make your move and take the shot.</u> (Read "Scent cone & Making the Move").

Bad Idea: Aside from stalking <u>with</u> the wind, there is really only one other highly stupid thing that you might do as regard wind and scent. That is in a situation where the terrain and cover cause the deer trails to funnel through a fairly narrow area. This happens more often in patches of mixed woods and farmlands. If the prevailing breeze at that time also happens to be going up or down that funnel, and if you are stupid enough to put your stand right in the middle of the funnel, you will have reduced your chances of seeing a deer by about fifty percent. In the case where the deer have made a habit of using this trail primarily in one direction at that time of day, you may have reduced your chances to nearly zero. Funnels offer a good hunting opportunity if you account for the direction of the wind and back off the trails far enough not to spoil it, while remaining within range for a good shot.

*Trick: I have **not** tried this. A hunter has told me about using an article of his scent-covered clothing to create a diversion. He tied it to a bush at a key distant spot that would likely cause the deer to alter their path toward him rather than continue on a path away from him. This is interesting. It seems feasible. But it would require careful thought, predictable conditions and it seems like it could go wrong in a whole bunch of ways. **I'll probably stay away from this one.***

Scent Cone & Making the Move: Please take another look at the happy hunter diagram as we go through different scenarios for making the move. The happy hunter in my picture appears to be a left-hand shooter. For him the easiest move to make will be for a deer approaching from his right on the trails labeled Comet, Cupid and where the Blitzen trail joins in. *(For a right-handed shooter it would be the opposite. Deer approaching from the left would be the easiest move.)*

The trails labeled Dancer, Dasher and Prancer are somewhat harder for this left-hand shooter to make his move. However the wind is not a factor and he can wait for the best opportunity as the cover and terrain provides. The importance of the rules "listen" and "use your eyes" is that you detect deer farther out. The additional time, terrain and cover that the deer might pass through gives the hunter more opportunities to get into position. A crossing deer will give more time and will pass more terrain and cover and offer many more opportunities for the move than one coming straight on. The Vixen trail is also not a real hard move. The problem is that it comes straight at the hunter. Therefore it offers the least amount of cover for concealing the move. The hunter then needs to make his move at the earliest good opportunity. This may be O.K. if this particular deer is slowly foraging its way undisturbed. However, if this deer is at a trot it may close ground very quickly. It may stop or slow down nearly on top of him or pass by before the hunter has a chance to make his move. In that case, rather than rush the move and give away his position for sure, he might think about remaining perfectly still until after the deer has passed. If it continues to trot, the hunter has not lost anything by waiting. He still has a possible quartering away shot. Often though, these deer do stop to check the back-trail for whatever spooked them. They also may stop after they enter the back edge of the hunters scent cone. This means that the hunter must make his move in the few intervening seconds immediately after the deer has passed and before it stops to look back. This is a very tough call and takes nerves of steel. To avoid this problem, it would have been better if the happy hunter had located his stand a little farther away from the Vixon trail.

Worst Case Scenario: Due to the wind direction and his scent, the happy hunter does not have a high expectation that deer are going to approach him from behind on the Vixen trail. He has generally conceded this approach area in favor of focusing on all the rest. However, there is no reason why deer might not be expected to approach from either direction on the Rudolph trail behind him. The worst-case scenario for this hunter is a northbound deer approaching from the south on Rudolf trail. (*For right hand shooters it would be the opposite, a southbound deer approaching from the north on Rudolf trail.*)

This is bad for two reasons. First it requires a very big move. His weapon and shoulders, hips, knees and feet all need to turn nearly one-hundred and eighty degrees to get into shooting position. The second problem is that Rudolf is coming in close enough that he's going to nail the hunter for sure once he enters the scent cone. In this case it's better to take the chance on the <u>best available</u> move opportunity before Rudolph gets too close. The logic here is that it will be impossible to make the move without getting caught once Rudolph has entered the scent cone and is staring straight at him. If the hunter hasn't already made the move he will end up with a running shot at best. He doesn't lose anything by taking the best chance to make the move sooner. If he doesn't get caught, all is well, wait for the shot. If he does get caught, he still may have the running shot.

Note: If a deer is moving through on the run and doesn't appear as if it will give you any good shot opportunity, the oldest trick in hunting is to give a single sharp whistle, some guys also do this using a predator call. The deer will often stop to try and locate the source of the sound. **This works sometimes, and sometimes not.**

Thermal Air Currents: If you hunt near a ridgeline or on the side of a valley, be aware that your scent can be carried uphill or down even on days when the wind is dead calm. This depends mostly on the sun, the time of day, and which side of the hill you are on. In the morning and in the late afternoon the sun strikes the ground on one side of the valley more directly while the other side is in shade. The ground then heats the air on the sunny side which causes the air to rise. The rising air is replaced by drawing in heavier cooler air. Your scent goes along for the ride. An experienced hunter told me that a similar thing can happen if you are in a well shaded tree-stand located next to a sunny clearing. He said he used milkweed seed pods to confirm this. He released some of the tiny dried white parachutes and watched them carried down from the tree, into the clearing and up on the thermal drafts. I have not tried this, but it seems feasible if the sun is directly overhead.

In my opinion <u>it would be rare to have to alter a chosen stand based solely on thermal drafts.</u> My reasoning is this. If there is any crosswind at all, it basically overpowers any affect of thermal drafts. So, you only have to worry about them on sunny days when the wind is dead calm. Even so, they are temporary and the direction that your scent might be drawn on these currents is hard to predict. If you've chosen your stand well, there are a number of other good strong factors which favor staying there. So I wouldn't let a weak temporary and unpredictable factor chase me away from an otherwise good stand.

Ground Scent and Your Scent Trail: Up until this point I've been writing about airborne scent. Now let's give some thought to ground scent and your scent trail. The short story of my opinion is, "don't worry a whole lot about this either." But a lot has been written about how important this is and I expect I'll get a lot of grief if I don't explain. So, here goes.

Have you ever wondered how it is that predators such as wolves or bird dogs and beagles are able to follow a ground scent trail? How do they always know the correct direction to follow? A favored theory these days is that the scent is dispersing with time at an exponential rate. This means that with time the intensity of the scent is getting weaker in one direction of the ground trail at a rate of a hundred or a thousand fold. All a predator has to be able to detect is which direction the scent is getting stronger rather than weaker. Thousands of years of survival (*dinner*) has depended on this skill. Predators have become very good at it. Some, predators and different breeds of hunting dogs depend more on airborne scent while others primarily use ground scent trail in order to find "*dinner*".

There is no doubt that deer have an excellent sense of smell. However, deer generally seem to respond with little more than curiosity about most human <u>ground</u> scent. What many authors seem to forget is that deer do not chase down and kill their food before eating. They are not predators. They have had very little need to develop a skill for tracking down food by a ground scent trail. (*Leaves, and nuts do not run away much. Yes, I know that a buck can follow a doe trail when she is in estrus and is laying down scent from her urine and her interdigital gland, but there's a damn good reason for that and I don't believe this skill transfers over to tracking down humans.*) Compared with predators most deer are very inexperienced as far as what to do with a ground scent trail. Add to this the fact that there are nine-hundred-thousand other smelly humans tromping around in the woods and you have some seriously confused deer.

For these reasons I recommend that you don't waste much time worrying about your ground scent. If it's not too recent, it will most likely cause a deer to stop for a moment out of curiosity. This curiosity may be to your advantage as it may provide a good shot opportunity. In some cases I've purposely left my scent on the deer trail at the point were I had a good shooting lane for exactly this reason.

I'm not saying that you can go ahead and meander around stinking-up the place with your scent. But you don't need to wear a chemical warfare/biohazard suite either. Use reasonable caution. Avoid brushing up against low vegetation if possible on the deer trails in the immediate area where you are hunting. It's best not to use primary deer trails as your path to and from your stand on days that you intend to hunt. Cross over the deer trails when you have to. I know I said the deer were inexperienced with ground scent when compared with predators. But, that doesn't make them complete idiots. Why alert them if it's so easy to be a little bit careful?

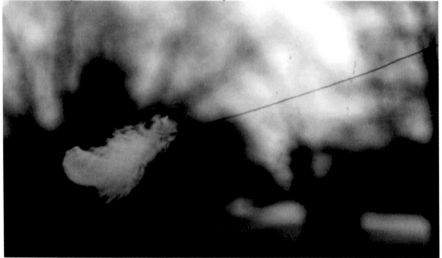

Scent Direction Indicator: This is especially important for ground-stand archery hunters who need close range shots. Even on days when it feels like the wind is dead calm, air currents are moving around you. When a deer is close, and you are trying to decide when to make your move for the shot, it could be very important to know the direction of those imperceptible air currents. So, try this. If you happen to see a flock of geese in a local park or field, go out and collect some of the down-feathers they leave behind in the grass.

You can easily collect dozens of down feathers in a few minutes. A feather that puffs outward in all directions like a Para-shoot is better than one that is mostly flat. Tie a piece of sewing thread to the tiny pointy nub. Suspended from a few inches of thread, this very sensitive device will tell you the direction of the air currents. I like it better than using bubbles or a powder squeeze bottle because it works at a glance without any movement on my part. Tie it to your weapon or hang it from a twig at your stand. (*I take no credit for this invention; it's probably at least 400 years old.*)

Sometime around about the 1992 archery season a nice buck entered the opposite side of a bowl shaped valley where I was seated half way down the western side in good cover. I watched it gradually browsing counterclockwise around the valley toward my position. As it came closer the goose-down wind detector tied to a twig, told me exactly when the imperceptible air current might give the deer my scent. I needed it to turn the circle a bit tighter. In a few more yards it would be within range. I just needed it to alter course a little. It was supposed to head for the heavily browsed area in front of me, with the nice deer trails leading into all that tasty vegetation, where the air currents still favored me, and with two clear shooting lanes. With all my mental energy I willed for it to turn. I prayed for it to turn It didn't turn. It continued toward my left. A shooting lane was there, but it was two degrees on the compass past where the little goose-down feather was pointing. I came to full draw hoping somehow that it would not detect my scent or that the air currents might shift back the other way. But they didn't shift. He moved into my scent cone twenty yards out, still inside heavy cover. Two more steps were all I needed. He stopped, licked his nose, twitched his tail and looked directly at me. He didn't panic and run. He just looked at the area with the certainty of a bird dog on point. "*I can't see you, but I know you're there.*" I had cut my fingers on my broadhead earlier that morning and wondered if it was me, or the dried blood on my glove-fingers that he smelled. In any case, the deer didn't like it. He turned and calmly walked away.

Note: In the vast majority of cases I simply take a quick glance at my little feather on a thread. It assures me that my scent will not be an issue. I can wait for the best opportunity to make the move and take the shot. That's its real value.

Scent-Blocking Clothing: This subject is a little tricky to write about. It might seem like I'm going both ways at the same time. So, I'll have to use a lot of ink and paper. As extremely picky as I am in my advice about a lot of small details, it may surprise you that I don't think scent blocking clothing is of much value for the vast majority of hunters. But note that all of the extremely fine detail in my advice is at little or no additional cost to the hunter. Scent blocking clothing cost a lot and provides only an extremely small potential benefit to a very small and select group of hunters. These are probably those "fortunate few". *(I have no axe to grind on this issue. If you can afford it and want to use it, go ahead, live your life and be happy. I really don't care. This is just my opinion.)*

If you were my young nephew, who's on a tight budget and yet is rabid about deer hunting, and if you asked me if I thought you should spend the equivalent of your next monthly car payment on scent blocking clothing, I would say "don't do it". I'd advise you to focus your budget on less costly items which go directly toward helping you keep the seven rules. Remember the "Big Rock Theorem". Scent blocking clothing won't do you any good if you don't already have the seven "big rocks" in the box first. But I'm just a regular meat and potatoes working class deer hunter and I've already had good success without scent block clothes. I'm not desperate. I'm not a semi-professional hunter, or guide, or trophy hunter, or outdoor writer whose livelihood depends on getting a deer. If it was that important, I would use the stuff no matter the cost.

Notice that the story on the previous page about the buck that scented me like a bird-dog on point, <u>seems </u>like a good example of a time when scent blocking clothing might have helped. I doubt it, but just for the sake of argument, let's assume that it would have helped. Put this into perspective. This is an extremely rare event. In fact, over my lifetime of deer-hunting, it represents only one time out of what I can easily estimate to be over a hundred close encounters with deer. It's an example of how easy it is to get your *"brain twisted"* and with the *"problem of proof"* that I wrote about in Part 1.

Furthermore, think about all the things that had to happen simultaneously in that story. It was a rare combination of my stand location being a too close to the deer trail, *(my fault)*, and being on the ground rather than in a tree, *(my choice)* and the use of a close range weapon rather than a firearm, and a risk I took in knowing that the air currents in this bowel shaped valley might be a problem for that particular shooting lane, (*both my fault again*), and the chance movements of the deer into my scent cone at that particular time when the air currents shifted. If any one of those items had been different, the outcome would probably have been different. <u>Simply relocating my stand three yards farther back up the hill would have solved the problem and cost me nothing.</u> I'm still highly doubtful that scent blocking clothing would have prevented that deer from scenting me.

> *As a side note:* I think it was really kind-a neat what this deer did. It *deserved to walk away. I'm O.K. with that. I'll get another shot on another day. It's also a really cool memory I have from what is now 15 years ago. Hell, I've killed deer more recently that I don't remember that vividly. But rabid stage hunters, or dedicated trophy hunters or people whose livelihood depends on killing a deer, probably have the exactly opposite opinion.*

But what about where <u>you</u> hunt: In some cases I hunt on public land within a short drive from the suburbs. Due to all the non-hunting human traffic in the park throughout the year, these deer become accustomed to human scent as non-threatening. The deer might not be highly wary of human scent for the first few days of hunting season. But being close to the suburbs, these areas often have very high numbers of hunters per acre. So, the deer become wary of hunters in a matter of just a few days. But still, odd as it may seem, there can be so many hunters leaving airborne scent and ground scent all over the woods that the deer actually become somewhat desensitized. Imagine the analogy of a good bird-dog placed in a five acre field where someone has planted twenty five pheasant or quail the previous day. Scent from birds in the field is everywhere and will drive the dog nuts at first. But the dog quickly learns to settle down and to not get too excited about all of the less intense older ground scent. Instead, it only reacts to the fresh, highly concentrated scent coming from downwind of a nearby bird. *(I've seen this with my own dog and with my own eyeballs at National Shoot to Retrieve Association field trials.)* This situation is exactly analogous to the *"happy hunter"* diagram and it's often what happens with deer in areas of high numbers of hunters per acre.

I also love hunting in more remote regions of the National Forrest where the hunting pressure is much less concentrated. Over the years I've noticed that deer in these areas can be either much more, or much less wary. The coyote population has exploded in areas where it was nearly non existent twenty years ago. This seems to make the deer more skittish and at a higher state of alert to any movement, sound or scent. During the mid 80's there were signs of a lot of poaching in the area which made the deer extremely wary even in the early days of archery season. In the 90's there was about nine square miles of national forest closed to partridge hunters for five years because of a study being conducted by scientists from Michigan State. The reduction in hunting traffic made the deer seem much less wary in those years. Other times I've hunted on small plots of private land or on wooded lots in farmland regions where the deer are good at keeping a distance from people. But it was fairly easy to select a stand location taking advantage of funnels of traffic in limited cover and considering the wind direction.

These various different types of hunting areas I've mentioned probably describe the conditions faced by the vast majority of hunters. The important thing to notice is that in each case, the most predominant effect of wind and scent on your hunting strategy ends up being due to your scent cone. This is exactly as I've drawn it in the *"happy hunter"* diagram. It's fairly easy, costs you nothing, and you can be highly successful without scent blocking clothes, simply by *"hunting around"* the scent issue in the ways I have recommended.

Exceptions about scent-blocking clothing: (*Again, this is just my opinion*) There are two situations where I think success in killing a deer rises in importance to a point where scent blocking clothing would be worth the expense. First is in the case where it has become known by farmers, the mailman, the school bus driver, your wife's hair dresser, and everyone at the local café that a huge trophy buck is in the area. This buck will naturally draw a lot of attention as people want to get pictures of it, and set up trail cameras, or set out bait piles, or scout to try and "pattern" its movements. The more attention it gets, the more likely it is to become one of those "genius deer".

If you are absolutely raving fanatical about getting this trophy deer, you should probably consider buying some scent blocking clothes. Just promise yourself not to go nuts if this deer ends up being dragged out of the woods by some smelly old guy in a plain wool coat.

The other situation would be if you're planning a trip to a trophy game ranch. Trophy-ranch deer might become "genius deer" because every third day there is another hunter somewhere in the woods trying to get a shot at them. They might learn that every encounter with any human scent is a threat. That's why the ranch guides will almost certainly be adamant in advising you to wear scent blocking clothes. It's not so much about your success as it is theirs. Their business depends on the customer success rate. They would much rather have you kill the deer than to provide it with a free education on the danger of human scent. That would only end up making the deer harder for the next customer to hunt. If you've traveled a long way and paid a ridiculously high price to hunt for a few days on a trophy game ranch, it wouldn't seem to be out of line to spend a few hundred dollars more for scent blocking clothing.

A few Words from Dad: During my first seven rabid years of deer hunting I had never gotten a deer. Dad knew that in those days I rarely had more than two nickels of disposable income in my pockets. Yet I was all fired up from some advertisement in a magazine and was talking about how I was going to buy some expensive gadget that I was sure I needed for the upcoming deer season. It was some ridiculous thing that would have probably caused me to miss a payment on my pickup truck. Dad knew how insanely rabid I was and how nearly impossible it is to reason with anyone in that state of mind. Finally, in a voice that indicated he was a little disappointed that I didn't remember, he said; "ya can't buy one ya know".

The pure truth of this was like a splash of cold water on my face. Dad checked my eyes to confirm that his words had cut through the crazed fogged-over look. I nodded, to let him know that I understood. Those few words were familiar and had a powerful effect as he intended. I was a little embarrassed, but he didn't judge me for it. I guess we all have been there once or twice.

That deer-season, I killed my first Buck. No expensive gadgets, just old fashion, authentic hunting. Ya can't buy that. All you can do is put in your time in the woods.

Hose the place: As I mentioned at the beginning of this chapter, among the more widespread pieces of hunting folklore from the 1980's, was the belief that serious hunters concerned about their scent should never pee near their deer stand. So a lot of guys started peeing into jars. Nothing identifies a rabid stage deer-hunter with more certainty than peeing into a jar. Yes, I admit, I did this myself. It's amazing how quickly two cups of coffee turn into four quarts of urine. I'm sure that the hunting gods were absolutely rolling on the ground with laughter at the sight of so many guys peeing into jars.

Anyway, the truth is that peeing in the woods does no harm at all to your hunting. In fact, some noted outdoorsmen are now convinced that it may be as good as commercially available scents to attract deer. Go ahead and hose the place if you need to. It won't bother the deer one bit. Don't make me draw a diagram. The idea is to keep your boots dry. You'll figure it out. But for God's sake, don't let yourself be seen carrying a jar full of your own urine around in the woods.

Good hunting.

Reading Sign
Part – 6

Over the years I've read articles claiming that there are at least three different types of deer trails, two types of rubs, and five different types of scrapes. Some writers seem to insist that you should plot every scrape, rub, deer-trail and poop-pile in four square miles on a U.S.G.S., TOPO Map. Others might have you examining deer droppings way too close or have you looking at tracks on your hands and knees with a micrometer. You might become a part-time botanist as you look for the eighteen different types of wild plants and the fourteen different crops that deer like to eat. All this horse-manure is re-heated and shoveled at deer hunters as if it's stuff you absolutely must know. It's not. As far as actually improving your chances of killing a deer, it's nearly useless. You don't need to be a deer biologist, botanist, or strategic military genius in order to be a highly successful hunter. All you really need to know are the **basics of reading sign and to understand how to use it to your best advantage**. That's what this section is about.

Beds. I bumped up two doe off these beds. Even without snow the beds would be fairly easy to see in flattened leaves or grass. Doe beds are usually smaller and are more often found as groups.

Buck beds are typically longer but it's a hard detail to compare just with your eyeball. They're more often single or paired up with a doe late in the fall. So what? Don't get all excited about finding deer beds. **My general advice is, don't try to hunt directly in or close to the edge of a bedding area.** Take a look around when you find some beds. Notice that the location would be very difficult to get close to without being detected. (*The beds in this picture were on a hilltop with heavy cover on all sided.*) So even if the deer is bedded down, you still have little chance at getting into the area without spooking them. Also, deer don't necessarily return to the same bedding area regularly. It might just happen that a good stand location is near some deer beds, but don't make it a criterion that you look for. (*Be sure to read the section called "Reverse ambush".*) **However,** bedding areas can be a hub of deer activity **especially as the rut approaches**. Bucks may circle downwind to scent-check the area for estrous doe. **So, if the rut is starting you might consider finding a stand along the trails away and _downwind_ of the beds in good cover.**

Licking Stick: I don't have a picture of a licking stick. I've only seen a couple while scouting and I mistakenly thought they were just oddball occurrences from young, half crazed bucks taking out aggression against a small sapling. But, I learned from the book Way of the Whitetail, by Dr. Leonard Lee Rue III, that these are actually much more common. Their importance is yet to be understood but they seem to attract a lot of deer   I've probably walked past more of these than I've noticed.   Basically it's a sapling that has been chewed and twisted off at about thirty to forty inches above the ground and is missing its bark around the top few inches.   Bucks leave scent on these.   Based on what little we know about licking sticks I'm not going to make any guesses about hunting near them.   I would probably look for all the other criteria for a good stand location in the area and hunt it about the same as a hot scrape.

Droppings. Doe droppings are supposedly less in total mass and individual pellet length then buck droppings. Deer poop is about the same size as rabbit poop but is more closely bunched-up and the pellets are elongated and dimpled rather than round. They can be brown or black and the shape can sometimes change depending on changes in their diet. Do not make a science project out of finding droppings. They really don't tell you a hell-of-a-lot.

Author's apology: I was surprised to read recently in a major outdoor publication, that taking careful measurement of the deer droppings in order to determine if it was from a buck or a doe has actually caught on in some areas.

I was just a little boy, along on a scouting trip in the deer woods, when my father first invented this whole thing. He had bet my Uncle Dennis five dollars that he could get my cousin Billy to go pick up some deer shit. I regret that what started out as a slightly sick, twisted, hunting joke on my poor dumb cousin, may now have spread to claim hundreds of other victims.

Sorry about that.

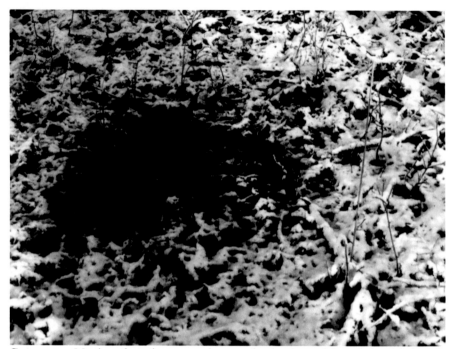

Scrapes: Notice that the snow has melted. A rookie might think this is a hot, active scrape. It's not. The leaves in the scrape are matted down and have been there since the last rain. Within this scrape, snow melts sooner due to contact with the warmer bare ground. But the layer of leaves outside the scrape provides an insulation barrier from the ground. **Scraping activity begins about three weeks prior to the rut, peaks during the rut and then drops off quickly.** Scrapes that don't have an overhanging branch, and are smaller than a paper plate, are usually not something to get too excited about. Early in the season they might be worth checking on once in a while to see if they grow and turn hot. A mature buck may scrape a week or so earlier, will be on average about 30 inches in diameter, and will almost always have the overhanging branch showing signs of being hooked, twisted and rubbed or chewed. A single buck can have dozens of scrapes in his range. Several bucks can overlap ranges and more than one buck may visit a single scrape. Bucks visit their scrapes much more frequently during the night, but hunting near scrapes during the day can still be well worth considering. **It's best to hunt near these during pre-rut before the buck has paired off with a doe.** Freshly tended scrapes with the leaves brushed out are better. You might find large buck tracks in a freshly tended scrape, but don't be discouraged if it shows visits from a smaller doe too. **If it smells musky-foul from four feet away, it's the best of all sign. This might be the one sign that would cause me to think about changing my already chosen stand location.** Don't set- up right on top of the scrape. Locate your stand a bit further away and downwind. Look for the same other qualities for a good stand location. Some hunters add commercially available buck or doe urine to scrapes hoping to aid in attracting deer. I don't have a strong opinion about that. Try it if it makes you feel better. Some guys have recently written about making mock scrapes. This involves removing the scent covered overhanging branch from a real scrape and relocating it to a fake scrape made where they have a better stand location. <u>I can not overemphasize, and I can't even count the number of ways that I think this is a dumb-ass, dumb-ass, dumb-ass, thing to do.</u> Either hunt the scrape where you find it or walk away.

Browse damage: Notice the leaves missing all around the top of this bush. The bush tried to recover with new green growth but the leaves were picked off again. Tiny frayed white tips are from recent browse. Brown tips are from older damage. **Browse damage like this is a very good sign and a lot of guys walk right past it.** The damage to low vegetation is different from rabbits. Rabbits have upper and lower teeth that snip cleanly like scissors.

Deer have no front upper teeth. They clamp down and pull causing a torn, frayed edge. You might not see a lot of browse damage along some of the major deer trails where deer mostly just pass through. But favorite browse areas will show a mix of old and recent damage and a network of small *"spider"* trails. **Often there are a couple main trails leading in and out. These can be very good places to look for a stand.** In areas where deer are over-populated you can see browse damage in the wood-line from a hundred yards away. Especially near the edges of fields. From a front view the forest will have a horizontal browse-line that looks almost perfectly straight about four feet up from the ground. From the end view you'll notice that it's concave. You may be able to see deep into the missing lower foliage. In the Fall, vegetation and deer feeding habits can change quickly. Make sure you are not hunting in a browse area that has been abandoned by the deer. Look for fresh browse and recent droppings. If there are oak trees anywhere in the area, forget about the browse and get into the acorns.

Rubbing (opposite page) begins and peaks several weeks pre-rut. Most writers believe that a rub on the side of a small tree is from a small buck. A rub on a tree larger than three inches in diameter is thought to be from a mature buck. I don't think this is highly reliable or very useful. Often a small tree might be used by a large buck in order to get at the small space behind the antler in-between the antler and the ear. While a larger tree might be chosen to rub and to test the strength of the main beams and points. This might be partly out of aggression and partly for exercise to test and build the fighting neck muscles. A bunch of rubs in one area is thought to be several bucks still in the bachelor group of early fall showing off to each other. I don't get highly excited about rubs. Rubs only tell you that at least one buck is somewhere in the area.

Buck Rub. Rubs are encouraging about the general area early in the season, but they're not the type of sign that would cause me to change my favorite stand location within that area.

This urine spot is from a mature doe. I bumped her up off her bed. She moved off about twenty yards and squatted very much like a female dog. The urine is behind the rear tracks.

The urine stain from a buck would be forward of the rear tracks, more spread out and there may be dribble marks along the tracks for a few feet. This sign is only useful for tracking / stalking hunters who need to know if they are following a buck or a doe. Otherwise it at least might be a clue that a buck or a doe is visiting the area.

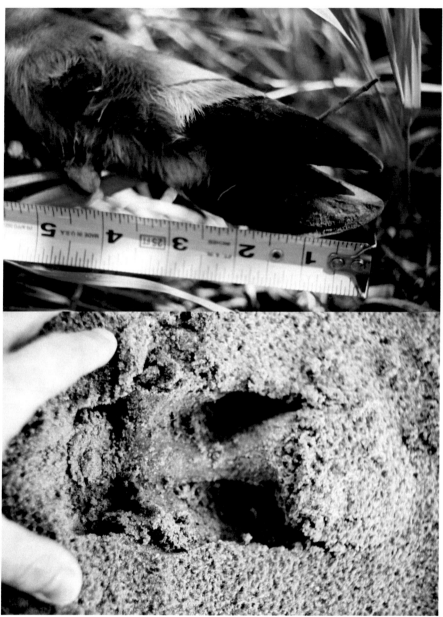

This track is over 3-1/2 inches wide. *Notice how the weight of the deer spreads out the hoofs forming a wide smooth saddle in the middle. This is partly due to the soft soil and partly due to the weight of a large mature deer. Dewclaw marks from both the front and rear are visible and slightly offset. A second deer crossed this trail at the same time leaving tracks that were only about 3/4ths this size.*

Tracks and Tracking: During my "Rabid stage", I was a fanatic about all the information I thought I could gain from reading deer tracks.   As the years have passed, reading tracks gradually became less and less important as part of my hunting.   Tracks can be fascinating, but if you hunt in the style that I've been describing, tracks are not all that important.   Mostly I just try to make mental notes of the general number of tracks in the area, their size, direction of travel, and if possible the approximate time of day when they might have been made.   The main things that I look for are simply <u>encouragement</u> from the deer trails having perhaps a few <u>mature sized tracks or recent scuff marks in the leaves that indicate use within the last day or two</u>.   This is usually a quick casual look while I'm walking. I might stop to study for a minute or follow a short distance if they seem unusual or if a trail gets my curiosity for some reason. On hard ground you might see only a simple heart shaped track without any dewclaw marks. Both bucks and doe have dewclaws on the front and back legs. These marks will show depending on how deep the tracks sink into the soil which depends on how heavy the dear is, how soft the soil is and how hard the deer is pushing off.

Without snow, and depending on the type of ground cover and conditions, even large heavy deer can leave almost no easily visible sign that they have passed. You might be lucky to get a few clear tracks in a row. These can be followed, but it's very slow going. The technique is similar to following a poor blood trail. You'll lose and find the tracks for several yards at a time, as you fan forward in careful semicircles. You may come upon a well worn deer trail that shows few if any clear tracks. It might be a bare compacted path with only scuff marks, or parted weeds, or a pattern of disturbance in a leaf-covered trail.   Use your eyes to pick up the disturbance in the leaves or ground cover. Sometimes it's just a slightly different shade of color in the dew or frost on the grass. It helps your eyes if you take a different angle of view. As you move, scan to the sides with your eyes and crouch down occasionally. Move forward quickly toward any clear soft crossings like dirt roads, tilled fields or soft creak beds where the trail is easy to pick up. **This is a valuable skill to develop for finding a downed deer with a poor blood trail, but it's not something I use in the actual pursuit of deer while hunting.**

About all you really need to know about tracks is that the pointy end is the direction the deer is traveling, and that bucks tend to be larger and heavier than doe, and therefore leave larger and deeper tracks. But, there's a lot of variability and overlap on that point. Don't get hung up on it. It's not that important. Recent tracks are good. Large recent tracks are great. Maybe it's a buck. Maybe it's not. Don't spend a lot of time trying to read this from the tracks. The point is simply that these are good signs of recent and regular deer movement through the area. **But the tracks are not as important as the trail and general area they pass through. Stop looking at the tracks! Get your head up and start looking at what's around you**. Ask yourself, does the area show signs that the deer come through regularly? Does it look and feel "bucky" to you? Does it provide cover or food or easy escape routes? Is it a pathway between cover and food? Is there a nearby intersecting or parallel trail? Is it a nook in the landscape that seems like it might be overlooked by other hunters? Is there a good place for a stand? Do you get a good strong gut level feeling about this spot? If the answer is yes to most of these questions, there is a very high probability that a buck will be among the deer that return to this area. This is much better than spending time trying to tell if the tracks are from a buck or a doe.

The best books on tracks is: THE TRACKERS FIELD GUIDE, By James C. Lowery, Copyright 2006.

If you want to develop an eye for track age, take special note of some that you know are fresh. A good way to see a lot of clear, recent tracks in a short time is to drive the dirt roads in deer country early in the morning. Stop and look carefully at dozens of different tracks. Especially look at tracks where you actually have seen the deer that made them. Try to follow them for a while just for fun and for practice. Check back on these tracks a couple times over a few days. Notice in detail how they change and begin to fade. Take into account the soil type and its condition when the track was made. Think about what the weather conditions have been in the past day or two and how it would affect the tracks in this type of soil. The sun along with a dry breeze or just a little rain will age sandy tracks much more quickly than tracks made in clay. Did it frost or freeze overnight? Was there recent snow, rain, wind or leaves falling? All of this gives you clues for estimating the age of the tracks. It's actually kind-a fun. **But even if the details of "track theory" were all true, and if you had a very sensitive eye and nearly perfect tracking conditions, it still doesn't really do you a hell-a-lot of good.** Don't spend a lot of time on your hands and knees studying the tracks. Even if you could say for sure that the tracks are from a big buck, it may have been a one time deal. The buck may have been forced through an area once, and is not likely to return. It might be in survival mode and not simply following a daily routine. **So, don't choose a spot based solely on a set of huge fresh tracks. Worse yet, don't rule out an otherwise great location based on the lack of huge fresh tracks.** (Besides, *even if the large tracks you're looking at were actually made by a doe, and this fooled you into locating a stand here, the doe could very well end up helping to draw a buck into the area. In that case you have double-out-smarted yourself and it still ended up working in your favor anyway. Go figure that one out.*)

In the past fifteen or so years I've chosen my stands based almost solely on the trails and terrain and cover without much concern at all about finding any tracks. The buck comes into the area because it's a good "bucky" area. The hunter who recognizes this area is there for the same reason and not because of any particular sets of tracks.

Fourteen signs it "*might*" be a very big buck.
1. Individual tracks are noticeably larger and deeper than others. (*Width more so than length. Varies greatly depending on ground*)

2. Dewclaw marks are noticeably wider. This may indicate a more massive leg bone needed for supporting more weight. (*This is a very fine details and is hard to measure*)

3. Hoof marks flatten and spread out. Not pointing into the ground like a lighter weight deer. (*Obvious*)

4. Dewclaw marks farther rearward from the hoof marks leaving the impression that a steeper angle from the rear legs and a more forceful levering action was needed to push the additional weight forward. (*This one is impossible to explain any better. Sorry. I really tried*)

5. Distinct and wider center line forming a saddle between hoofs tapering outward due to the added weight. (*Much more so on soft soil or wet snow than on hard ground*)

6. Length of walking stride is notably and consistently longer. (*See my notes on this in Theory vs Reality*)

7. Traveling alone, or following a doe, but not usually with a group. Avoids open areas, tends to keep low profile, and stays in cover if possible. (*Especially in late fall*)

8. In early season, may be reluctant to go through extremely tangled brushy cover that other deer go into, but will instead choose to pass nearby this cover. (*When antlers are in velvet or have just recently come out of velvet. This would be prior to hunting season and so would only be useful in pre season scouting*)

9. Later in the season, it is more willing to go into tangled thick cover. Look for twigs in the snow broken off by its antlers. This is unlike a small buck or a large doe which could easily slide through the thick cover without much disturbance.

10. Urine stain in snow is not in a small neat circle concentrated even with or behind the rear tracks. Urine stain is somewhat spread out and is concentrated forward of the rear tracks. Urine may also show dribble pattern along the path side to side for a short distance.

11. Tracks sidestep the trail at a narrow point between two trees where other deer normally pass through.

12. Bed is noticeably larger, more often located alone or with one doe. Bed, may show stain more toward the center third in the area where the rear legs are folded under and may smell very musky.

13. Antler imprints may be in the snow where the deer had to put its head down to get acorns or also sometimes near the edge of the bed.

14. Deer stopped and rubbed it's antlers on a large tree or visits or makes one or more large scrapes.

It's a mistake to fixate on just one or two of these signs or on absolute fixed measurements. But all together these may help you build a reasonably strong case that the deer is a huge buck. You should be able to find several of these signs in a quarter mile of tracking. **However, for hunters anywhere in the Midwest, my best advice remains, <u>not to track or stalk the deer.</u>**

On My Hands and Knees: I went through a decade or so in my "Rabid stage" when maybe I read a little too much about deer hunting and I believed just about everything I read. I'd look at a few sets of tracks and then start making some long speech about how this deer must be a buck or it must be a doe for this reason or for that reason. My dad would stand there look'n at me a little sideways wait'n for the speech to be over, and then he'd always say *"Ya can't eat tracks ya know'.* He repeated this phrase exactly the same way, every time, every deer season.

After the first book was published I realized that I had treated the tracking issue too lightly. I also realized that most of what I believed about deer tracks was stuff I had read or heard, but that I couldn't actually prove. So, I made it my mission over the winter to get field data to prove the big buck track theory. **I observed and studied only the tracks of real, live, wild, deer that I had actually seen with my own eyeballs.** I made three dozen trips into the deer woods taking about a hundred pictures and all kinds of measurements. I looked at length, width, depth, walking stride, running stride, and drag marks in snow. I carefully studied the location of the front print relative to the rear print on the left and right side of the centerline. A good deal of time was spent on my hands and knees in the snow with a tape measure, camera, and notepad. At times I recognized that this was ridiculous and how obsessed I had become. I envisioned the hunting gods laughing at me like they did when my cousin Billy was tricked into picking up the deer shit. I kinda had to laugh at myself too. But still, I kept on going.

On three separate outings I was fortunate to find a nice buck paired with a mature doe and with snow on the ground. One became the cover photo of this book. These provided the perfect situation to study and compare tracks. There was no guessing or theorizing about "if" it was a buck or a doe or how fresh the tracks were.

This nice sized doe paired with a big buck provided a good chance to compare a lot of tracks of both deer side by side in the snow.

I started out trying to get pictures in support of what I thought I would be writing about deer tracks. But instead, **I was stunned to find that almost everything I believed about big buck tracks could not be supported by the evidence.** So, this entire new section of the book was created. I hated to use up all the ink and paper for it, but it couldn't be avoided.

Big Buck Track Theory: Take a look at the walking gait track diagram on the next page. Assume that these are sets of tracks you've found in the woods. It's best to have at least three or four good sets in a row. First, stand straddling the tracks facing the direction the deer was traveling. Next, find the centerline. This is an imaginary line that divides the tracks so each set falls to the left or right of the deer's line of travel. Each track set might appear as if it's a single print. It's not. Each set is actually the (left front and rear) -or- (right front and rear). The rear hoof often lands almost exactly on top and perhaps a little behind the front hoof. If you look closely you might be able to see this offset in the prints. So, at this point you know the deer's left and right, front and rear tracks.

Take note of the general length of the walking stride. Take more careful note of the individual track width and depth. Pay special attention to the width and shape of the center split between the hoofs. If possible see if the front tracks fall toward the inside or outside from the centerline compared to the rear tracks. Notice the possible presence of dewclaw marks, their distance from the hoof marks, depth, angle of entry and their spread.

With all of the above information you "*supposedly*" can tell if it is a big buck versus a doe. You do this by plugging the information into the "*big buck track theory*" which involves six points that I will describe next in "Track Theory vs reality" .

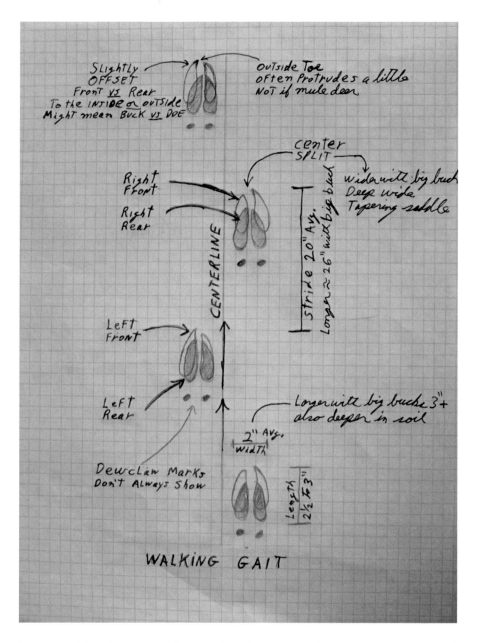

Slightly OFFSET
Front vs Rear
To the INSIDE or OUTSIDE
Might mean Buck vs DOE

outside Toe
often Protrudes a little
NOT if mule deer.

center SPLIT

wider with big buck
Deep wide
Tapering saddle

Right Front
Right Rear

CENTERLINE

Stride 20" Avg.
Longer ≈ 26" with big buck

Left Front

Left Rear

Longer with big bucks 3"+
also deeper in soil

2" Avg. WidTh

Dewclaw Marks
Don't Always Show

Length 2½ ≠ 3"

WALKING GAIT

The combination of wider tracks, deeper tracks, longer stride, and _perhaps_ the front track offset to the outside of the rear track _might_ help determine that it's a buck. **Use caution, read track facts**

Track fact: The photographs on page 131, are from one of three occasions when I had excellent tracking snow along with a nice buck paired up with a mature doe. The situation could not have been more perfect. I placed my hat on a branch to mark the spot where I started tracking the buck. The two deer moved mostly in parallel staying within about twenty-five yards of each other. They moved to cover ahead of me and then waited to check their back-trail. I worked very slowly, often on my hands and knees, measuring and photographing the buck tracks. The two deer gave me several more good looks at them. I returned to collect my hat and then started following and measuring the doe tracks for about the same distance. This produced the clearest tracks and the best measurements yet. During all of these outings I estimate that I followed a mile of big buck tracks and probably five miles of mature doe tracks.

Track Theory vs. Reality: The following six points are what you'll most likely read in popular hunting publications about how to tell a big buck track from a doe track. Up until a couple months ago I believed most of this stuff was true. It's not. In the blue italics are my counterpoints and opinions versus the theory.

Front print outside from centerline versus rear print: A number of different sources have claimed that the front tracks of a mature buck will land slightly to the outside (*away from the centerline*) versus the rear track. The reason is supposedly that a mature buck has a wider front chest area than a doe. ***This is not true on a consistent enough basis to be of any real practical use to a hunter.*** *The tracks of a **mature doe can also show this**, and with about the same frequency as a buck. Even with perfect tracking conditions this sign is **often hard to determine with certainty** and shows up almost randomly in only a few track sets. **While tracking the same deer, a known buck or doe, I found the front tracks sometimes fell to the outside or inside of the rear track. I suspect that this is actually the deer making small adjustments for balance as might be required by the uneven terrain.** This sign alone is certainly not a good indicator of a big buck versus a mature doe.*

Wider tracks: Typical whitetail deer tracks range in width from about 1-5/8 to 2-1/8 inches, and are 2-1/8 to 3 inches in length. Track width is thought to be a better indicator of a big buck than track length. Some hunters use the known length of a rifle cartridge laid across the track as a handy measuring device to judge its width. Most authors believe that tracks wider than 3-1/4 inches are a good sign of a big buck. *This I believe is **partially true** but you have to <u>be very careful</u>. It's easy to find doe tracks that are this wide too. It's also possible to have a nice buck leave tracks that are not as wide as you would expect. The width varies along the trail of an individual deer and depends a lot more on the ground conditions (hard ground versus mud, sand, snow,) than the size of the deer. In order to use this as a reasonably decent indicator it would be very helpful to have several different deer tracks made at the same time in the same type of soil for comparison. It can be a moderately useful indicator but it's certainly not foolproof all by itself.*

Tapering wide Hoof split: The heavier buck will show a wider split between the hoofs. Rather than being close and sharp, the ridge spreads wide and taper to the sides forming a saddle in the middle. ***This is partly true.*** *It's a judgment call. A large doe can leave a print like this and a nice buck might not look much different. The wide tapering center split between the hoof marks spreads out in sand, mud or soft wet clay. To a somewhat lesser extent it can also spread in wet thick snow. But a heavier deer will show this to a higher degree. A big buck might be on average 25% heavier than a mature doe. So it will sink in deeper and force the hoofs to spread wider. A very heavy deer may show this even on hard compacted soil. It won't be as deep and the center saddle might not be as prominent, but the surface scuff mark will spread wider. This detail also has to be used carefully.*

 *Suppose for example, that large doe in the area weighs 160 lbs and that an average buck weighs about 200 lbs. Can you tell the difference in the tracks of these two animals if they walk across soft ground? It depends on your eyeball and your experience with looking at a lot of tracks in different conditions. In any case it's quite possible that you could get crossed-up about the tracks of a nice 200 pound buck versus those of a 160 lb doe. But you're not likely to mistake the tracks of an average doe with an **above average buck** weighing 225 to 300 lbs. **You'll know-em when you see-em.***

Longer walking stride: The walking stride is typically 14 to 22 inches and tends toward the longer side on bucks versus doe. *This varies enough along the trail of each individual deer that it is **of little practical use** to a hunter. If the walking stride is consistently in the 22" to 26" inch range it might be helpful. But it's certainly not foolproof. A large doe could be close to that range too. This actually might be more due to the fact that the stride of deer lengthens going downhill and shortens going uphill, just like it does with the stride of humans.*

Wide dewclaw marks: Dewclaw marks that are wider apart are thought to be from a more massive leg needed to support a larger deer which might be a big buck. *This could be true, but in order to tell this from marks left by a large doe **you would need a micrometer** to measure the difference. It is **of no practical use** to a hunter.*

Drag-marks in snow; Years ago some guys wrote articles in major hunting magazines claiming that drag marks in the snow were more likely from a buck than from a doe. ***This is not true** and almost nobody believes it anymore. All deer leave drag marks in the snow at least some if not most of the time. This depends mostly on the depth of the snow.*

My advice about tracks remains the same as it was in the first book. The tracks are not as important as the trail and general area they pass through. Stop looking at the tracks! Get your head up and start looking at what's around you. Don't choose a spot based solely on a set of huge fresh tracks. **Worse yet, don't rule out an otherwise great location based on the lack of huge fresh tracks.**

All those times in the past, when I had not actually seen the deer, and when I was making some long speech about everything I could tell from a few sets of tracks, was all just plain-old horse-poop. For twenty-odd years I had read, and believed this stuff. I adopted it as the truth. I spread, preached and believed my own bull. That's probably what my dad was really thinking. In the future if someone starts giving me a long speech about a few sets of tracks, I might not say "*prove it*" and I might not say what I'm really thinking, "*yer-full-a-horse poop*", I'll probably be a little more polite and just say what my dad always said. "*Ya can't eat tracks ya know*".

Good hunting.

Making the Good Shot
Part-7

> *This section is intended to be short, general and relevant to both archery and firearm hunters. Separate sections for archery and for firearms give much more detail.*

Cornerstone Point! You don't need to be a superb marksman in order to be a highly successful deer-hunter! You just need to be good enough. This is exactly opposite of what other writers would lead you to believe. So, let me explain.

This rule provides a cornerstone point at which you can see how the other six rules contribute as a total package. If you're good at obeying the first five rules (*be still, be silent, listen, use your eyes, resist the urge to move quickly*), then it's not hard to have a deer come within range. Add a little skill with rule seven (*Find a good stand*) and the effect is multiplied again.

The fact that most of the deer approaching your area <u>do</u> end up coming within range of your stand is not an accident. You planned for it when you chose the stand. You read the signs. You looked at the trails, the topography, the cover and the various choices for a stand. You set up within range of two crossing trails or between two parallel trails so you could cover plenty of real estate with less concern about the wind direction. You used your skills and maybe a bit of instinct. So, it shouldn't be a surprise to you when at the end of the day, ninety percent of the deer you saw passed well within your range exactly as you had anticipated! I'm not saying you can predict that deer will move toward you from a mile away. I'm not saying you can predict how every deer will approach. What I am saying is, for those deer that do happen to be heading in your direction, as they get closer, the trails and terrain begin offering fewer other likely alternatives. Their route becomes more predictable within that smaller area. It becomes increasingly probable that the deer will continue to move in your direction. **At that point all you have to do is <u>not mess up</u> with rules one through five!** If you do mess up, you are likely to see nothing at all, or perhaps a fast moving tail bounding away. Then, even a great stand location and being a superb marksman does you no good whatsoever!

But, the big payoff from obeying the other six rules is that the shots are generally not that difficult! So, you don't necessarily need to be a superb marksman. A second important bonus of making a good shot is that you will have a much easier recovery of your downed deer.

How good do you need to be? The classic broadside shot at a deer offers a kill zone that's roughly eight inches in diameter. It's reduced to about six inches for quartering shots. Frontal shots give you only about four inches. Depending on the distance, hitting a target this size isn't hard to do. You don't have to be a world-class thousand-yard target shooter. The critical question for both archery and firearm hunters is this: *At what distance are you capable of putting a very high percentage of your shots inside that four, six or eight inch diameter?*

For firearms hunters, depending on the weapon and the marksman, the answer might typically be anywhere from fifty-yards to three-hundred yards. It shouldn't be a problem to find a stand where a very high percentage of deer come within those distances. For shotgun and some of the older muzzle-loader rifles, fifty to seventy five yards might be about the best you can do. That's fine. Just locate your stand with the intention to take shots inside those limits. With iron sights, even at forty-yards, in low light conditions, and with a target that blends in with the background, it's sometimes hard to find that four or eight inch area. But, even with a scope on a superb rifle and being an excellent marksman, I think it's a poor hunting strategy to try and cover a vast open area with three hundred yard shots in both directions. Deer generally avoid crossing these areas unless forced. Then they cross quickly into heavy cover.

In my experience in Michigan, Illinois and Wisconsin and in the type of terrain and deer-cover that I like to hunt in firearms season, most shots are less than one hundred yards. So, for practical purposes, one-hundred yard capability is adequate. Although this is considered short range for target practice, it's a good practical distance for most hunting conditions. For a decent rifle and with a modest amount of practice this is not too demanding. If you follow the advice in the next section "Getting Good with a Rifle", you should have no problem out to ranges of two or three hundred yards.

For archery hunters, from a practical hunting point of view, you need to develop enough accuracy and precision **with your broadheads to have a good, twenty-yard kill shot**. Many shots are in the range of twelve to fifteen yards so this gives you an added margin for error. Developing a kill shot at thirty-yard or beyond is nice, but not absolutely necessary. Mostly it just increases your confidence for the more frequent shots you'll get inside twenty-yards.

Once in a while you'll meet someone who takes shots out to fifty yards or farther. A small percentage of the best archers, usually shooting compound bows, have developed an excellent kill shot capability at those distances. In theory, I suppose there is nothing wrong with that if you can do it. But there are also a small percentage of hunters who attempt those shots knowing full well that they don't have the precision and accuracy. It's more of a shoot and hope approach. They basically don't really give-a-shit if they wound a deer. It's stupid and unethical.

There's nothing wrong with pushing your skills to develop a fifty yard kill shot. But remember a few things. It's rare in the deer woods that the available cover requires you to locate your stand at distances that would force you to make shots at beyond twenty or thirty yards. Longer shots require overhead clearance for the arrow trajectory. From up in a tree the overhanging foliage often blocks the shooting lane making these long shots impossible. It becomes critical that you know the exact distance to the target which probably means using a range finder. It adds arrow flight time, which means a deer could jump at the sound of your release. Furthermore, it's fairly easy to find good stand locations within twenty yards of crossing or parallel deer trail. This doubles your coverage area. Thirty or forty yards capability is nice, but the vast majority of real action takes place between fifteen and twenty-five yards.

Mental shooting ritual checklist: Most hunters will get a bit excited at the sight of the deer. I've met a couple hunters who told stories of severe cases of what is referred to as "buck fever". This is a level of excitement that destroys their ability to perform. The technique of developing a mental shooting ritual checklist does a couple things to help overcome this. First, it's intended to give you something that's familiar. This has a calming effect and may give you enough time to get your breathing and heart back to normal.

Second, it gives you something mechanical to go through that will help you do it right. This is exactly the reason why emergency medical people practice doing CPR by the numbers. It's like a ritual checklist. They practice until it actually would be hard for them <u>not</u> to do it right even on their first ambulance run.

For the rifle, my mental ritual checklist is, *safety off, gun up, kill zone, gentle squeeze.* "Safety off" means that I've made the first part of my move to get the gun into my lap and that I am about to move the safety to the fire position. *Be aware that on some rifles it may be necessary to muffle the metallic click sound of the safety if a deer is extremely close.* Do it before you bring the gun up to your shoulder. "Gun up" means that I have decided to make the second part of my move to get into shooting position. "Kill zone", means that I have the sights on the exact aim point. "Gentle squeeze" reminds me that this is still important and to do it right even in the last millisecond. In order for it to become familiar, it's good to practice saying it while you are shooting at the rifle range.

With the bow my mental checklist is: *Draw, lock-point, sight on, kill zone, gentle release.* The first couple times that deer came within bow range, all of my strength seemed to leave me. The excitement or nervousness made it seem like the draw weight had quadrupled. Part of this is the fear of getting caught making the move with the deer so close. So, the first item on my list *(draw)* was intended to acts like a mental command to focus my mind and strength on only one thing, making the draw. The next item was to remind me to check my **lock-point** (***anchor point***). This is a key part of archery shooting form. It's the thing most likely to get screwed up due to excitement and can contribute the most to shot error. **But, if the anchor point is right, the rest of my form is probably right too, or at least it won't contribute enough error to bring the shot out of the kill zone**. Once I reach this point in the countdown I begin to feel a calming effect. The hardest parts are done. The next step, "sight on" reminds me to check that I am using the correct sight pin for the distance. The mental command "gentle release" is <u>allowed</u> only after the sight pin is centered on the "Kill Zone".

The countdown sequence of the checklist often takes less than ten seconds. But sometimes it gets interrupted and needs to be re-started. Practice it a few times before you go hunting. Give it a couple rehearsal trials after you first get settled in at your stand without actually shooting. A ritual checklist that you faithfully follow will make it very unlikely that you would be out of the kill zone even if you are a bit excited. Try it. It really works.

Fine Tuned: Realize that not only are your shooting skills with a gun or bow fine tuned, but also that these weapons are individually fine-tuned to you, and you are tuned to them. On several occasions I've been out shooting with my brothers Dale or John, or with my nephews Steve and Jeffery. Dale and John are both excellent marksmen. Steve is getting to be quite good with his fathers' deer rifle. Once in a while, just for fun, I would take a few shots using someone else's rifle. It was embarrassing. My shooting degraded instantly and noticeably. There was something that felt very strange to me as I applied pressure to the trigger. I remembered also a time when I owned two superb shotguns. One was used for skeet and the other was for trap. The problem was that if I got good with one, I was horrible with the other until I burned through a full box of shells to make the switch. I've also had a very similar thing happen with archery. My point is this. **Even though you may have gotten to be very good with your gun or bow, it's unlikely that you can simply pick up someone else's and be as good with it as you are with your own.** In the process of getting good, you have become married to it, and it to you. You know the weapon in very intimate ways of which you may not even be conscious. These intimate details are what make you good together. That's why someone else's finely tuned weapon might not shoot exactly the same in your hands. Yours might not shoot precisely the same in their hands either. Don't flirt with a dozen different weapons. Stick with the one you love and learn to love the one you're with.

Choose your weapon: Humans have successfully hunted deer with spears, crude bows, high tech bows, shotguns, hand guns, mussel-loaders and modern rifles with telescopic sights. The point is that they all work in the hands of someone skilled in their use provided that they shoot inside the weapons effective range.

The mistake for any of these weapons is to push the distance of the shot beyond the point where the trajectory or energy and accuracy starts to fall off rapidly. All you need to do, is know what those limits are for yourself and your weapon, and then simply accept them as part of your hunting. But, there's no way in hell of making a good shot beyond those limits. It's unethical and simply stupid to try in most hunting situations.

Now I have a couple short stories to illustrate some other points. When I was in college, I worked the night shift as an Emergency Medical Technician in a hospital E.R. near Ann Arbor Michigan. One night, some nutcase was out on a shooting spree with a twenty-two rifle. A couple of patients walked into the E.R having been shot once or twice. They were O.K. Another guy came in by ambulance even though he could have walked. He was shot something like five times and was basically not in serious condition.

On another occasion somewhere around this same period of time I watched a friend shoot a deer *(illegally)* with a twenty-two rifle at a distance of about seventy yards. What was astonishing was the speed with which this deer dropped like a sack of rocks from a single shot to the brain. My point is this. It's not about power, and it's not about how many shots you can get off, it's about shot placement.

I do not advise use of a twenty-two rifle, which is illegal for deer hunting in all states that I know of. I also do not recommend attempting a brain shot since the kill zone is extremely small. These comments were only in order to make my point.

Shot placement: Many articles and diagrams and even paper targets are available that show the kill zone on a deer. Three-D targets are also good because they get you thinking about the different aim-points from different angles that will cause the arrow or bullet to pass through vital organs. If you've never gotten a deer and have a chance to watch someone else field-dress one, it's a good way to learn some anatomy. Before the field-dressing gets too far, look for the location of the heart, lungs and liver. Make a special mental note of where they are in relation with body features, especially in relation to the front leg. Another key thing to look for before it gets severed is the location of the diaphragm. This is a sheet of membrane-like muscle that basically separates the body cavity into front and rear compartments with some plumbing going through it. Note the location of the diaphragm in relation with the outer anatomy. Basically you need to try and avoid hitting the back compartment containing the stomach and intestines while hitting in front of the diaphragm containing the vital organs.

Not necessarily the heart shot: In the case of a classic broadside view look for the point where the front leg has a sudden backward crook in it that makes a backward pointing "V". Inside the point of that "V" is the aim point for a heart shot. This point is low on the deer's chest area. It's at about "six-o-clock" on the kill zone. The problem with this aim-point is that if your shot is in error just a little low, you might simply clip some hair or wound a front leg. So, you need to be very sure for this shot. I suggest that a better aim point is about two inches above the "V". It gives you a little room for error by putting the shot more toward the center of the kill zone. For archery, stay away from that big heavy front shoulder bone. But, with a rifle this is an excellent spot since the deer will go down instantly.

Fire away: You might choose to hunt with an old muzzle-loading rifle or a simple re-curve bow or an extremely high tech. compound bow or a modern rifle with a fine telescopic sight. Some guys who went all the way out to high tech. have become a bit more seasoned and returned to the appreciation of simpler, more primitive weapons. The important thing is to accept as part of your hunting, the capabilities and limitations of whatever weapons you choose.

Of course there are any number of things in the deer-woods that might make the shot more difficult. Brush, trees, hills, wind, lighting, movement of the target and distance all contribute. Distance is always a key factor because it amplifies any mistake the shooter makes and adds a trajectory problem. Mistakes at this point are mostly due to the excitement of the moment. Most everything else can be worked out through practice at a range prior to the season.

Good hunting.

Dad. *In the 1970's 80's and 90's you might have bumped into a one-armed man in the Huron National Forest, Southeast of Mio Michigan. He liked to talk with hunters passing by on the trails and was sure to ask if you "seen any". He was a superb marksman. He said my first book was "pretty good".*

"Getting Good with a Rifle"
Dedicated to my father
Part - 8

In Dad's view, shooting well was not simply a nice thing to be able to do for recreation. It was important. As a youth, near the end of the Great Depression, he helped provide food for his younger brother and two sisters after his father had been killed. There was no such thing as Social Security in those days. He sold extra game meat, mostly rabbit, pheasant and duck, to local restaurants in Saginaw, and made some money from the small bounty on birds that would swarm over farmer's crops. Shooting skills served him well as a teenage combat veteran of World War II. After returning from the war, he lost his right arm below the elbow in an accident at the foundry. In the woods at Mom's folk's farm, he re-taught himself to shoot left handed. It was like a sort of therapy I guess. If he could shoot, there was still a chance that everything would be O.K.

For most of my youth, the only guns he had for hunting were the old .22 rifle and a blunder-bust of a 12 gage side by side. He had long dreamt of owning a fine deer rifle. Tucked away next to his EZ-chair, was a dog-eared, two page centerfold picture of a rifle in a magazine. He almost wore the picture out from looking at it over the time it took him to finally save the money to buy his rifle. I was about twelve years old and happened to be with him on that day. It was a used rifle, but in excellent condition. He examined it closely, bending over the counter to check the serial number as if it had to match a number in his mind. Only then, would this rifle be meant for him. In a low tone, talking mostly to himself, and partly I think, to the rifle, I heard him say "*Belgian steel*". His voice made the words sound like magic. Dad was a rugged man, not easily shaken. That's why I remember this so clearly. He placed an envelope on the counter and held it down by the edge with his hook as he counted out the bills. Finally he scooped up the money and told the man at the store to count it again to make sure it was right. The bills trembled in his hand across the counter. I'd never seen that before. Then, I recognized the special profile of the rifle. It was the one from the centerfold. They had found each other. This was the happy marriage between a superb marksman and a superb weapon. It lasted forty-some years and became the stuff of legendary tails at deer camp.

Dad was first of all, a real bear about gun safety. He didn't bullshit around about it either. He expected his instructions to be followed, and without a whole lot of explanations. He liked the idea of starting a youngster with a .22 rifle rather than a BB-gun. He thought a BB-gun would teach a lack of respect and carelessness, as if a firearm was a toy. I think his opinion stemmed from an incident in the late 1950's, when an unsupervised neighbor boy, playing with a BB-gun, shot Mary in the face, hitting her just below her right eye. According to legend, Dad busted the BB-gun, spanked the brat, and "tuned-up" the kid's father too.

Dad taught all five of us boys and my sister Mary, to shoot when we were young. There was a benefit from having only one rifle being shared among two or three of us at a time. As one shooter was handling the weapon under dad's direct instruction, the others were watching and listening. This was much better quality instruction and much safer than having multiple students with multiple weapons. My older brothers, Dale and Larry, were shooting with dad in the back yard, when I finally must have begged long enough, that he let me take my first shot with the .22 rifle while sitting in his lap. The rifle was too heavy for me, so he helped steady it at the forearm. I snuggled up to the stock, aimed as he had told me, and squeeze the trigger. I still remember the astonishment and delight of a child, at seeing a small glass baby-food jar, ninety feet away, suddenly shatter. Since that day I have enjoyed shooting. All of us, each in turn, came and went, from school or military service, to jobs, to marriage, and to kids of our own. Twenty, thirty and forty hunting seasons have passed. In all those years the outdoors provided the background for many of our most memorable family stories.

When Jim got sick, the family came together to do what we could in a hopeless situation. Dad sold his rifle in case the money might come in handy for Jim. But we knew that selling his rifle was never really about the money at all. I'm also certain that Dad knew he could not bargain with God. It was only a small symbolic offering, tossed into the collection plate, accompanied by the deepest of prayer.

I like to believe that there's a hell-of-a good man somewhere in Michigan, still walkin the trails with that great old deer rifle. Hope he left the marks in the forearm too. Gives it character.

My sense of things nowadays is that a lot of young hunters might not have a Dad who can teach them. So, I'd like to recommend the next best thing. It's a short, simple, easy to read and perfectly illustrated book, published in 1972, that contains everything my dad taught us about shooting. The fundamentals of marksmanship have not changed. Even if you've been shooting for many years, and especially if you're teaching a youngster, go to your library and ask them to find this book. **Marksmanship, by Gary L Anderson.**

I will touch on a few points from the book here, but I will not attempt to repeat them. The book was not written with hunters in mind. It was more intended for the Olympic competition type of shooting. There are major differences. Hunters often can't take one of the classic shooting positions, don't have a fixed stationary target at a precisely known distance. Preparation time for making the shot is likely to be much shorter. Also, the bull's eye didn't blend in with the terrain, and there weren't a bunch of obstructions in the way or low light conditions to deal with. That's hunting. Get used to it pilgrim.

Getting Started: I think it's a common mistake with dad's nowadays to start their youngster too early and then try to move them along too fast. You can see it immediately in the young shooters body mechanics, movements, posture and attitude. There's no sense of harmony or comfort between the shooter and the weapon. I saw this again yesterday at a shooting range. Three young guys were obviously uncomfortable with handling a shotgun that was way too big for them physically and in recoil. Their body mechanics were completely screwed up, tense in anticipation of the recoil and embarrassed in front of their dad and their piers because they couldn't hit a slow flying clay pigeon. It wasn't the kid's fault.

It's not a bad idea to start out shooting as a youngster. But this has to depend on the kid's maturity, physical development, coordination and their ability to follow instructions. I think this might be anywhere between eight and twelve years of age. A good test might be to watch how the kid does with handling a fishing pole. If they can follow instructions with the fishing pole, hold it like you tell them, cast, retrieve, and walk along a path by the river without getting fowled up every ten yards, it's a good sign that they might be ready to learn to handle a firearm.

> **If you don't have an experienced and trustworthy friend to teach you, contact the NRA, DNR, State Rifle association, Boy Scouts or a local gun club to get good training for handling firearms.**

If you are acting as the instructor, it helps if you are comfortable, relaxed, calm, friendly and firm. Don't be in a hurry. The basics of safe handling of all firearms are the same. Teach that first. Don't introduce too many mechanically different types of guns at one time. Don't expect youngsters to get it all, and retain everything from a single lesson or from shooting once a year. It's better to have repeated instruction and exposure (*maybe* 9 or 10 *times*) with shorter time lapses in between. Start with nothing larger than a 22 rifle. The idea is to develop excellent shooting style and to get very comfortable with the weapon. This is easiest with a rifle that has very little recoil. I was happy shooting a .22 for many years before I was old enough to start bird hunting with my first shotgun, a single shot twenty gauge. That's the next step up in recoil. But it ain't the same as shooting a deer-rifle. Moving up to a rifle that has a bit of recoil adds a whole new problem for a young shooter. If the recoil is too much, a complete mental attitude shift takes place. It goes from one of "*I love shooting and look how tight my groups are,*" to a totally different attitude, "M*an this hurts and my groups are terrible."* The difference is between being very comfortable and enjoying shooting, versus tension fear and pain. That mental shift will quickly degrade their shooting ability. The reason for starting with the 22 rifle is that good shooting habits are already in place. The youngster already has good confidence in their ability. So, they won't get discouraged easily. They go at it knowing they can shoot well and that all they need to do is learn how to handle the recoil. Ultimately they need to get back to the relaxed state of harmony with the weapon. Then the tight shot groups will return.

There's no such thing as a "natural" shooter who's an excellent marksman without having practiced. There's nothing natural about placing your face and shoulder against something that you know is about to jolt you with two thousand foot-pounds of energy. For practical purposes the hunter needs to be able to do this while placing the shot inside a moving kill zone that is "X" number of yards away. This requires disciplined shooting that is achieved only with adequate practice.

Probably the most common mistake of gun-hunters is simply not practicing enough. Getting to the level of accuracy needed may take a lot of rounds. But once you get there, maintaining the ability may only require a few pre-season practice sessions. So, especially for rookies, I strongly recommend that you join a local gun club, at least for the first couple of years. This will quickly accelerate the process of becoming a good marksman. Otherwise, with only a few casual practices it might take a very long time and **you'll have missed deer because of it**.

As a young man I was allowed to shoot my dad's .22 rifle in the back yard provided that I could buy my own bullets. So, I saved my coins for ammunition instead of candy bars. Over the time of about eight years I probably put four thousand rounds through that rifle. During later years, when getting to a rifle range was not as easy as walking out the back door, and while I was more focused on archery, I took my shooting skills for granted and allowed them to deteriorate. A trip to the rifle range showed me how those skills had rusted. A hundred careful rounds with the .22 helped sharpen the skills again before bringing out the deer-rifle.

A lot of deer-hunters create a bucket load of problems for themselves by selecting a caliber that's way more power than they're comfortable shooting. A deer is not a three thousand-pound rhinoceros. What in hell are you trying to prove by shooting a gun that kicks the living crap out of you? If it hurts to shoot, you're not likely to practice enough and will also probably have a nasty flinch. This means you have no chance at accuracy and precision. Accuracy and precision are more important than power every day of the week.

I'm purposely staying away from the endless argument over what is the best rifle caliber for deer hunting. Ideally it would be great to go through a mental exercise and look at some ballistics charts before we buy a rifle. Most references I've seen recommend that you should have at least 900 to 1000 foot pounds of kinetic energy remaining in the bullet at the point of impact. But, most of us just shoot what our fathers or grandfathers used and that's probably fine. Still, it's a good exercise. Think about the type of terrain you are going to be hunting in, and the distances at which you are likely to shoot. The terrain might limit most shot opportunities to less than 100 yards. Low velocity cartridges such as the .30-30 Winchester, .35 Remington and .300 Savage are fine inside that range. For these, it is

149

especially important to understand the drop off in trajectory and energy, to sight in accordingly and to keep shots inside the effective range. In areas where shots are more likely to be 200 or 300 yards a medium caliber high velocity cartridge is better. These include the .270, .280, 7mm, .308 and .30-06. But, if you will not be shooting at anything heavier than a white tailed deer, and if recoil causes you trouble with accuracy, you might be better served with a high velocity smaller caliber such as a .243. This is at the high end of the varmint class rifles. It will give less recoil, has great accuracy and has plenty of energy for deer hunting. Performance can be adjusted somewhat for all these cartridges by selecting different bullet weight. The rifle caliber that is the most popular for deer hunting, is in fact way more power than is actually needed. There is a good and practical reason for this. If you're considering your budget and are going to buy only one rifle that might someday be used for heavier game or for hunting in areas requiring shots at longer distances, it makes sense to go with more power. This might be for the once in a lifetime dream hunt in some far away place. In either case, as long as you are accurate, it doesn't matter much to the deer.

If possible I suggest that you follow a progression similar to what is listed in the next few pages. This is not done in a single day or a single year. It's a good way to progress with a young shooter over several years. Keep it safe but also try to keep it fun.

Trigger: First, work to develop a very smooth gentle squeeze of the trigger. For most hunters there are two things that affect shooting accuracy and precision more than anything else. One is trigger jerk and the other is flinch. Regardless of whether you're an iron sight shooter or if you use the finest telescopic sights available, trigger jerk and flinch still need to be controlled. It does you no good to go out and buy a very expensive and more powerful scope. This might help you see better, but it doesn't do a thing to solve your shooting problems. Once you have a good sight picture steadily and gradually add pressure to the trigger. You may notice that no matter how still you hold, your sight seems to float very slightly around the perfect aim point. Don't be tempted to try and *"steel the shot"* by quickly pulling the trigger when the sight appears perfect. This will destroy the steady addition of pressure and cause a trigger jerk. This will most likely pull your shot off. It's better to let the sight float slightly around the perfect aim point as you add steady pressure. You might notice movement of the sight caused by your breathing and your heartbeat. Remember to hold your breath at the end of your exhale, but not for more than a couple seconds. Once you have the sight picture and begin adding pressure, don't take more than four to six seconds for the shot. This is where small caliber practice may help to develop good shooting habits. **I strongly recommend practicing for accuracy and precision with a good quality 22-caliber rifle.** It allows you to shoot many rounds at low cost and without the punishment of a deer rifle or shotgun. This does not mean buying a fifty-round banana clip for your semi-auto and hosing the place with 22 bullets! It means taking the time to shoot for a group that is in the bulls-eye and is as tight as possible. Start at close range until your bullet holes are touching. Then move to longer range and shoot to tighten the group again.

Relax the Shoulder: Many young shooters fight the recoil with a very tight stiff shoulder. This causes the shoulder to get sore with just a few shots. I recommend that new shooters should progress to clay pigeons with birdshot in a 20-gauge shotgun. This has a little recoil and makes a bit more noise (*and its fun*). But, the reason I suggest it, is because it's easier to teach them to relax the shoulder during recoil. This is because they are focusing on the clay pigeon and on the fun of shooting rather than on the kick of the gun. After getting comfortable with this you might step up to try a 12-guage.

Back to a rifle: If possible the next step up might be to a varmint class rifle (*low caliber, high velocity*). Some calibers in this class are perfectly fine for hunting white-tailed deer so long as you are very careful about shot placement. These rifles look and sound similar to a deer rifle but without the recoil. If a varmint rifle is not available, use the lowest bullet weight for your caliber of decr rifle.

Controlling Flinch: Flinch is entirely different from trigger jerk. It's a sudden tensioning of the muscles in anticipation of the shock from recoil. My Dad's complete instruction on this point is "*don't flinch*". If you want more detailed instruction he would say, "*do not allow yourself to flinch*". The truth is that these simple instructions are exactly what you have to do. There is no secret. It is a conscious act of discipline using the force of will. For me, it helps to phrase it in a positive way. Instead of thinking to myself "don't flinch" I think "*smooth gentle squeeze*" while adding steady pressure to the trigger. Somewhere along the continuum of time and pressure the weapon fires almost by surprise. Don't try to steel the shot. That just add trigger jerk on top of flinch. You may have no flinch while shooting the .22 rifle since it has practically no recoil. However, it only takes one or two rounds out of a big gun to suddenly develop a nasty flinch. Within four or five rounds your shoulder may be sore enough that you need to stop shooting. This means that you will not get enough practice with the deer rifle, your flinch will get worse and your accuracy will be gone. For these reasons I very strongly recommend the use of a shock absorbent shoulder pad and the lightest weight bullet available for practice. Make sight adjustments if you switch to heavier bullets during the hunting season. (*Here's something that's true, and that many hunters will tell you, but it seems a little odd to write. I barely notice any recoil at all when I am shooting at a real deer instead of a paper target. Perhaps this is due to the level of concentration on making the shot.*)

One way to check for flinch is to have a shooting partner give you the gun without <u>you</u> knowing whether a live round is actually chambered. As you aim at a target and squeeze the trigger on an empty chamber, any flinch will be very noticeable. This is called dry-firing. **I would never do this with an old vintage weapon**. But due to advancements in design and in steel, it won't hurt the firing mechanism in modern rifles if you do this once in a while. If trigger squeeze and flinch aren't problems, you're probably shooting well already. But if they start to develop while you are shooting the higher caliber weapons, go back to the .22 rifle and work it out. It's always good to keep your skills sharp with the friendly little .22 rifle.

Remember your body mechanics in each of the shooting positions starting from the ground up. **Be sure to develop a good steady kneeling or seated shooting position.** These are the ones you'll use the most in the deer woods. You'll basically be trying to make a tripod out of your body. One of the legs is made from your back down to your butt. The other two are made of the arms with elbows resting on the knees. Everything is anchored solidly to the ground. This might feel a little uncomfortable at first and might not seem very steady. With repetition it gets more comfortable and you start to make very small individual adjustments to your body position. You'll find just the right angle of your legs and the best spot for your elbows to lock into your knees. An advantage of a scope is that it helps magnify your own wobble which helps you quickly fine tune these body adjustments until you get a nice steady sight picture. Once this happens keep practicing so the position gets locked into your body memory. I have never had a situation in deer-hunting where the prone position was of any use.

Follow-through: Get the mental attitude that you are not finished with the shot until you see where the bullet has hit. Try to see the target immediately as the gun settles back down from the recoil. Even the little .22 rifle does this just slightly. (*You can't actually see the bullet hole in the paper at long distance, its just that this is the mental attitude that helps with follow through.*)

It's more fun and it's more instructive to shoot at something that reacts instead of just poking holes though paper. It helps if a little dust flies or if something breaks or falls over. This gives you instant feedback about the shot. The idea is to focus on the target during, through and immediately after the shot as you're looking down the sights. Your eyeball sees the recoil take the sights off target slightly for just a split second. The mental attitude of wanting to see the impact actually helps you concentrate on the target through the shot. It reduces trigger jerk, reduces flinch and insures good follow-through. It's actually much more important than it might seem.

Concentrate on the target: One of my good friends, an excellent marksman, told me that he doesn't think about any of the above stuff while shooting. He is totally concentrating on his target. The shot simply seems as if it just happens. He's exactly correct. The physical skills required for shooting well have become so deeply rooted that he doesn't actually think about any of it consciously. He is concentrating on the target while this other stuff is all happening automatically on a subconscious level.

Ballistics (Important): Now that you've worked to become a good marksman, you could still screw this up and miss a deer that you should have killed if you don't have a good understanding of trajectory and ballistics. I expect that most readers of this already own a rifle or shotgun for hunting. Even so, a lot of guys never take the time to study their weapon's ballistic performance.

Basically there are three things that are constantly being tinkered with; the mass of the bullet, initial velocity, and caliber which is basically the diameter of the bullet. These all work together to give a weapon its range performance. *There are other things like the bullet shape, sectional density, ballistic coefficient, coating that change the bullet drag-coefficient, different powder loads and burn rates, and changes in the density of air due to temperature or altitude, but these are reserved for true full-time gun-nuts and thousand yard snipers, not for the average recreational hunter.*

First do this mental exercise. Let's suppose you have a golf ball and a ping-pong ball and they are exactly the same diameter (*caliber*). Now suppose that you throw each of them as far as you can. Both are accelerated to the same speed and are launched at the same angle as they leave your hand. Why does the golf ball go fifty times further than the pin-pong ball? The answer is kinetic energy. A mass moving at a given speed has kinetic energy. This energy is used up in doing the work of fighting against gravity and pushing its way through the atmosphere. Since the golf ball has about fifty times more mass, it has fifty times more kinetic energy when it leaves your hand. So, it can do a lot more work pushing the atmosphere out of its way. The ping-pong ball doesn't fly as far because it uses up the little kinetic energy it has very quickly. To make it go farther all you would have to do is fill the hollow inside with the same heavy mass that's inside the golf ball.

The same thing is true for your bullets. If the diameter (caliber) and initial velocity are the same, a bullet with more mass will have more kinetic energy and will therefore travel farther down range with a flatter trajectory. Since the diameter of the bullet is fixed by the weapons caliber, more mass is simply achieved by adding slightly to the length of the bullet. So, a particular caliber of weapon may have bullets available in several different weights. The advantage is that you can select a bullet weight that's best for the type of game and the distances you are shooting while also taking into account the recoil. The heavier bullets will punch a bit harder at both ends of the gun. For deer hunting most recommendations would be to have at least 900 to 1000 foot-pounds of energy remaining in the bullet at the point of impact.

A whole bunch of calibers can do that inside of 100 or 200 hundred yards. Other calibers reach out to over 300 or 400 yards with enough energy. The energy/distance question is one thing. The trajectory/distance question is something else to think about. At some distant point the trajectory starts to drop off quickly. With shotguns, muzzle loaders and some of the heavier slower velocity rifle cartridges it's especially important for you to know the trajectory and range performance of your weapon. For most hunting situations it's stupid to try and shoot beyond that range. Hunt inside it, or get a different gun.

Shotgun: A slug being launched out of a shotgun doesn't have great velocity compared to most modern deer-rifles. But, it does have a huge amount of mass and therefore it has great kinetic energy. Its large diameter causes it to use up energy quickly in pushing against the air. That, coupled with lower velocity, causes it to have a huge trajectory arc. Range is also limited by the fact that a shotgun has inherently less precision. The good news is that you don't have to worry about the wind. It would take a hurricane to blow the slug off course. Also, inside its effective range nothing hits with a more devastating impact. For a shotgun, fifty to eighty yards might be about all the range you get. That's perfectly fine. Just hunt within that range. Experiment with different types of slugs to improve precision. A slug barrel with slug sights or a low power scope will help. If your budget forces you to use your regular upland game barrel with a standard front sight bead, simply adjust your hunting to shots that are within its limits. That might be less than fifty yards.

Experiments might get you a little more range due to improved precision, but it doesn't do a thing about the trajectory problem. Since shotguns have a fairly large trajectory arc, it's a good idea to work with the shotgun at different distances on paper targets in order to understand its trajectory. Remember that open sights versus a scope may make a big difference on how you work with the trajectory. The scope places the line of sight higher above the barrel. Everything that applies toward sighting in a rifle also applies toward the shotgun. But, the maximum range is less and the rise and fall of the trajectory arc is more severe. So, it's important to know how the slug patterns at long range, midrange and short range.

This might surprise you. But it's best not to find out about it after you have missed a deer. Similar to my recommendations about archery hunting, you might want to have distance markers on your shooting lanes. Hunting regulations in most states take advantage of the trajectory drop as a matter of public safety by requiring the use of shotguns rather than deer-rifles near populated areas. Black powder rifles may also be allowed in these areas for the same reason. If given a choice I would prefer to use a black powder rifle since they have recently been made to be much more accurate and have more range.

Sighting in a Rifle: Many of the rifle calibers commonly used for deer hunting have trajectories that are good for beyond 300 yards. But, a lot of rifle ranges are set up only for one-hundred yard shooting. **Don't sight-in these rifles to hit "dead-nuts-on" at one-hundred-yards.** If you do, you will probably lose about thirty percent of the range performance for that rifle. Look carefully at a ballistics chart for the caliber and the weight of the bullet you are shooting. Every rifle caliber and all the different weights of bullets for those calibers has different trajectory. Sight it in accordingly.

Also note: If you had a scope mounted at a gun shop, chances are that it was "*bore-sighted*". Be aware that "*bore sighting*" only means that the weapon should be able to get bullets onto the paper target at something like about fifty yards. **It does not mean, and was never intended to mean, that the weapon was precisely sighted in and ready for hunting.** Get it zeroed in starting at close range.

The correctly installed sights or scope on your rifle is set up so that when you aim downrange the bullet is launched out of the barrel with a slightly upward angle. If you raise the rear sight, it causes an increase in the upward angle of your aim and of the launch. This angle gives the bullet a slightly upward force. That force is what allows the bullet to temporarily overcome the downward force of gravity. So, the bullet actually rises during the first part of its flight path. Odd as it sounds, the first "dead-nuts-on" aim point may be as close as twenty-five yards as the bullet rises to intersect with your line if sight. If you know this exact distance, it's possible to quickly check your "zero" at very close range. The bullet may still be rising by a few inches out to perhaps one-hundred-fifty or two hundred yards.

Then, as the bullet has used up all of its upward force, gravity causes it to drop at an accelerated rate. At some distance downrange, it has dropped so that it again passes through the zero point. This second zero point is perhaps two-hundred yards out. At some distance beyond that, the bullet begins to arc more severely towards the earth. **The trick is to make the most use of the flattest part of the trajectory path in order to get the greatest range from the rifle**.

Here's how to do that. Look at a ballistics chart and find the weapon caliber and bullet weight that you plan to shoot. For example: the chart may show that your bullet needs to hit between one-inch and two-and-a-half inches high at one-hundred-yards in order for it to drop back into the bulls-eye at two-hundred-yards. This means that you are in the kill zone all the way out to two-hundred-yards without adjusting your aim-point on the deer. The chart may also show that at three-hundred-yards the bullet has dropped something like five to nine inches. So, your aim-point is still on the fur, but five to nine inches high. Even two individually excellent marksmen may find that a particular weapon shoots slightly differently in their hands. Also, every individual rifle will shoot a little differently depending on how it is set up. The rifle needs to be fine tuned to the individual who is shooting it. **So, don't rely solely on the ballistics charts to zero your weapon.** Use them as guidelines to start with, but not as a replacement for going out to the range and shooting so you can see the trajectory on paper at longer range with your own eyeballs. Remember that the diameter off your shot group will spread out with increased range. So, you need to know that you can hold a tight enough group to take shots at these longer distances. Another thing the chart will show you, is the approximate range where the trajectory starts to fall even more rapidly. Don't try a hunting shot beyond that range. For most deer rifles the flat part of the trajectory reaches out far beyond the distance that you are ever likely to have to shoot at a deer.

Safety: By far the most dangerous point in any hunting trip is at the time when a group is together at the vehicle loading and unloading their guns! This is simply due to the increased possibility of an accidental discharge with a whole bunch of people close by. Several things can contribute to this. Larger groups might have several "Bambies" and "Yearlings" who might be a bit nervous and excited. They could be using a borrowed weapon that they are not as familiar with as they should be. People may be trying to manipulate a rifle in the dark using the light from the vehicle or from a flashlight. Unlike the gun-range, there is no convenient place to set the weapon down and there is no designated "downrange direction". Some weapons require more manipulation than others to load and unload. Senior members of the group might be focused on getting their own weapons loaded. They might also mistakenly assume that everyone is as comfortable, proficient and safe in handling a weapon in the field as they are. Often several hunters are loading or unloading their weapons near the vehicle in the dark at predawn or in the evening. **One thing that I have found to be very helpful is a head mounted flashlight.** This allows me to have two hands available and light on my work. In addition, walking in and out of the woods with the light on helps insure that some goofball doesn't think I could be a deer.

Senior hunters should take the initiative to immediately designate safe downrange directions for all muzzles pointing away from the vehicle and away from the other hunters. Have people move a few steps away from the vehicle to load and unload. Then, if someone needs to go to the vehicle, they will be behind the line and don't have to walk in front of anyone's muzzle. Observe and assist young hunters as they load and unload. Sometimes a cartridge doesn't slide in like it should with cold fingers or a breach is hard to open. This is a time when young guys might make a mistake with trigger safety and muzzle direction. It's a good time to demonstrate how to deal with a problem safely. Before you put your rifle back in its case, set a good example by properly clearing it and then calling out *"clear"*. Have the young ones in the group do the same. You'll be surprised how quickly this gets to be a really good habit. Do not be shy about telling any member of the group *"watch your muzzle"*.

Other stuff with the rifle:

- How good you are from the bench-rest doesn't mean a lot in the deer woods. Practice sitting and kneeling shots.
- If you don't have a sling, get one. A sling is used for a lot more than just carrying the weapon. Used properly it is a major aid in marksmanship.
- Never use a new untested rifle straight out of the box without sighting in. Avoid using a borrowed rifle unless you have the time to test fire it. Make sure you have permission if you need to adjust the sights.
- Do not try to steady your aim by resting the barrel or forearm of your rifle <u>directly</u> on a hard surface like a log or rock. This can drastically change your impact point. If you must, cushion it with something, your gloved hand at least.
- After you've worked to become an excellent marksman, you may tend to believe that these skills are fixed within you. But in fact, your shooting skills will degrade over time if you do not practice. How much you practice depends on how good you want to be. More is better.

For ninety percent of all hunting shots, your weapon probably delivers enough accuracy and precision just as it comes from the manufacturer. But, if you are good enough to begin pushing up against the limits of the weapons capabilities, and if you're just plain fussy enough and want to push the limits out to farther distances and tighter shot groups, a good gunsmith can probably do several things to make your rifle more accurate.

One last thing: I've heard stories told about some old red neck morons who think its funny to hand an unsuspecting youngster a high caliber weapon, you know... just to see how they react to the recoil. This young shooter will have a lot of problems, not just with shooting. If your father or uncle did this to you as a young shooter, I'm sorry. It's not funny. It was an asshole thing to do.

Good hunting.

The story of searching for this deer is told in the section "After the shot, following <u>no</u> blood trail.

"Getting Good with the Bow and Arrow"
Part – 9

If you don't intend to hunt with a bow, there is no reason for you to read this section. Skip it.

> *Archery is a fascinating and complex subject. I won't pretend that these few pages contain everything you need to know.* Rather, my *idea in this chapter is to help you solve, or avoid, a whole bunch of problems commonly faced by archery hunters.*
>
> > *If you don't already have basic archery skills, I urge you to seek competent instruction from a trusted friend, a proshop, a local archery club or an archery organization which may have instructors and equipment available. Check the internet for (*your State archery association and for organizations such as; NAA, NFAA, IBO, FITA, JOAD, NASP

I love archery hunting even more than rifle hunting. In recent years my success rate with a bow has been higher than with a rifle, but it hasn't always been that way. I started with a forty-five pound recurve bow in 1974 and didn't really have a clue about what I was doing. My brothers and I learned archery mostly on our own, in the back yard, shooting at cardboard boxes stuffed with newspaper.

In 1984 I bought my first compound bow from a friend. It was high-tech for the time, but would be considered a real clunker by today's standards. I've upgraded every decade since then. I love shooting these high-tech bows, but things are not so simple and the price can get crazy. It's now common to see bows that cost as much or more than a good rifle. But rifle design, performance and technology have long stabilized; a high quality rifle, five or ten years old retains or even grows in value. Archery equipment is just the opposite. It's emerging from an era of rapidly changing design, performance and technology. This means that expensive high quality bows, five or ten years old, may be worth only half to a third of their original cost. The good news for newcomers is that a lot of perfectly good, high quality, used equipment is available at a relatively low cost. If you're just getting started in archery with a used compound bow, be sure to have it checked out for safety and properly setup by a competent archery pro-shop.

Traditional Archery: One of my young nephews now shows up at deer camp each year with my thirty-some year old recurve bow. I pick it up and hold it like an old friend, recalling simpler times. Recently there is a trend away from high-tech bows, back to traditional archery (longbows or recurves). These bows are simpler, lighter, quieter, and less prone to finicky problems. They can be just as deadly. Traditional archery hunters take pride because it requires more skill and more practice to shoot accurately. In the hands of most archers, the range of shots might be limited to less than twenty-five yards. But that's fine, just hunt within the limits of the weapon. As I've already said, a very high percentage of shots are in the range of fifteen to twenty yards anyway.

If you start with traditional archery and learn to shoot "instinctive style", it's relatively easy to change to a compound bow. However, the reverse does not seem to be true. If you start with a compound bow with sights, it's hard to switch to the shooting of traditional archery.

The greatest difference in hunting technique has to do with making the move to take the shot. Unlike compound bows, which allow a hunter to hold back at full draw while waiting for perhaps two minutes to release the arrow, traditional bows are usually released in a single fluid motion or held back for no more than a few seconds. **This means that traditional archers need to be very good about rule five; Wait for the right moment to make the move**. I made this mistake as a young hunter one year when a nice buck was approaching a shooting lane. I drew my bow a bit too early. The deer stopped behind a tree. I held back the forty-five pounds of force, hoping the deer would step forward. My arm began to shake as muscles started to fail. The deer seemed to enjoy this game. It was messing with my mind. Finally I had no choice but to let the bow down. The deer walked away, acting casual, with a snotty attitude.

The majority of what I write in the rest of this section pertains to shooting compound bows. I don't feel qualified to write more about traditional archery since I've been away from it for so long.

High-tech archery: The old rule about complexity shows up here again. By pushing the technology, force, and speed, out to new limits, it means that there are two dozen new ways to screw up. To start with, **don't do what I did.** Don't go poorly informed and in a hurry to purchase equipment. Visit a few good archery pro shops. **The <u>newer</u> you are to archery, and the <u>more serious</u> you are about <u>shooting well soon</u>, the <u>more important</u> it is for you to purchase equipment from an <u>archery pro shop</u> and not off the rack at a discount store.** Half an hour with a good archery pro will prevent you from making a whole bunch of time-consuming and costly mistakes. It will enable you to focus on shooting, rather than spending time fiddling with equipment and trying to solve technical problems. A good archery pro will find your correct draw length, make recommendations regarding draw weight, arrow length, arrow weight, spine, and arrow balance, and properly attach and adjust your accessories. He'll help tune your bow and give you plenty of worthwhile advice in the process. You may rely on them for help with parts, repairs and maintenance.

The best thing you can do to improve quickly, is join an archery club or shooting league. **This has tremendous advantage over practicing alone in the backyard.** Aside from encouraging you to shoot more regularly at safe and convenient range facilities, a club exposes you to different equipment, shooting techniques, and more experienced archers. When you see someone who shoots exceptionally well, watch them closely for a while. Pay attention to how they come precisely to the same anchor point. Notice their string hand in the instant before and after the release. Watch how their bow hand stays in position after the release. Ask them to watch you shoot and give you a few pointers.

Unlike me as a beginner, you should **read!** Read about improving your shooting-form, tuning your bow, diagnosing and solving various problems. **Twenty minutes of reading may save you days or weeks of frustration trying to figure it out on your own**. Don't just read archery hunting magazines where the advertisers and authors mess with your brain. Read actual books about archery. It wouldn't kill-ya to make a trip to your local library. You might be surprised at what they have on archery, <u>and it's free.</u>

Choosing equipment: Today's archery hunters are blessed with plenty of choices from seven or eight good manufacturers. Even backing away from the highest end of the price range, the quality and reliability among them isn't bad. It's now rare to hear about major equipment failure in the field. Performance isn't bad either. It's well within range for what most hunters need. So, long as you get the big things right first, draw length, draw weight, and correct arrows, you're not likely to be disappointed with a bow from among any of the top seven or eight manufacturers. You're likely to find two or three within your price range that will serve you quite well.

The issue now is more about individual shooting preferences. These preferences depend on a list of detailed specification and features of each bow. For example: Length, weight, brace height, type of cams, a soft valley at the back wall, or a hard back wall with no valley. These all have an effect on performance, but more importantly, they make a bow feel and behave differently as you draw and as you release the arrow. These might make two bows of the same draw weight feel as if one is heavier than the other. It might mean a trade-off between one bow being faster but more finicky and another being slower but more forgiving. A good archery pro may let you shoot a demonstration bow so you can feel the difference.

Beyond selection of the bow itself, I recommend your purchase of front sights, a rear peep sight, a trigger release and an adjustable arrow rest that will allow for fine-tuning. It's generally better to select these accessories individually rather than buying a prepackaged deal which often involves a poor compromise for at least one of these important items. Silencers on the string and an arm guard are also good additions. The arm guard will help keep bulky clothes from getting in the way of the string. I prefer a "string loop" for use with the trigger because it improves my accuracy. But, many hunters prefer to use the trigger directly on the string serving, because it's a bit easier to use in the field.

Avoid "*junking up the bow*" with a lot of other stuff. I strongly advise against using a "string tracking device" while hunting. I'll explain why later. I also prefer not to have a large capacity arrow quiver mounted on the bow. It adds weight and potential noise while reducing maneuverability in heavy cover. It also positions the arrows to create the visual effect of a "*picket fence*" when you make your move. For most situations, capacity for three arrows is plenty.

I have doubts about the advantages of the circular whisker style arrow rests. I worry that it might interfere with the natural flexion of the arrow, may cause an unnecessary loss of speed, and could cause an arrow to appear to shoot well during paper tuning when in fact the bow could be poorly tuned. This would affect longer range accuracy. However, I know other hunters who think the circular whiskers are fine. I don't favor the use of a *"drop away"* style arrow rest if it requires additional tuning and timing with the release or if it drops away prematurely due to a small amount of forward creep which sometimes happens as a hunter maneuvers to get a shot. This is likely to cost you a deer and it could be dangerous. I also try to avoid using a stabilizer on my bow while hunting. They can be expensive, they add a lot of weight and make very little noticeable improvement in precision. I know that stabilizers help extremely competitive shooters who are trying to shave a half inch off their already excellent shot group. But, it's not going to make a poor shooter much better, and if you already have a 100% kill shot at twenty or thirty yards, you won't find the improvement to be worth the extra weight and expense. But, some archers do find that the stabilizer makes an immediate and noticeable improvement. Borrow one from a friend and try it out before you buy one. Consistency with the correct bow hand grip costs nothing, weighs nothing, and might be all you need.

As a beginner, a decent set of relatively inexpensive arrows will suit you fine so long as they are the correct length, weight, balance and spine. You're going to bang these up a bit anyway as you learn. But once you've gotten past the introductory phase, buy the best arrows you can reasonably afford. Arrow materials and the quality of their manufacture has most recently been the area that has pushed the new technology. The better you get, the more you will notice the difference in arrows.

In our earliest years, my brothers and I would toss our bows and arrows in the back of the truck, sometimes piled-on and bounce around with the rest of our camping gear. Now I am horrified by the thought of this. We were just too young and dumb to be concerned for the problems this might cause. With reasonable care a soft case for the bow is often enough protection. But I recommend a hard case to protect the arrows.

Never "dry fire" a bow; That is, never pull it back to full draw and release the string without an arrow knocked. All of the energy stored in the bow has to go somewhere. With no where else to go, it gets absorbed back into the bow limbs. This is very bad for the bow.

Avoid String flinch. If the string smacks your arm, stop shooting immediately! <u>Do not shoot one more stinking arrow without an arm guard.</u> Be sure the bow is the right draw length and that you are holding it correctly. It's a huge mistake to think that you'll correct the problem later or that you'll just have to be tough enough to put up with the pain. Your body has a pain response that might root a flinch deep in your shooting form, one that can't be detected without the aid of a high speed camera. In one session, you may develop a flinch that will take weeks of work to overcome once it's implanted. How do you determine your correct draw length? Measure your wingspan from fingertip to fingertip of your fingers and divide by 2.5. A half inch plus or minus is O.K., but if you're unsure, it's better to be a little short than a little long.

If it's your very first time: Start as close as five or ten paces from a large target. This way you can <u>focus on getting the arrows launched with good technique</u> and not worry about hitting the bullseye or spending time searching for lost arrows. A partial list of what you need to work on includes: proper stance, grip, and wrist and arm position, consistent anchor point, sight picture, head position, back tension, release and follow through. No bow on earth will shoot well in your hands if you don't lockin consistent shooting form.

As you begin to develop consistent shooting technique, your arrows will start to strike in a group. It's fine if this group is six or ten or fourteen inches off the bullseye at this point. The important thing is, <u>it's a group!</u> This is what allows you to start adjusting your first (top) sight pin. <u>Don't start adjusting anything on the bow until you have a consistent shot group.</u> Once you do, you can adjust the top sight pin to bring the group closer to your aim point at the center of the target.

"Follow the arrows." For example; if the arrows are hitting right and high, follow the arrows by moving the sight pin right and high as it would appear to your eye while aiming.

As the diameter of your shot group gets smaller, you can work your way back from the target in increments of five or ten yards. Gradually add and adjust sight pins for each longer incriment. The top sight pin is used for the closest range shot. Each lower pin is for a range farther out. For hunting, it's best if the pins occupy the area close to the center of the sight, allowing better visibility in low light conditions.

Beginning archery hunters create a dozen problems for themselves by practicing with too much draw weight. In a desire for more speed, you may push your equipment into an area where a lot of very touchy little things can have a big impact on your accuracy. Neither your body muscles nor your shooting technique nor your understanding of the touchy little things are ready for this. If you strain to draw your bow and begin shaking as you hold it back, it will be very hard to get any kind of tight arrow pattern on target. It will also prevent you from focusing on good shooting form.

Hunting bows are usually adjustable for draw weight in a range of ten pounds. Ranges are 40 to 50 pounds, 50 to 60 pounds and 60 to 70 pounds. By practicing at the lower end of the draw weight, you can focus on good shooting technique, you can shoot more arrows per session, gradually building strength in your archery muscles. But shooting with high draw weight in the beginning, slows down your improvement because you are using your bow as an exercise machine and must wait until your muscles build up. It's a bad idea. After you get to be good, and after your muscles have built up, adjust your bow to the higher draw weight.

Progression: Let's suppose that your equipment is basically O.K. and that you've gotten past the introductory stage where half your arrows end up in the grass. Let's say that your 20-yard group of six arrows has a diameter of 18 inches on the face of the target. This is not very good. You are not ready to go hunting. This significant lack of precision is telling you that something big is wrong with your shooting, most likely caused by the largest and most complicated accessory attached to the bow. That is you, the shooter. At this stage, improvement in your precision is going to come from the development of highly consistent shooting form, not from the addition of some new special accessory.

Keep practicing and the first 50% reduction in the diameter of your shot group will occur almost by what seems like magic. But it's not magic, it's just good practice. Let's say that your 20-yard shot group has now improved by 50% to about 9 inches in diameter. That's still not great. Most hunters want to have a margin for error and take more pride in their shooting ability. So we either take closer shots or keep pushing for more precision at 20-yards. The next 50% reduction in your shot group will be harder to achieve. But still it's mostly due to the shooter improving, achieved through more practice. In my opinion, this 4.5 inch shot group at 20 yards would be O.K. for hunting, allowing an almost twofold margin for error in an eight inch kill zone. More importantly, it means that most of the variations in you, the shooter, are now well under control.

At this point the equation changes for just a moment and you, the shooter, are no longer the major limiting factor. The limiting factors now might be your equipment or accessories. A new set of matched arrows, a better sight, a different type of trigger release or a trip back to a pro shop for a careful bow tune-up might help. These very picky things may help you get the next 50% reduction in the group diameter down into the range of two inches. **But, if you are not doing the big things right in the first place, these little things won't make that much difference.**

This change in the equation is very short lived after you've improved the equipment. With its added ability to deliver precision, the bow begins to teach you again. The equation quickly shifts back to the shooter being the limiting factor. Keep improving until your shot group is inside the kill zone from whatever distance you are shooting. But now the bow is showing you what happens with even the smallest variations in your shooting form and you are good enough and sensitive enough to notice it. At this stage, you probably have enough precision to extend your 4 inch group out to forty yards.

Hunters score: It's a good idea to shoot for a score at least once during your practice sessions. This will help you gauge your progress and will force you to take each shot more seriously than you would during casual unscored shooting. Do this after a warmup round, but before you start to get fatigued. Use a formal archery scoring method, or try this simple way to keep score that is especially good for hunters.

Take ten careful shots (two groups of five) at a fresh, unused paper target. Draw three circles around the cluster of holes in the target so that the first contains eight of ten shots, the second nine of ten and the third all ten holes. These circles tell you, you have enough precision to put 80%, 90% or 100% of your shots inside that diameter from that distance. Repeat these groups at different distances out to the farthest that you intend to shoot. Now you know exactly what your kill shot percentage is from whatever distance you are shooting. It's up to you to decide what your ethical limits are for taking a shot at a live deer.

Remember that you often scout to set up near trails so that a twenty yard shooter actually has forty yards of real estate to cover north to south and east to west. That's a good sized chunk of land.

Listen to the bow: At some point after you're able to get decent groups, your bow will start talking to you with each shot you release. The strike point of the arrow gives you immediate feedback. Be sensitive and avoid background noise caused by too much draw weight and by fiddling with gadgets on the bow. This "noise" makes it nearly impossible for you to hear what the bow is saying. Sometimes, it's talking loud and clear: "Bad release." Other times, it's a whisper: "A little too much heel pressure on the bow hand grip." If shot groupings suddenly spread out after the third or fifth set of arrows, the bow is probably telling you: "Too much draw weight". Get sensitive. Listen to the bow.

Torque and your bow hand grip: Try this sometime, as an experiment. Bring your bow to full draw and take careful aim at a target through your peep sight. Then purposely apply too much heel or too much palm on your grip. Don't shoot. This is only a visual experiment. What you'll see in the sight window is an extreme example of torque caused by your bow hand grip. The small amount of twisting force will appear to shift the sight pin left or right inside the peep. If you are not highly sensitive, you may not be aware that you are doing this to a much lesser degree while you're shooting. Contributor to torque problems might be your percentage let off. A sixty pound draw, with 80% let-off, means you are holding back only 12 pounds. At such a light weight, it is easier for unintended torque to go unnoticed. You might do better with a bow that has a lower percentage let-off. The added tension may help everything line up better.

If you are not highly sensitive and consistent with your bow hand grip, you may make small adjustments to your head and eye position so that the shift in the sight picture will *appear* *perfectly* *good* again. Don't be fooled by this. The symptom is usually a shot group that is much wider than it is tall, or an inexplicable shift in shot groups that you "chase after", with sight pin adjustments. Even when you're fairly consistent with the torque you apply, it's possible to get a tight shot group that has drifted to the left or right of center. You would then simply adjust your sight so you're arrows are in the bulls-eye again. But this only masks the problem. It will show up again as soon as you back up ten paces and notice that the arrows have drifted out of center for no apparent reason. To further complicate things, an incorrectly positioned launcher, or unnoticed canting of the bow could cause the same symptoms. You might spend half a day messing with the launcher and still never notice and never correct the torque problem. This will drive you nuts.

The grip that works best for you and your bow is likely to be different than what works for someone else and their bow. Experiment carefully with small adjustments in your grip until you find a position that is most stable and eliminates torque. Don't strangle the bow. Don't add too much palm or heal. Some guys shoot well with a small "gooseneck" hold with pressure mostly inside the "V" of the hand and thumb. Some shoot with fingers open rather than wrapping them around the grip. I prefer a "fat" hold with pressure coming directly back into the thick heel of my hand. My first two fingers wrap around, touching my thumb, but not actually gripping the side of the bow.

Draw Weight: An experienced hunter told me of his surprise at seeing a deer taken with only thirty-five pounds draw weight. He said the arrow penetrated up to the fletching. In my opinion this draw weight is too light. It's a touchy subject and an ethical question without a clear cutoff line. Check your state regulations for the legal draw weight.

The ribcage of a deer is not nearly as thick as a slab of beef or pork you cook on the Bar-B-Q. In fact, it's surprisingly thin and easy to penetrate. If you're careful about shot placement you can hunt ethically and get good penetration with a low draw weight. But things happen which can reduce penetration and affect the humanness of the kill. These things may mean the difference between a good blood trail versus no blood trail and a downed deer that's impossible to find. My advice is to hunt with the <u>most draw weight</u> that you can pull <u>without excessive strain</u>. Forty pounds is a reasonable minimum draw weight for deer hunting. More would be better, but don't get crazy.

The first deer I killed with a bow was with fifty-two pounds draw weight. I had never actually seen a deer shot with a bow, so I was surprised that the arrow went completely through the deer as if it was no more than a paper target. It passed through the ribcage and stuck in the dirt leaving a very good blood trail. Based on this one experience years ago, I probably would have written that there is no need to be shooting higher draw weight. But a few years later, when I was hunting with sixty-three pounds draw weight, the arrow struck the nearside shoulder-blade and angled forward stopping in the heavy shoulder bone on the opposite side. Even though this was a good kill zone hit, the blood trail didn't start for about thirty yards and was extremely difficult to follow.

My point with these two examples is a little contradictory. In the first case, fifty-two pounds was plenty. But in the second case, sixty-three pounds was almost not enough. The truth is that it was <u>shot placement</u>, not draw weight that made the big difference. Although I know this is true, and I am very careful about shot placement, I still favor hunting with as high a draw weight as I can <u>reasonably</u> pull simply because it means fewer chances for trouble and more chance at a complete pass through shot.

Penetration: Some folks go half nuts with three pages of physics equations in order to try and understand the issue of penetration. The arguments involve the contributions from force, mass, velocity, kinetic energy, density, resistance, momentum and mechanical efficiency. All of these have very precise definitions and are related to each other by equations in physics. You can follow these equations from small contributing pathways into the main route and eventually gain an understanding of penetration. Because of all the variables involved, it's a tricky subject. Kinetic energy ranging from 40 to 50 Ft/lbs is often recommended for hunting white tailed deer. Some physics purists argue that it's actually momentum and not K.E. that contributes most to penetration. This gets coupled with resistance and mechanical efficiency. O.K., fine. **"Now please, let's all step away from our calculators before someone gets hurt."** These arguments, calculations and equations are the long and difficult way around the barn for the vast majority of hunters. The values for K.E. and momentum are not easy to find upfront. First you need to have the total mass of the arrow (which depends on shaft length, inserts, fletching and broadhead.) and its velocity which you also won't know upfront. The mechanical efficiency of the bow and of the broadhead is also difficult to know. You can't simply walk into an archery shop and ask for a bow with 40 Ft/Lbs of K.E or 50 Lb/Sec of momentum. But you <u>do</u> easily know, up-front, the maximum draw weight that you can reasonably pull. This isn't a bad place to start because draw weight roughly leads down the main pathway to K.E. and momentum and therefore to penetration. I know it's not a precise and exquisite physics formula. But it's a practical way around the barn. Furthermore, the density of the target, your deer, can make it either very hard or very easy to penetrate, depending on the <u>shot placement</u> which mostly depends on <u>accuracy.</u>

The real penetration thief is an arrow that is "porpoiseing" or "fishtailing" or "corkscrewing". This happens with a damaged, improperly spined, poorly balanced, extremely fast, or light arrow. It's bad enough that it robs you of accuracy and energy during its flight through the <u>air.</u> But it's even worse when it robs you at the instant of impact with something denser. Even a small "fishtail-angle" of five or ten degrees can cause a huge loss of penetration. The physics nuts are technically right about this point; it's momentum more than K.E. Momentum depends on the arrow impacting with its

172

axis <u>in line</u> with its path of flight. The best way to ensure good penetration is to make sure your arrows fly straight. This in turn preserves accuracy which helps with shot placement which is the other "big gorilla" contributing to good penetration.

> **Experiment:** Take a sharp new pencil and drop it pointing straight down into a tub of butter at room temperature, from a height of eighteen inches. Repeat except this time, drop the pencil off-axis so it falls and impacts at an angle. (Yes, I actually did this.) With five repetitions each way, I found that the penetration is over $1/3^{rd}$ deeper with the straight drop. This could very crudely translate to mean that the penetration of a 60pound bow, shooting arrows that porpoise, fishtail or corkscrew, might be reduced to effectively equal that of a 40-pound bow with arrows that fly straight.

Need for speed? A ton of marketing money is spent to convince you that you need more speed for hunting. Speed is a great thing for competitive tournaments when you're shooting field tips that will fly straight. But, for hunting, these very light, very fast arrows are not necessary and they may cause of a lot of problems, especially with broadheads.

First of all, you probably already have plenty of speed for hunting. For example, suppose that a heavier arrow has a velocity of 220-feet-per-second; that's about 150-miles-per-hour. Fast enough, don't you think? Now, suppose new lightweight arrows might increase your speed to 240-feet-per-second. For a deer standing twenty yards away, the actual difference in time to impact is about 2/100ths of a second. This is not going to make any difference in your success rate.

Some of us math geniuses remember the formula that force equals mass times acceleration. So we think we can either increase the force or lower the arrow mass in order to get more speed. We buy the lightest arrow on the selection chart and figure that kinetic energy and penetration should stay about the same. But it's not that simple. The combination of too much force with too little mass is likely to make the bow hard to tune and finicky to shoot. Arrow flight is likely to go erratic with broadheads and a lot of K.E., momentum, accuracy and penetration ends up being lost.

With increased speed comes an increase of a force called "shear drag" which acts against forward motion. Shear drag causes "eddies" of air turbulence, which in turn creates "form drag", which acts at <u>right angles to the arrow</u>. Form drag increases <u>with velocity squared.</u> This force causes oscillation, (fishtailing or porpoiseing), so the combination of extremely high speed and extremely low mass is your enemy.

Two weeks before deer season is a bad time to discover that your new lightweight arrows don't shoot worth a damn once you attach your broadheads. Your twenty yard kill shot is not nearly as tight as it should be. The thirty yard shot is very doubtful or maybe completely gone, along with your confidence. Forty yards is out of the question. No amount of bow tuning seems to help. The best chance you have to quickly recover your accuracy and precision is to reduce the draw weight. But then you lose the speed. Crap! That was the whole reason for using the lightweight arrows in the first place. A heavier arrow will be less affected by "shear" and "form" drag and will better tolerate the effects of switching to the broad head. It's less likely to porpoise or fishtail. This will give you better penetration and a tighter shot group inside the kill zone at longer distances. Trajectory is solved simply by adjustment of your sight pins. **My advice is to give up a little speed in favor of good arrow flight. Hunt with a heavier shaft**.

3–D tournaments are a lot of fun and will definitely improve your archery hunting skills. They involve shooting a series of life-like foam animal targets, stationed at varying distances, and scoring points based on how close the arrow is to the center of the kill zone. 3-D tournaments are a great exercise with your hunting gear. However, a hunter shooting mostly just for fun and improvement, is in a different class than a very serious, highly competitive, Three-D shooter.

Most Three-D tournaments require you to estimate the distance to the target which may be as far as 65 yards away. Part of the challenge is that misjudging the distance by only a couple of yards can make a huge difference in the score. Speed is a critical advantage due to flatter trajectory. It means that misjudging the distance will cost fewer points. Remember, these arrows have field tips that still fly straight at high velocity.

My preference is to enjoy shooting with my hunting bow for my own satisfaction and not get caught up in the competition. If you're a "stalker hunter" (which I advise against), or if you take an unexpected opportunity for a long shot at a very uncertain distance, (which I also advise against) then three-D tournaments start to resemble hunting. If you set up your stand and mark the distances on your shooting lanes in the way I've recommended, Three-D tournaments are nothing at all like hunting. It's best to keep these two approaches to shooting completely separated in your mind. When you're hunting, a kill shot is a kill shot. Nobody is forcing you to take a ridiculously long shot at unknown distances with a high likelihood of wounding the animal. So, why guess? Why take a shot like that? Why not let'em walk? You'll get another shot another time.

Arrows: Very touchy little things: All the laws of physics for ballistic flight apply in archery as well. But arrows have a couple other characteristics that affect how they fly. Some of these touchy little things weren't so important for older, slower bows of the past, but modern archery equipment is shooting lower mass at a higher force. This means acceleration to speeds that are typically two times faster, pushing arrow technology into place as the new critical factor. You'll go crazy messing with your bow if you don't understand arrows.

Get it straight: Straightness is another thing that can drive you nuts when it comes to arrow flight: it's especially important during high-energy acceleration. Imagine hammering a long, thin finishing nail into a piece of hardwood. If the hammer hits it straight, and without too much force, it's likely to go into the wood. But once the nail becomes bent, it can no longer withstand even light force and it becomes nearly impossible to drive. Likewise, if your arrow is slightly bent, the spine is drastically reduced. In some cases, the variation is hard to see with the naked eye. The problematic arrow will most likely be the one that is consistently somewhere outside of your shot group.

It's a good idea to take a permanent marker and number your arrows. In this way, you'll be able to tell if one of your arrows tends to fly a little wild.

Spine: It's important to understand spine in order to avoid a lot of other problems that might develop with your shooting. An arrow needs to be stiff enough but not too stiff. A correctly spined arrow actually flexes and bends as the string pushes it forward. It also vibrates slightly and recovers in the first few yards out of the bow. This flexing and vibration is not visible to your eye without a high speed camera and it should not be confused with fishtailing or porpoiseing.

The following experiments will help illustrate the concept of spine. Suppose that you take a marble, a golf ball, a baseball and a bowling ball lined up on a table and you have a plastic straw which you will use like a pool stick to push the balls. Point the tip of the straw against the marble and strike the back end with a flick of your finger. The sudden acceleration of the straw will push the marble forward without a problem. The straw may also push the golf ball forward. But the straw is likely to bend radically when you try this with the baseball and it's no surprise that the straw will not push the sixteen-pound bowling ball. It bends radically because it can't withstand the force at its rear, which is trying to accelerate against the large mass at its tip. You have surpassed the straw's spine. The situation could be even worse if the straw is bent, cracked or kinked to start with. This would destroy its spine and drastically reduce its ability to withstand any acceleration force.

What about too much spine? What if the straw was a steel tube rather than plastic? Yes, it would push the bowling ball, but there's another problem, illustrated by this "tight-rope" experiment. Imagine that you have a strong cord tied horizontally between two posts and that you're carefully holding a steel tube at the top standing upright in the center of the cord. Now push down against the cord from the tip of the tube. As you push with more force it becomes increasingly difficult or impossible to keep the tube in line with the cord. The cord wobbles and starts slipping sideways. This affect would be magnified by a longer tube, and by more force. Imagine if the tube was a 28 inches arrow and the bow string had 40 or 50 or 60 pounds of force. Too much spine will cause the bowstring to start slipping sideways and steer the arrow from the rear, off line with the center of axis and off-center with the arrow rest. This causes poor arrow flight.

The type of material, thickness of the arrow walls, diameter, length, draw weight, mass at the tip, and the type of cams on the bow, all affect the selection of shafts with the right spine. The trick is to find a nice harmony between all these. Shaft selection charts are very helpful, but a little experimentation doesn't hurt either. Stay away from the extreme edges of too light or too heavy, too thin or too thick, too stiff or not stiff enough and you will be O.K.

Paper Tuning: A procedure known as "paper tuning" is a good idea. It involves shooting the arrow though a sheet of paper stretched over a frame and suspended about four feet in front of a target. The idea is to make small adjustments to your bow (most often the arrow rest position or the knock point) so that each arrow makes an almost perfect hole in the paper rather than a tear. This technique is well known and described in many archery books and magazines. The instructions for paper tuning will tell you that if the arrow knock tears the paper in a certain direction, you should adjust the arrow rest or the knock point in a certain other direction. This is probably not a bad way to start. But, don't be too dogmatic in following the directions, which have in my experience sometimes made things worse rather than better. When that happens, don't be afraid to reverse the instructions. Sometimes, it really is a matter of tinkering around until you get it right. If you have nice arrow flight and tight groups at twenty, thirty or forty yards don't go nuts over trying to get a perfect hole while paper tuning. A small tear may simply mean that the arrow is still recovering from its normal flexion at close range out of the bow.

It's also a good idea to do "walk-back tuning"; start at close range and move back to shoot from longer range to make sure arrows don't drift left or right out of center. If they do drift, it could be a symptom of a torque problem or of canting the bow. But it also could be due to the launcher position too far in or out. Note that while paper tuning, with a circular whisker type arrow rest, it is possible to get very nice looking arrow holes from a poorly tuned bow. Walk-back tuning is a good way to cross-check for this.

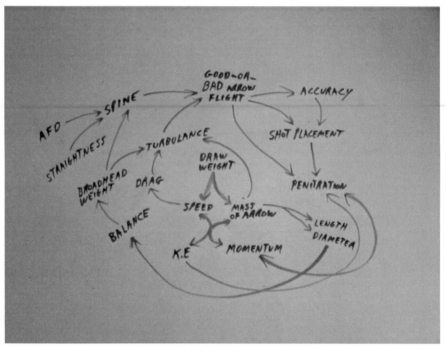

No matter how you draw it, the lines and arrows always end up looking like a plate of spaghetti because everything is connected with everything else.

Connected: Getting your broadheads to fly well often seems more like magic than science. That's because, in archery, everything is connected to everything else. It's a mistake to focus on one thing, such as speed or draw weight. If you mess with one thing, you're messing with several other things, too. Draw weight is connected with mass and speed, which connects with K.E. and momentum, which connects with penetration, which depends mostly on good shot placement and good arrow flight, both of which depend on spine, balance, straightness, arrow fatigue, broadhead weight and the effects of turbulence and drag on the arrow, which are connected with mass and speed and draw weight. The key is to find the harmonic comfort zone where all of these things work well together. The harmonic comfort zone gets disturbed when you push things to the extreme.

You ain't ready yet–broadheads: Regardless of the claims made in advertisements, I can almost promise that your broadheads won't fly the same and won't hit with as tight a pattern as your field tips. There are ways to work around this fact and improve the pattern so you'll have plenty of accuracy for hunting. Some folks believe that you can tune your bow so the broadheads will fly the same as your field tips. I think this would be a rare and lucky occasion, a perfect harmonic convergence of all the variables involved. It's usually a lot of work. I prefer to simply zero in my broadheads.

Be sure to check the flight of your broad-heads long before the opening of hunting season. Forget about your field tips. You've already shot plenty of field tips all summer. More practice with them, right now, is not going to help nearly as much as having your broadheads shoot well. Shooting broadheads can be a pain because they're a lot more trouble to pull out of the target. Accept that the pace of this will be much slower. Don't even try to do this when you're in a hurry. Plan to take your time. Plan to do some fussing with small stuff. Plan to be a little frustrated, but try to enjoy the process anyway. It's part of the sport.

Several things cause broadheads to fly differently, or poorly. The broad-heads may be longer than the field tips, which means that a significant chunk of mass is hanging out farther over the front of the launcher. This affects the arrow's center of balance (weight FOC) and its spine characteristics. Broadheads also have little wings (blades) and field tips don't. These wings might cause erratic flight because of the turbulence of air passing across their surface at over 150 miles per hour. "Shear drag" and "form drag" are increased with broadheads at the square of speed. Broadhead misalignment with the shaft's center of axis can be a big problem. It means that a large chunk of mass is not in line with the force that is pushing it, due to poor fit of the threaded inserts or from undetected damage to the broadhead. Accumulated Fatigue Damage could be an unseen factor that destroys the arrows spine characteristics. In all of these cases, it's a force versus a mass thing, or a force versus strength thing. Whatever the forces are, they will have the greatest effect on the lightest or weakest arrow. From the opposite side, it means that the forces will have less affect on the flight of a stronger heavier shaft. In any case, you just have to deal with the fact that the broadheads will fly differently. If the difference is fairly minor and the grouping is still O.K. you may simply need to adjust your sight pins. But if the grouping is completely erratic you may need to do some work with the bow and with the arrows

Inexplicable changes: For a couple years I used the ~~same set~~ of a dozen arrows for hunting as well as for competition in Three-D and field archery tournaments. These arrows worked fine with my favorite broadheads simply with minor sight adjustments before hunting season. In the third season, I began having a lot of trouble getting them to shoot well with the broadheads and ended up buying a new set of arrows. These worked well for a couple of years until the same thing started happening again. At twenty yards, most of the arrows flew borderline poorly; Two arrows flew very nicely and two others flew radically bad. By radically bad, I mean that at twenty yards they took twelve inch corkscrew dirt dives. This was extremely frustrating since I had been drilling targets all summer from much farther distances using these same arrows. It was destroying my confidence in making hunting shots. I couldn't figure out what had happened. The arrows all appeared to be in excellent condition. They all shot bullet holes during paper tuning with field tips. The fletching was good. They were straight and had no visible damage. It was maddening. So, just for the hell of it, I started to experiment by interchanging broadhead tips, all the exact same type and weight. A few came from my reserve supply of new tips in my archery tackle box and some were simply switched between different shafts. During this process, I found that two of my broadheads caused a good shaft to fly poorly and a borderline shaft to fly even worse. I set those broadheads aside. I also discovered that the two extremely erratic arrows would not fly well even with a broadhead that seemed fine on another shaft. I set those two shafts aside. After that, I was surprised at how quickly I was able to get the remaining arrows to fly very nicely, simply by interchanging the shafts and broadhead tips. Soon, I had a matched set of five for the hunting season.

Note: By matched set, I don't mean simply that all the shafts and all the broadheads are the exact same type, _which they should be anyway_. I mean that individual arrows are **matched and married** with individual broadheads and they all strike in the same relative location. These remain married for the duration of the hunting season. After sighting them in, the only change I make is to replace the dulled practice blades and insert new sharp blades into the body of the broadheads.

Accumulated Fatigue Damage (AFD): _I just made this acronym up myself so don't expect to see it in common usage anywhere else._ Here's my theory about AFD: High energy repetitive impact causes microscopic damage to the arrow shaft and the broadhead. The excess vibration on impact from being shot hundreds of times into high density foam and the occasional arrow striking another arrow during practice, could cause Accumulated Fatigue Damage. A broadhead shot into another broadhead or cutting into the shaft might also cause unseen damage. The axis of the threaded broadhead might be slightly off due to repeated impacts. Micro stress fractures in the shaft may reduce or destroy the arrow spine. You have no way to easily detect this damage, which may account for "inexplicable changes" in how certain arrows might fly when matched with certain broadheads. The combination could make the arrow take an unexplainable dirt dive. Don't leave this up to chance. Match and marry the broadheads and arrow shafts.

Here's how to match and marry your shafts and broadheads: Use a marker to label your shafts with a number or letter. Have a paper tablet and pencil handy. Carefully shoot one arrow at each of three or five separate bulls-eyes on the target face. This will avoid damage from being shot into the same cluster. Start at close range from a large foam target. If a particular arrow flies very erratically, ditch that arrow and possibly also the broadhead. Don't try to use it for longer range shots. It will only get worse. Before you pull the arrows out of the target, make notes of their location versus the bulls-eye. Repeat this so that each shaft has been shot three to five times.

Your notes may show that a few shafts repeatedly tend to hit at the same relative place on the target. For example; shafts A, C and E might all tend to strike at 11;00 O-clock, 4 inches out and in a fairly tight pattern. This might be the start of a family. Keep track of these and set them aside. Shaft B might tend to hit at 5 O-clock, 3 inches out. Shafts D, F, and G might be a bit more erratic but still perhaps recoverable. Try "mixing & matching" these shafts by interchanging broadheads or replacing with new broadheads of the same type and weight you have been using. From among your original dozen or so arrows, you should be able to add a few new members to the family, that all hit at the same relative location on the target. At this point you can make sight adjustments to bring these arrows into the bull's-eye. Then, shoot to adjust your longer range sight pins. Install a new set of sharp blades. Keep them safe, sharp and protected for the entire hunting season. This will give you a very high degree of confidence in your hunting shots.

I think it's a mistake to either credit a particular type of broadhead for a good blood trail and good penetration, or to blame it for a poor blood trail and poor penetration. These are more matters of the shot placement and the amount of fat tissue the deer has which may or may not clog the entrance and exit wound. Most importantly the blades must be sharp –sharp –sharp!

Problems, problems: Ya buy new, expensive, super-light, super-thin arrows to get more speed. Ya buy mechanical broadheads because the advertisements say they give better penetration and fly better than fixed blades. Then ya discover that yer prong style arrow rest needs to be adjusted closer together for the super-thin arrows. But that causes erratic arrow flight due to interference with the fletching passing through. To solve that problem, ya gotta go back to the store to buy an expensive drop-away launcher. Then ya discover that the launcher requires ya to fine tune the timing with your release. If ya manage to get past all this, ya discover that it can drop away prematurely with the slightest forward creep. Ya also find out that mechanical broadheads don't fly any better, and that neither speed nor penetration was the problem in the first place. Sorry, pilgrim. Don't feel bad, we've all been there.

Quick tips if your broadheads fly poorly: Before you start cranking on all kinds of screws and trying to fine tune your bow, be sure to check your arrows, thouroughly.

1. Check for wobble at the tip by laying your arrow in a roller/spinner. If it does wobble, try a different broadhead or a different shaft.
2. Check the balance point of the arrow with the broadhead attached. It should be about 10 to 15 percent forward of the actual center. This is called the "weight FOC". The easiest way to change this point of balance is to attach a different weight broadhead. It may also change slightly with different fletching.
3. Consider having your arrows re-fletched. The purpose of fletching is to create a slight drag at the rear of the arrow, and may also have a slight twist to create spin. Too much or too little drag, can cause problems with arrow flight, and too much twist robs the arrow of energy speed and trajectory at longer range and can also cause trouble with clearing the launcher. With prong style launchers, try fatter arrows which allow wider adjustment for the fletching to pass through.

Tracking by String, is a no-no; There are devices that attach to your bow and arrow which act much the same as a fishing line. The string feeds off a spool as the arrow pulls it toward the target. The idea is, that if the deer runs with the arrow in it, the string continues to feed off the spool for several hundred yards enabling you to track the deer by following the string in the event that there isn't a good blood trail. In past years, I've found a couple of these strings winding their way through the woods, but I've never used one myself. In my opinion, these are a dumb-ass, dumb-ass, dumb-ass, thing to use for a whole bunch of reasons.

First, it adds drag to the arrow by expecting it to tow a small cable as it flies. That small cable gets heavier as it gets longer creating even more drag, and after a certain distance, the arrow is going to start dropping toward the ground with the trajectory of a dead duck. Next, you have no way to practice taking multiple shots, because once the string is out, you're done and there isn't an opportunity to adjust sight pins for the new "dead duck" trajectory. This means all your previous work, practice and fussing is thrown out the window.   Finally, I suspect that the string itself, being pulled through the woods, is brushing against leaves and branches; causing the deer to believe it's being followed.   So, a deer that would otherwise have lain down within a hundred yards and been easily found, will instead be frightened into running much farther and might never be found. You didn't need the thing in the first place. Have some confidence in yourself. You can avoid all this by simply doing everything I'm telling you in this book. You don't need a string tied to your arrow. Drill the deer in the kill zone and it will lie down and die within a reasonably small search area. In a later chapter, I will advise you on finding a downed deer.

You still ain't ready;–Tree stand shots: If you hunt from the ground, be sure to practice plenty of sitting or kneeling shots. But if you plan to hunt from a treestand, you need to practice shooting from a treestand. Twenty yard shots from a stand are usually not a problem because your body mechanics aren't all out of whack. **It's the close shots that cause the most trouble**. These are the shots that cause a guy to walk back to camp muttering *"I can't believe I missed a deer, 5yards from my tree"*. The trick is to shoot from a tree without screwing up your body mechanics. Bend at the waist so that your upper body position, relative to the bow, is exactly the same as when you shoot at ground level. Achieving this is hardest for very short shots from above. You can't simply point your bow downward as if you're shooting at the dirt in front of your feet. Your body mechanics and normal shooting form will be completely out of whack causing your arrow to go radically different.

A good way to get lined up right is to start out by pretending you're shooting at something straight out across from you, up in the trees. **Be sure to feel the tension of your safety harness supporting you at the waist before leaning forward!** Keep your upper body form locked in as you lean forward and bend at the waist to come on target. This can be a bit unnerving. It feels like you're about to take a twelve-foot dirt dive onto your face. Practice before deer season. You'll get used to it. **Better yet, avoid these shots by setting your tree-stand a little farther away from the deer trails.**

*Selecting a tree-stand: There's always a three way trade off between weight, size and cost. If you hunt where you can leave the stand up, and within a close walk, or if you use an ATV, weight might not matter so much. But if you backpack in, weight matters a lot. Reducing the weight means either driving up the price, or sacrificing size. Size usually contributes to comfort, which contributes to the ability to sit still longer. Lighter stands with less mechanical junk are faster, easier and less of a wrestling match to go through while climbing a tree. If the seat height is too low it makes it difficult for you to stand up. It should be higher than your knees by at least a couple inches. You might forgive a stand for being a little small, or a little heavy, or even too expensive, **but the <u>one unforgivable trait</u> of any tree-stand is if it makes noise when you go for your move.** This will cost you a deer in the last moment. A few drops of silicone grease and nylon or Teflon washers between joints might help.*

Understanding how and why a bow might shoot differently from up above versus at ground level requires analysis involving physics, geometry, the acceleration of gravity, projectile motion, the Pythagorean Theorem and vectorforce analysis. Lucky for you, I ain't smart enough to do all that. Instead, here's my best advice. **Prove it in your own hands, with your own bow, and with your own eyeballs.** In many cases, the difference in the point of impact might be so small that it could be ignored. The theory and physics might say one thing, while reality could say something else. Go with reality. Practice shooting your bow from up above. Don't start adjusting your sight pins after two damn shots, either. Shoot enough so you know your body mechanics are correct and you have an actual shot group.

Back off; Rookies sometimes make the mistake of selecting a tree that's almost on top of a deer trail, thinking that closer is better. It's not. It leads to very difficult shots from high overhead. It's far better to back off the deer trails in order to minimize these shots. A fifteen or twenty yard shot is much easier. It's more likely that you'll have a broadside shot with a much better angle of penetration through a larger kill zone. It also gives you the chance to cover more than one deer trail.

> *Height: My tree stands are usually about 10 to 14 feet up depending mostly on having enough foliage to break up my outline as seen from below. Some guys go 25 feet up but I think that's just nuts.*

You're almost ready:–Distance: Here's a simple and inexpensive way to take the guesswork out of the distance question. Either set your sight pins to shoot according to your pace count, or calibrate your pace count against real yardage and practice maintaining a uniform pace so you can repeatedly hit the correct distance. Pace off and mark the distances on each of your shooting lanes. I carry small orange stickers or ribbons to use for markers. Some guys get all worried about leaving scent in the area, but I've never had this cause a problem. On the contrary, deer often stop to smell these markers, at which point, it's too late for the deer. Take a good look at the markers once you get settled on your stand. When a deer approaches, these marks eliminate the need to guess at the distance. From up in a tree your perception of the distance to the markers might seem skewed. They might appear to be farther or closer, but don't let that fool you into using the wrong sight pin.

Clearance: Remember that your arrow is traveling on an arch above your line of sight for a good part of the way toward the target. An arrow is not a laser. It needs clearance overhead to fly along the arch. Even if the thirty yard pin looks clear to the target, make sure that an overhanging branch twenty yards away isn't in line with your twenty yard sight pin. If it is, you don't have clearance for the thirty yard shot and the arrow will end up hitting the branch. Remember that in the first few yards of flight, the arrow is traveling below the line of sight and needs clearance there too.

On rare occasions, you might be able to take advantage of this arch. A low branch about half way to the target might be exactly in the line of sight for a thirty yard shot. But the arrow path is actually going to arch slightly above that branch. Aim as if this obstruction is not there. The arch of the arrow will pass over the branch and hit your target. It's a little tricky. Try it in practice at a Three-D outdoor range a few times.

Mind games: Years ago I worked on my shooting to move from a thirty to a forty yard kill shot.   I had never actually needed to use the thirtyyard shot while hunting and didn't expect to use the forty either.   I just wanted to push the limits out a little farther.   That fall, on the evening of the second day of archery season, I heard a deer approaching from behind my tree.   It slowly worked its way through heavy cover fifteen yards to my right while stopping to eat.   I passed on two possible shot opportunities because of brush.   The light was fading quickly and I thought I might have to watch this one walk away.   But, finally it looked as if it were going to take a left turn and come out of the brush into my forward shooting lane.   I made my move and waited a few seconds.   It stepped into the open.   I looked for the kill zone through my peep sight; it appeared as if this deer was a mile away.   For a moment, I simply did not believe that I could make this shot.   I checked my sight pin and looked for the distance marker.   The deer was standing nearly on top of my thirtyyard marker.   It was a mind game; I had to tell myself that I had at least a ninety percent kill shot, to ten yards beyond this distance, and that the percentage on this shot was much higher.   This gave me the confidence to take the shot.

Two more picky things: If you do all your practice in the summertime or at a nice warm 72-degree indoor range, you may have to make some adjustments for cold weather shooting.   If your finely tuned high-tech bow is shooting near the edge of the technology limits a temperature drop of thirty or forty degrees could have a significant impact.   My theory is that it might effect the limbs recovery speed, the string length and tension and the arrow spine characteristics.   Shoot some in the cold and make last minute sight adjustments.   You'll probably need an arm guard to help keep your heavier clothes out of the way of the string.

Another picky thing is vibration.   The long drive to the woods exposes the bow to vibration which could cause accessories to loosen and sight pins to move.   It's a good idea to carry a foam field target with you in order to take a few practice shots and make last minute sight adjustments before you hunt.   Don't shoot good sharp broadheads for this.   Keep a few well-marked old ones with dull blades specifically for this final practice.

And finally, the humaneness of the kill depends on a well-placed shot with <u>surgically sharp broad-heads</u>. A sharp blade causes much more bleeding than a dull blade. It makes for a faster kill, a shorter distance to follow, increases the likelihood of a good blood trail and your chances of recovering the deer. After all the effort you put into getting the shot, it would be a shame to lose a deer for such a simple reason. If you don't feel the need to be extremely careful while handling your broadheads, it means they're not sharp enough.

The arrow may pass completely through with such speed that the deer doesn't even realize it's been mortally hit. I have seen this happen twice. Both times the deer were actually startled by the arrow striking the ground on the opposite side, apparently without understanding that the arrow had just passed threw their own ribcages. They reacted almost as if they had been stung by a bee, running a short distance in a semicircle and returning to munch on vegetation. I was puzzled for a moment both times and wondered if I had missed. But I clearly remembered seeing the fluorescent knock of my arrow disappear exactly in the kill zone. Within less than a minute, the deer appeared to be feeling weak, decided to lie down, and then lost consciousness. This is not so bad as most other ways there are for deer to die.

However, a poorly placed shot or dull broadhead can turn into a horrible nightmare. Spend the time, shoot the arrows, and become a good marksman. Keep your blades surgically sharp. When selecting a stand or taking a shot, be aware of your abilities and limitations. A deer does not deserve to be shot at with the same attitude that one shoots at a bail of straw. It's not the end of the world if you have to let one walk away.

You'll get another shot another time.

O.K. now you are ready.

Good hunting

Why Not Other Hunting Styles
Part-10

First, I need to take a detour into the world of fishing. Stick with me, it's relevant. I grew up in Bridgeport Michigan, a half mile north of the Cass River. As a kid, I used worms or sweet-corn on a hook to fish for Carp. I used this technique because I was there, and they were there, and that's what worked best. In this region, Carp are not highly regarded as a sport-fish or as an eating fish either. But I was too young and dumb to know that there was any social status assigned to different kinds of fishing. As I grew older I expanded into different waters and all kinds of game fish. I used all the different techniques and even became a fly fishing snob for a while. I loved it all. But I learned that even the same species of fish requires different techniques depending on the time of year and the type of water and a whole bunch of other factors. I also learned that there is a bit of snobbery that occurs between different types of fishermen. Dry-fly fishermen somehow seem to hold claim to the highest form of the art. Somewhere along the rest of the continuum, are guys who use ultra-light tackle, spin casting, live bait and trolling. At the bottom of the social status, are the poor worm dunking Carp fishermen.

The relevant part is this; all of the above about fishing is the same with deer hunting. In my opinion, **the best technique to use can be regional depending on a whole bunch of factors**. A technique that's good for mule-deer out West or for trophy white-tail in the Northeast might not be worth a damn in the Midwest for a whole bunch of reasons.

There are also a lot of regional attitudes customs and values attached to deer hunting. My Dad recalls in the old days, when some gas stations and hotels in northern Michigan had signs posted, saying *"doe hunters not welcome"*. That attitude has slowly changed over the years due to a better understanding of good deer-herd management. A certain degree of snobbery also exists between different types of deer hunters. It might be the modern compound bow hunters versus the stick bows, or the scoped rifle guys versus the iron sight muzzle-loaders, or the trophy-only buck hunters versus the meat hunters, or the stalkers and trackers versus the ground blind or tree stand hunters. It's kinda stupid, but that's the way it is.

My point is that every one of these methods holds the joy of hunting. They each contain advantages or disadvantages and require different skills to be successful. The style known as "stand hunting", is what I believe works best for Midwest White-tail in most situations. That's what this book is about. **There are other techniques used in other parts of the country that in most situations I simply don't recommend for white-tailed deer in the Midwest.** Elitist snobbery and superiority is not any part of this opinion. It's simply that different regions have different deer population, hunter population, terrain or weather, that affects what style makes the most sense. In any case, you're here, the deer are here, use what works here.

As a side-note: I have not fished for carp in many years. But I've read that in some parts of the world it is considered the highest gentleman's sport to outsmart one of these big old fellows. So, for the record, as a kid, it was a thrill to hook into one of these large under water tractors. So, to any fly-fishing elitist snobs, I would like to say a hearty and exuberant "screw you"! I had a blast.

Glass & Stalk: In Western States, mule-deer hunters use binoculars to carefully scan for the deer out in the brush and on the distant hillsides. They might see a deer or perhaps just its giant antlers sticking out from the brush as the deer lay down seeking shade in the mid-day. Then, the hunter carefully stalks up on the deer to within range for a shot. As a Midwest white-tailed deer hunter, this approach seems astounding to me. Yet, I'm sure it works, out West on Mule-deer. Well pilgrim, you ain't in Kansas and these ain't mule deer. The terrain and cover in most of the Midwest doesn't lend itself well, to the use of binoculars for spotting deer while hunting. The deer don't cooperate much either after opening day. Midwest White-tailed deer have become much more alert to approaching hunters especially in more recent years. Also, there are a lot more hunters per square mile. Even if this technique did work well here, we would end up with twenty nine guys trying to sneak up on one deer. This technique is not a good fit for hunting Midwest whitetail.

Still Hunting: It seems odd to call this "still hunting" since it involves quite a lot of movement. Basically it works like this. The hunter moves very carefully and quietly into the wind and into good deer cover for eight or ten paces and then stands perfectly still for several minutes while looking for deer. The process is repeated many times until the hunter finds a deer without spooking it, and then gets into a position for a shot. This style relies far more on your eyes than on your ears. It may seem odd to say that this style of hunting uses all of the Seven Rules with a little modification. Instead of *"be still"*, you need to be still during the time when you are not moving. I know that sounds stupid. But it's true. Think about it. Remaining still and silent while carefully scanning the cover is critical. Then, everything depends on the ability to move forward eight to ten paces with <u>absolute stealth</u>. The hope is, that deer won't detect your movement. Stealth is a good general hunting skill to develop anyway, even for just walking down the trail.

It helps if you have damp conditions so you can move quietly. On breezy days the movement of branches may help to mask your own movements although this also tends to make the deer skittish. Rifle hunters might be more favored by hilly terrain and with snow and with mixed pockets of dense and less dense cover. This allows for better visibility and a longer open shot in case the deer is spooked. I hunt in hilly country so on occasion if there is snow I do a version of this that I call "ridge popping". It also helps if there are a lot of deer per square mile and very few other hunters in the woods. So it probably favors larger chunks of private property. This approach also seems to appeal to a certain personality type. I had a good friend who simply liked this technique because it was more fun than sitting still on a stand. He accepted the fact that he would have less success and that he would mostly just end up seeing deer tails as they *"skee-daddled "* over the next hill. Anyway, depending on all the above, the odds might begin to tilt so that still hunting is worth trying.

Drives: Be sure to check the game regulations to find out if drives are legal in your state. This is a common technique in other parts of the world. It also works well in the Midwest if you have enough guys and a large section of private land. It's probably best if there is a small section of excellent cover that you can predict the deer will try to move into once the drive begins, or if there are predictable routes of escape. A few guys are posted at these key locations while the others push through the area from the other side in hopes of moving the deer. The posted guys need to follow the seven rules. An advantage is that they may not need to sit very long waiting.

A hunter who has only one or two days might feel better about the possibility of seeing deer using this method. But there are also some disadvantages. I don't think this is the best technique for large regions of public lands because of all the other hunters and because it's rare to know the area well enough to cover the endless number of escape routes. You might also end up quickly forcing a lot of deer out of the area and toward other hunters. Some of those deer might be doe that are the whole reason a few nice bucks might be attracted to the area. So, it's possible that all you have done, is perhaps spoil it for yourself.

Tracking / Stalking: Out in the Northeast some hunters prefer tracking especially for mature trophy bucks. This means actually picking a set of fresh tracks and following them in order to get within range for a shot. This requires some great hunting skills, woodsman-ship and stamina. I think a number of factors favor this approach in the Northeast but do not favor it in the Midwest. The deer population in the Northeast is spread out into pockets of wilderness areas. I suspect this is partly because of the habitat and the large moose population. Some regions might have few if any deer at all. So, it would be stupid to just walk out into the woods without at least seeing some deer tracks. The good news is that the Northeast can damn near depend on snow in November for deer season which is a huge advantage for tracking. So, it's not a bad idea to drive some wilderness roads early in the morning until you see some large fresh deer tracks in the snow. The reason for starting out early, is because you might end up tracking this deer all day long over many miles.

Since these deer are relatively fewer in number per square mile, and also since there are fewer hunters per square mile, tracking might be a good technique. Basically it requires that you use the terrain and cover to gain ground on the deer as quickly as possible. Then, based on reading the sign and terrain, switch to a very slow "stealth mode" so as not to spook the deer. For rifle hunters this approach seems to make reasonable sense. For archery hunters I think this would be the ultimate test of every hunting skill you have.

For the exact opposite set of reasons I don't think tracking is a good technique for the Midwest. On the night before opening day every deer hunter in the Midwest is praying for snow by morning. Still we only get it less than a fifth of the time and in less than a third of the region. But, lucky for us, our deer are well populated just about everywhere. So locating a region that contains deer is generally not the problem. The problem is that there are many more hunters per square mile. By tracking a deer, you will most likely push it out in front of a whole bunch of other hunters. They'll have a far better chance of getting the deer than you will. Chances are good that you will track it right up to a gut pile. However, late in the season with a better chance for snow and when most other hunters have abandoned the woods, it might be worth a try if you have a large tract of land.

Still there is one more problem. After intently tracking this deer for six and a half hours, while looking down at the snow, you may feel a sudden sharp whack on the top of your head. As you stumble backwards and the tears clear from your eyes, you'll see the cause of your pain. It's the sharp corner edge of a great big sign that says "*no hunting or trespassing*." If you listen carefully you might also think you hear the sound of a deer snickering from the dense cover over on the private land. I hate it when they do that. So, I don't think this technique is a good fit most of the time for the Midwest.

Good hunting.

After the Shot
Tracking a Downed Deer and Field Dressing
Part -11

There are things in this section that you need to know in advance. Don't wait until you've shot a deer and then pull out this book to read this section. Read it now.

In many cases the deer will drop with stunning speed right where it stands or perhaps run a very short distance. Often though, they can run seventy or a hundred yards even with a vital wound. Usually they leave a clear blood trail that can be followed without much difficulty. On occasion, even with a well placed shot in the kill zone, a deer can leave very little or no blood trail to follow. This is more frequent with archery but it does also happen sometimes with guns. Deer biologist have done studies reporting that the average distance a mortally shot deer runs is 109 yards for archery, and 77 yards for a rifle. A double lung or heart shot, results in death in as little as six seconds. Hunter retrieval rates of mortally wounded deer are in the range of 83% to 91%. Making a good shot means less distance to follow and probably a 99% chance of recovering the deer. My advice on finding a deer is a little different. You should expect that by now.

Immediately after your shot: If the deer runs and doesn't appear to be going down, **get control of your brain quickly.** This can be tough because you're probably excited. It helps if you have already given this some thought in advance. As the deer is running, remain still and silent. **Focus on remembering three things.** First is a landmark of the location of the deer when you made the shot. Second (*and often times even better*), mentally mark any point where you might have seen the deer stop for a few second and then resume running. This can be a good spot to find a blood trail. Third, mentally mark its last known location and direction as viewed from your stand. Later it might be very helpful if you can sit at the stand and direct a hunting buddy to any of these locations. If it happens that you had an opportunity for a shot while walking through the woods rather than at a stand, place a marker at the location from which you shot. It might be helpful later.

First waiting periods, Judgment call: The first waiting period is often only about five minutes, depending a lot on the cover and terrain and your estimate of how far the deer might have ran in the first minute or two after the shot. In some cases a mortally wounded deer will run only forty or fifty yards and then stand still in cover looking back to find out if it's being pursued. It's to your advantage not to push this deer. Keep watching and listening for the deer to either start moving again, or lay down on its own accord. If it seems that the deer might have stayed very close, you need to remain still and silent at your stand even into the second waiting period if necessary. The length of the second waiting period depends on how certain you may be about the shot placement. It could be ten minutes or it could be another half hour or two hours.

But most often, within the first minute after the shot, you'll have a good idea that the deer has continued to run farther and that the terrain and cover won't allow the deer to see or hear you if you're reasonably careful. In that case it wouldn't do any harm, and it probably would be to your advantage, to go check for the blood trail after about five minutes. Based on what you find, you can then better decide about the length of a possible second waiting period.

I'm <u>not</u> saying that you'll actually begin <u>trailing</u> the deer in five minutes. I'm only saying that the deer has moved away far enough so that it can't see or hear you. Therefore it does no harm for you to <u>quietly move to look for the blood trail.</u> But on the other hand, if you wait an hour in your stand without checking the blood trail, you can't get that hour back if you need it later due to running out of daylight or bad weather that might wipe out the blood trail.

Second Waiting Period, Judgment call: After you've seen the blood trail you can decide if you should follow sooner or have a longer second waiting period. This might be a half hour or it might be two hours. It's a judgment call based on a combination of ingredients. The most important ingredient is your own level of confidence about your shot placement. The next major ingredient is how hard or how easy it's going to be to follow the blood trail. You also might need to factor in how much daylight is left, the availability of lanterns, what the weather is doing, your knowledge of the terrain, and possibly getting help from a hunting partner.

Consider three possible outcomes: The first is in the case when you're certain that you've made a nearly perfect double lung or heart shot. This favors a decision to follow the deer as soon as you wish regardless of the quality of the blood trail. The deer is down, probably within a hundred yards, and it aint gett'n back up.

The next outcome is if you believe the shot placement was good but not perfect. (*single lung or liver*) This knowledge would be coupled with either a good, or not so good, blood trail. The deer will most likely slow down or stand in heavy cover and eventually lay down with its fatal wound. This is the case where you do not want to push the deer by following it too soon. Therefore a good blood trail would favor a decision of waiting perhaps as much as an hour or two longer since the trail can be followed quickly to find the deer. However, in the case of a sparse blood trail, it might favor a decision to start tracking the deer a bit earlier since the tracking process itself could easily slow you down plenty enough.

The third case is a shot that you think was outside the kill zone. This is not likely to be fatal. The deer might keep going forever. Your chances of finding this deer are low to start with. But if you did happen to hit an artery, there might be a good blood trail and the deer would eventually lie down if not pushed. This would favor a decision to wait as much as four hours or even overnight before starting to track the deer if the weather will allow. Still it could easily take three to five hours of tracking to catch up with this deer. Bring your compass.

Finding and Following a Blood Trail: In some situations it helps if you can stay on your stand while you direct a hunting buddy to the location of the shot and to the spot where you last saw the deer. This is usually not necessary for archery hunters since the shots are much closer. But rifle hunters shooting a couple hundred yards across a valley can have a tough time crossing that distance and then finding the right spot. Hopefully you got control of your brain quickly after the shot and have chosen at least one good landmark for a starting point. Mark this location with something easily visible and start looking for a blood trail by making slow expanding semicircles in the general direction that the deer was headed. Sometimes (*especially with archery*) you will not find blood at the spot where you shot the deer. It might take ten or fifteen yards before it shows up.

With a rifle or shotgun there is often an immediate trail starting with chunks of blood, bone or fur.

Move forward slowly scanning the ground cover and the sides of trees or brush, and low hanging leaves. Use your eyes in a mostly forward, fanning, sweeping, expanding, semicircle type of motion.

In the dark, use the same kind of motion with a strong flashlight. You will often be able to see fresh blood drops on the leaves from fifteen or twenty feet away shinning in the beam of the flashlight. This helps you to move forward quickly and start scanning again. On an extremely weak blood trail you might need to place a marker each time another spot of blood is found, and then do a very careful expanding semi-circle search again. This could take a lot of time. Stay calm. Hunters orange marking tape is good for a marker. Toilet paper sometimes works well for this too.

The reason for semi circling your view to the sides, is that as you move forward, you might not find any blood, and this may simply be because the deer has turned sharply in a new direction. Fanning and semi circling to the sides helps you pick up these turns. Include in your scanning pattern a brief but careful look at the ground immediately in front of you before making a few steps forward. Sometimes you may find that the blood drops tend to show up at a regular interval of distance. A short interval is very helpful, but often the trail can be only a few drops every three or five or eight yards. This can help your eye as you scan with that interval in mind. If the interval shortens it may mean that the deer is tired and slowing down.

If you happen to know that a dirt road or field or soft stream bank is somewhere in the direction you are headed, it might offer an opportunity to shortcut the tracking process since these are easy places to pick up the trail (tracks or blood).

Look carefully to notice a few drops of blood on the leaves.

I found these blood drops at an interval of about every ten to twelve feet. Although the shot was a double lung complete pass-through, it left what seems like a somewhat sparse blood trail. If you are highly confident that you made a good shot don't be discouraged by what seems like a sparse blood trail. It doesn't necessarily mean that the deer will run a long way or that you made a bad shot. The thing to remember is that the deer is running and covering three to five yards in a single bound. Even if it is bleeding quite a bit, the blood gets spread out over a long distance and seems sparse. A lot of bleeding may be happening inside the deer as well. An obvious large blood trail is a good sign that the deer will be found soon, but it's also not a guarantee. In some cases the trail can end suddenly and you may need to switch to a grid search. I watched from my tree-stand as this deer run in a large semicircle before it collapsed. I would guess that it took about six seconds to run seventy yard. I didn't find any blood trail for about fifteen yards past where the deer was hit. This is not unusual in archery hunting. It takes a second for the blood to come out and in that time the deer has moved a good distance. (*Even if you know where the deer is down, it's not a bad idea to find and follow the blood trail just for practice.*)

No Blood Trail to Follow: After I had climbed up the only tree large enough to hang my stand, I found that the dense upper foliage blocked my best shooting lanes. I was forced to take a ground stand at the base of the tree. I cut some small branches with foliage, sharpened the ends and stuck them in the ground to provide some needed cover. I sat still and silent for an hour imagining the perfect twenty yard silhouette shot on my twelve o-clock shooting lane. But it was a sound at my eight o'clock position that alerted me. At first, all I could see was the movement of antlers. I thought it was maybe a four point. Then, its head rocked a little sideways exposing the other half of its rack. I got a bit excited. Its head went down behind the slight rise in the ground cover allowing me to make my first move. A second and third deer were following. Both were doe. I decided not to risk the awkward movement needed for a kneeling shot. Instead I made my draw while seated on my butt-cushion just a few inches up off the ground. The buck moved along the trail a little more quickly than I had expected and stopped broadside exactly at my twenty yard marker smelling it curiously. He seemed like he was about to move again. I hurried through my mental check list. Everything looked perfect. I released the shot. The deer jumped like it was hit. But there was a very odd series of sounds "pop-snap-whack". *"What was that, I thought? Was that my arrow careening through the trees? Did I just miss a twenty yard broadside shot?* The buck stopped briefly after running about twenty yards looking to find me before disappearing into the cover. The two doe ran about ten yards and then stuck around for a while. I waited five minutes before checking for a blood trail. Nothing. Not a trace. No blood. No arrow. All I had was the scuff mark in the leaves where the deer jumped at my shot.

I moved to the area where the deer stopped. This would be my best chance to find blood. Nothing. Not a drop. A little voice told me to follow the narrow ribbon of heavier cover as I kept looking for blood. After carefully searching for about seventy yards I was worried about running out of daylight. I heard a deer snort at me from out in the marsh grass to the south and was drawn out to look. Three white tails bounded away in the dusk. *Was it the buck and the two doe?* I circled the marsh grass. No sign of blood. Again I returned to my stand. I took the same shooting position and came to full draw. Everything looked perfect. *What happened? What was that odd series of sounds?*

Then I looked down and noticed the branch stuck in the ground. *Was that what happened? Did my bow limb hit this branch?* Maybe that would account for the odd series of sounds. The arrow would have been kicked low. The deer must have jumped at the sound of it passing under its chest. That became my theory.

I drove home talking harshly to myself. *"Yes, this would be just my kind of luck. The branch that I sharpened and that I stuck in the ground for cover was the very cause for me missing a nice buck."* I couldn't sleep that night. I cursed myself for being such a dummy. *Why hadn't I thought about the clearance for the lower bow-limb?* I relived the shot a hundred times. It was something about the way the deer jumped that kept bugging me. I kept repeating to myself, *"it jumped like it was hit."*

But there was something else too that bugged me. It was a timing thing. After all the practice, especially at twenty yards, I think your brain gets accustomed to the timing of the sounds. The arrow impacts in a fraction of a second, and the sound of the impact is in your ear in another fraction of a second. Your brain gets used to it on a subliminal level from all the repetition at twenty yards. I finally realized that the thing that bugged me was the vision of the deer jumping. Impact would have been before the deer jumped and before the sound returned to my ear.

By morning I started to believe that I had not missed. Even with the possible interference of the small branch I didn't think my shot should have been off the kill zone. So I returned to search with plenty of good daylight. After a short methodical grid pattern type search, I found the deer. Although it was hit well in the kill zone, there was no sign of any blood or even any obvious wound. The arrow had penetrated to the opposite side where it stopped against a heavy shoulder bone. When the deer jumped, the scissoring effect of its nearside shoulder sheared off the arrow inside the fat and muscle layer completely sealing the wound. This accounted for why I found no blood and also for the strange series of sounds I heard. The deer was down within twenty yards of where I was drawn out into the marsh grass. If I had stuck with a grid style search I would have found it the night before in just two or three more passes.

Grid Search: If you're fairly confident that you made a good shot and yet you find no blood trail, consider a grid style search. Start with the premise that a deer hit in the kill zone will rarely run more than one hundred yard. If it's not well hit, it could go much farther, especially if it is pushed by the hunter who starts tracking too early. In the first few seconds the deer may be panicked and could run in any direction without any rational choice. Often they move toward nearby cover and familiar trails or areas where it feels safe from pursuit. It will either pass-out walking, or lie down and then pass-out and die. This all may happen in less than a minute or two.

There is always a possibility that the deer will turn left or right from its original escape direction, but you will at least know its general direction when you last saw it. **With no blood trail and no snow for tracking, the above information is all you have to go on.** It can quickly become disheartening if you believe that you're faced with searching four square miles of land without any clue about where to look. So, be encouraged that the deer is probably down somewhere within your grid search area of about one hundred fifty yards. This is a manageable search area, especially for two or three guys. But even alone it's not such a big deal. Start with a combination of your reading of the terrain and cover along with some instinct about where the deer headed from the point you last saw it.

If the careful fanning semicircle search fails to find any sign of the deer, it's better to try a grid style search. Take a compass reading from near the point where you last saw the deer and establish your best guess as to its general direction. Mark this spot and then begin searching 90 degrees to the left and to the right for about eighty yards each side. The pace of your search can be much faster since you are now looking for a whole deer rather than to find blood spots. At the end of each sweep, move twenty paces forward in the direction the deer was headed and begin crossing again. You may want to use markers at the ends of the sweeps to keep track of where you've already been. If you repeat the pattern nine times you will have carefully searched an area of one hundred and sixty yards wide and one hundred and sixty yards long. This is the highest percentage search area. If you don't find the deer, the grid can be expanded.

Field Dressing: The taste of your venison depends a great deal on this. It's generally agreed that venison tastes better if the deer went down quickly and was properly field dressed sooner rather than later. It should also be transported with care to keep it clean from road dirt and road salt. Don't make this into a science project. It should only take about fifteen minutes. Do it right. Don't cut yourself. Don't spoil the taste by spilling any of the content of the bladder, stomach or intestines onto the meat. If you do spill, rinse it off as soon as possible. Some hunters believe it's best to age the venison in a controlled temperature meat cooler for several days before it gets processed. This is the same principle for good expensive aged beef you buy in the store. My dad had worked as an assistant to a butcher as a young man, so we processed our own deer. We would hang them in the cold garage for a week before beginning. Be sure to have clean sharp tools and a clean place to work, butchers paper, and perhaps an electric meat grinder.

In recent years I've paid to have my deer processed. I've been generally happy with the result. Professionals have the tools and facilities and generally do a better job. The meat is cut, wrapped and labeled almost as if it came from the store.

> *Caution: Anybody with a knife and a box of baggies can hang a sign "Deer Processing", out by the roadside. Some places are much better than others, so be sure to get a good recommendation. The best are usually real professional butcher shops who know how to cut and handle meat properly.*

Knife: For field dressing, the knife needs to be sharp and stout enough to get through the rib cartilage. This is not as hard as you might think. A four to six inch blade length is plenty. On one occasion I had only a 2-1/2 inch folding pocket knife. It was not ideal, but it got the job done. The problem is that folding knives often have no hilt-guard and tend to get gunked-up inside the hinge. I prefer a knife with less than an inch from the back to the cutting edge. This helps to make the tighter radius turns. Avoid extremely pointy tips so as not to accidentally puncture. A drop-tine point is good. Avoid large "survival" knives. They're awkward at this job. It's better to have a good sized handle for griping and a hilt-guard to prevent slippery fingers from going forward onto the blade.

I carry a homemade field dressing kit in a Zip-lock baggie inside my daypack. It has two short pieces of cord, a paper towel and two more baggies inside. One of the inner baggies has a wet wash cloth with a little dish soap on it. The short cords are optional. They're used to tie off the upper and lower plumbing so none of the stomach or bladder content spills out onto the meat. Some guys also carry a small folding bone-saw for use on the pelvic bone. I find this to be messy and unnecessary because I don't cut through the pelvic bone. A hands free head lamp is another good idea for night work.

No, you do not need to "bleed" the deer by cutting the throat. That's an old idea which I believe originated from a common method used in the old days by farmers when butchering pigs.

Field dressing procedure.
These steps can be done in a little different order, or with slightly different technique, but the idea is still basically the same. This is just the way I do it.

1. **Buck:** Cut from front to back the folds of skin which acts as a sort of hanging envelope between the abdominal wall and the external sex organs without cutting through the plumbing (urethra). The urethra tube runs backward and then takes a sudden "J" turn inward between the hams close to the anus. Free the urethra tube without severing it and pull it back toward the tail. Then, make a cut that circles about an inch around the anus and includes going around the plumbing for the urethra. This is not into muscle tissue. It's soft skin and fatty tissue that surrounds the rear plumbing in the pelvic tunnel. Carefully dissect around the plumbing about 4 or 5 inches into the tunnel. Note that it doesn't go strait in, it turns up toward the rump. This cut will allow you to pull the plumbing out a few inches and tie it off with a cord. You can then sever the external sex organs outside the point where it's tied off.

  Doe: With a doe, it's a bit easier. The anus, urethra and sex organs are within a small region at the tail. Make a circular cut around them and proceed the same way to free them inside the pelvic tunnel, pull out a few inches and tie them off with a cord.

The idea for both the buck and the doe is that the rear plumbing is now basically all loosened in the circumference within the pelvic tunnel and is tied off. Later it will be pulled into the abdominal cavity through the pelvic tunnel and then out with the rest of the guts without spilling anything into the meat. This makes a much easier and cleaner job than hacking through the pelvic bone.

2. Lay the deer on its back. If you're alone, straddle the deer facing the tail and use your knees between its legs to help keep it in position. Feel for the spot near the base of the sternum where it turns soft at the abdomen. Pinch a section of fur pulling up to keep tension away from the abdomen. This helps prevent the knife from cutting into the stomach, or intestine. Make a small cut to allow two fingers inside under the abdominal muscle layer.

3. Insert two fingers keeping tension up and away from the abdominal contents. Insert the knife between the fingers with the cutting edge up and pointing on a shallow angle toward the rear. Extend the cut longitudinally stopping at the pelvic area. This is an easy cut with a sharp knife. Be careful near the pelvic region not to puncture the bladder. (*Some knifes have a special curved blunt tip blade with a recessed cutting edge for this cut. The two finger technique is good if you only have a regular blade.*)

4. Next, extend this cut forward alongside the breast cartilage near the centerline almost up to the base of the neck. This requires a bit of force, but it's not too hard. Insert the knife, sharp edge up, near the base of the sternum, and pull up and forward. The knife will tend to surge and stop as it cuts through the cartilage between the ribs.

5. Find the thin sheet of muscle (diaphragm) that attaches to the ribcage and circles around the chest cavity. You probably already cut into it while splitting the breast cartilage. Cut the diaphragm near the chest wall around one side to the spine. Roll the deer to do the same from the other side. This will relieve some tension and allow you to spread the ribcage open a bit wider which makes the next step easier.

6. Find the esophagus and windpipe but do not cut through them. Get the knife blade underneath and loosen them from the connective tissue running along the underside close to the spine.

7. Use a clean cord around the loosened esophagus and windpipe to tie off the upper plumbing. This will prevent stomach content from spilling out onto the meat later when you make the last cut severing the plumbing. If you don't have cord, be sure to grip tightly around the plumbing before making that last cut.

8. At this point you can finally cut through the esophagus and windpipe above the place where you have tied it off. With the deer on its side, pull outward from the esophagus toward the middle while also pulling from the pelvic area toward the middle and outward. All the entrails should come out together easily. If you used a cord to tie it off, you can roll the deer onto its chest and the entrails will all fall out without much trouble. However, you risk getting dirt inside.

My dad liked to keep the heart and/or liver to cook with butter and onions. That's what one of the extra baggie is for.

Clean your hands with the soapy washcloth from in the baggie and use the paper towels to dry off.

Next, tag-em and drag-em. An inexpensive child's plastic toboggan makes for a nice deer-drag. It works well even without snow and helps keep the meet clean. *Be aware that the game regulations may require you to tag your deer immediately, before field dressing.*

Tenderloins: On the inside of the cavity along the back there are two small strips of meat that run longitudinally. These are the tenderloins. They are the best and most tender cuts of meat on the deer. It's a good idea to get them out fairly soon after field dressing. That's what the second empty baggie is for. The tenderloins don't need to be aged or tenderized before cooking and eating. You might think about giving them to the guy who helped you drag the deer two miles out of the woods. It's a nice way to say thanks.

Voice Of The Hunting Gods....., The Eighth Rule
Part -12

There's one more extremely important rule. This rule couldn't be placed on the list because it's nearly impossible to explain in terms of "*do this*" or "*don't do that*". It's a matter of a spiritual nature about which I am at least half serious. It's not simple luck and it's not superstition. When you think back about your own hunting experiences you will believe that there must be at least some grain of truth to this. As a tool for understanding please use your imagination to envision for a moment the following description of hunters' heaven and the "Hunting gods".

There's a patch of snow in a small clearing surrounding a rickety little hunting cabin on a hill deep in the north woods. It has two small windows, a cracked cement floor and a beat up old tin roof. The structure leans slightly to the east so that the door wouldn't latch even if it had a latch. Inside is a smoking old wood-burner with a black chimney pipe that elbows up and out the wall.

The smell of gun solvent and moist leather is mixed with that of the wet wool socks and boots hung to dry by the warmth from the chimney. Four bunks with green wool army blankets are crammed in the back corners and a fifth against the wall behind the table. A hundred-year-old lantern hangs from the rafter providing light for the midnight card games. A small snowdrift has built up at the crack in the bottom of the door, which is held closed by the remains of a broken broom. A two-hole outhouse sits among the birch trees about 40 yards to the north from the back of the cabin. To the east down the hill is a cedar swamp through which runs a small stream that is the only source of water. The shack and land was passed on down and shared in the family of hunters for generations. If the whole place burned to the ground, the most valuable thing lost would be the vintage pin-up girls that someone stuck on the walls years prior to World War II. Certainly they could have afforded to fix the place up over the years, but some instinct keeps telling them not to change a thing.

Seated around the wooden table, playing poker are five of the crustiest old deer hunters that have ever lived. They tell hunting stories or talk about great guns or good dogs or women. They drink beer while munching on Pinconning cheese with venison sausage and crackers. These are hardy men, happy, cranky, peculiar men. They tell jokes and deal cards. These are the hunting Gods.

Three of the five might light up a fine cigar. One seems to have a touch of hyperactivity. The only time he's able to remain perfectly still is while he's on his deer stand. He does most of the camp cooking which always seems to have a slight wool sock flavor. He's the God most likely to stick-up for the newer hunters known with affection as 'Bambies" and their slightly older brothers the "Yearlings". Another of these five is heavy and strong as an ox. He has a quick wit and a great gift for telling stories. He wears thick glasses without which he couldn't find his way to the outhouse. This somehow does not prevent him from being a deadly marksman. He's the God who always sticks up for the old time hunters known as "Old Bucks". The tall one is known to be the most precise rifleman among them as a result of winning the annual "red M&M" shooting matches. This involves shooting the small candy coated targets at a respectable distance and then carefully examining the snow for chocolate and red powdery residue. He's the one who most usually champions the case of hunters who have "done it right". These are most often the hunters who are in the more advanced stages known as Rabid or Seasoned. Only one of the five is what most modern suburbanites might think of as normal. Every day he goes through a curious ritual of heating water that he has carried up from the stream and using it for the purpose of maintaining his personal hygiene. He's the only one wearing a watch. He's responsible, studious and concerned with order, rules and organization. He wants to know what time we eat lunch and what time we go to bed. He sticks up for the hunters who've followed all the rules. The other Gods kinda look at him a little sideways and regard his hygienic habits as maladies that he may someday overcome. He was the newest among them and was uncomfortable with the fact that there simply were no rules here at the cabin. (*Except for the thing about not eating the red M&M's.*)

In order to make the new guy feel more at ease, the tall one decided to make up some rules. He watched the new guy seated at the table curiously examining a black-powder hand gun, looking into the barrel and asking "*How do you load this thing?*" Someone quickly took it away from him.

"*First rule,*" the tall one said as he put up one finger – "*Do not shoot a hole in the cabin.*" The others nodded in agreement, "*Yes, yes this seems like a very sensible rule.*"

"O.K," he continued "*second rule,*" as he added another finger – "*Eat what you want when you want*". Again the others concurred, "*Good rule.*" Makes sense." "Yeah, I like it."

"*All-right then,*" he said as the third finger popped out, "*Third rule – sleep when you get tired*". Astonished at the genius of this rule, there was again agreement all around. No one could think of any more rules. Besides, he was holding a beer and a cigar and a chunk of venison sausage, which meant that he had kinda run out of fingers. These three seemed like a lot already anyway. Nobody wanted to have to write this all down. So that was it.

The fifth god is a gray haired old timer. He's heavy, missing an arm, wears thick bifocals and walks with a limp. He had two heart attacks and a small stroke. He can be a bit cranky. It's hard to predict what side he might be on from one time to the next. Mostly it seems like he favors letting the deer get away. As for the hunters, he just wants to see what you're made of.

Somehow these five characters have been bonded together over many lifetimes of hunting. They spend eternity at this cabin where deer season never ends. That patch of snow in the clearing on the hill isn't snow at all. It's a cloud floating in the sky. This is hunters' heaven and these old goomers are the hunting gods. We deer hunters are stuck with these five characters. From their cabin in the sky they're watching and listening to every deer hunter on earth. After a brief discussion or sometimes heated arguments, they're the ones who decide what'll happen to you when you go hunting. Sometimes it's hard to tell whose side they are on, the hunters or the deer. Perhaps it's both.

The decisions of the hunting gods are largely dependent on the actions and attitudes of the hunter himself. Perhaps they'll decide that a particular hunter won't get a deer this season. This isn't a big deal, and it's not necessarily any kind of punishment. This particular hunter may still have an enjoyable few days in the woods. Other times a hunting trip may seem cursed by the gods. This may not have anything to do with deer hunting. They might just be looking to see what kind of guy you are. They're testing and perhaps building your character. The important point of the 8th rule is that you should try never to give the hunting Gods any reason to step out of their cabin, go over to the edge of the cloud and piss in your general direction. When this happens you'll know it! If they're angry with you, they're usually not subtle about it. Everything that might go wrong does go wrong, big time.

It can be tricky trying not to irritate the hunting Gods. They're a peculiar lot, with an odd and quirky sense of humor. The hunting gods are the reason why sometimes it's the 16-year-old on his first hunt that gets a huge buck. They're also the reason why most hunting camps have at least one story of a guy who never saw a buck until that awkward moment when he had his ass hanging out, pants around his ankles and nothing but toilet paper in his hands.

The logic or fairness or reasons for the decisions of the hunting gods is far beyond human understanding. **But, countless successful hunting stories start out with a phrase such as "*some little voice told me to* _____.**" Perhaps this voice is the hunting Gods whispering to us, giving us a little extra help. Perhaps it's an extrasensory remnant of a hunting skill that was common in prehistoric man.

The hard part is in recognizing the true voice from the voices of wishful thinking. In my experience the true voice tends to be softer and subtler. It has a quality of purity that is unlike a thought that has originated from the normal inside pathways. Sometimes it tells you to do a very simple but maybe slightly odd thing. It may tell you to sit still five more minutes or to take a different trail, or to look over your right shoulder. The thing is, if you do what it tells you, something happens that you will not forget for a long time. Of all the hunting rules, this, the 8th rule, is the most certain. It's this. **"When you hear the voice of the hunting Gods.......do what it tells you."**

I would never pretend to be so wise as to predict what the hunting Gods have planned or what they will decide at the last minute. But, I do think that there are some general guidelines. My sense is that the hunting Gods don't like bragging, whining, greed, envy, stupidity or rudeness. I have noticed that most good hunters, when telling of their success, are not necessarily bragging. Some may comment about the bitter cold or the rain, but they are not actually whining. Seldom do they kill more game than they expect to eat, and if they do, it is shared generously with those who will eat it. Most are truly congratulatory when a fellow hunter is successful. Very few are rude. Despite the Hollywood stereotypes, hunters are statistically in fact better educated than the general population. This is well known by the demographic statistics kept for the advertisers of products sold by major hunting and outdoor publications. It also seems to me that the hunting Gods dislike liars, thieves, cheaters, jerks and slobs. As a percentage, hunters with these character traits are quite rare compared with the non hunting population. Most hunters are honest and polite. Perhaps this is due to the fact that everyone is armed. The hunting Gods tend to reward those who *"love it in its entirety"* and who put forth a good effort. Of course, I believe good effort mostly involves following the seven rules. Tremendous effort and hardships may be wasted if you break the rules. I also believe that the Gods tend to favor those who are in harmony with other parts of their lives. Don't even go hunting if things aren't right with your work, your kids, your parents or between you and your wife.

The question always arises about people who seem to try hard and do everything right year after year, but still do not get a deer. Why did it take me eight years to get my first deer? Had I somehow angered the hunting gods? The opposite question also arises about guys who stumble into the woods and get a deer their first time out. Are the hunting Gods that arbitrary and unfair? In frustration this may lead us to believe that the hunting Gods don't exist at all. New hunters such as Bambies and Yearlings and even many Rabids are susceptible to this. The problem is that most people tend to look at things in a short time frame and through a narrow window. Usually that window and time frame only includes the question "Did I get one this year?"

The hunting Gods are looking at things in a time frame that may include a full lifespan and through a window that includes a much wider view of your life and your character and of those close to you. They may have decided that "getting one this year" isn't what you need. Maybe what you needed this year, was to simply spend some time getting closer with your father or your children or brothers or nieces and nephews. The Gods may be preparing you for something entirely different. They may be blessing you with things that happen while in the pursuit of deer hunting, but which are totally unrelated to deer hunting. Most Seasoned and Ol-Bucks have learned to expand their view of things. That is their wisdom. Do I look back at those first eight unsuccessful seasons and wish that I had not had those times with my father and my brothers? Do I regret having the memories, or hearing the stories of those times now retold thirty-some years later? No. Not one, not for anything.

When I was in the rabid stage it seemed like "*getting one*" was all that mattered. I couldn't fully grasp the Ol-Bucks statement, "*I just like being out there.*" Neither do most non-hunters. They usually just ask, "D*id you get one?*" One night I actually had a conversation just like this with the husband of one of my wife's teacher friends.
"*Did you get one*? He said.
No, not today, I didn't even see any deer today".
"*God, isn't that boring*? He responded. "*How can you sit up in a tree all day long and not be bored out of your mind*?" In those days I used to try to explain to these types of people that it's much more than just sitting there. I would explain about the different things I might see and hear out in the woods. So I responded. "*Well actually some days can be a little boring. But this afternoon I was sitting in the tree, camo from head to toe, everything was dead calm in the woods. Suddenly I heard a strange sound approaching fast from my left rear and circling behind me to my right.*

212

My mind raced to think what that sound could be. Suddenly there was a pair of huge thick knurly claws on the branch right next to me. It swooped in and landed close enough I could have kissed him. The strange sound had been from the air passing through the wings of a Great Horned Owl. Out of reflex I turned my head to look at him just as he landed. He turned his sharp stubby beak toward me. The dark eyes surrounded by yellow saucers suddenly realized that I was not part of the tree. We looked each other dead in the eyes, each of us with the same "holy shit" expression. The only question was which one of us could get out-a the tree fastest. The bird did, but only because of my safety harness. Scared the crap out of me! It was great! You ever have anything like that happen?"

The guy just looked at me, blinked twice and said, "*no*".

But nowadays, mostly I just don't feel like try-n to explain it to-em. It's too much work and they won't get it anyway. Besides, half the times these people are just trying to bait me into a conversation where they hope to convert me into believing that what I've been do-n for thirty-some years is wrong and stupid and immoral. So anyway, I hear myself answering them with the short, simple truth, *"I just like being out there."* Maybe I'm getting to be an Ol-buck. They see and feel things with a wider view. They love it in its entirety. Even the small and simple things. Even just a sandwich on the tailgate and coffee steaming in the cold. Even just walk-n in at sunrise, or a surprise visitor passing through.

One season many years ago some shirttail relatives of ours had a young man hunting with them who was suffering from some kind of terminal cancer. He wasn't much older than I was at the time. He seemed like a real nice fellow. It was nearly certain that he wouldn't be around for the next deer season. As I sat at my stand I remember praying to God that this guy should get a deer. I asked that he even should take the one that might have been meant for me. He didn't get one though. I remember thinking how that seemed unfair. But, the last time I saw him, he had a hardy smile and color in his face. He was with the best of his comrades up north in the midst of a national forest standing next to the truck breathing deep the cold air.

From a distance as we drove out of the valley on the old logging trail, something told me to roll down the car window. It seemed a bit odd since it was cold out. It was also a little strange that my dad didn't tell me to put the window back up.

As our car turned to make the bend on the trail leading up and out of the valley I saw him standing by the truck with his buddy. His breath vapor filled the air along with the sound of his deep hearty belly laugh. It must have been a good deer camp joke. In that moment he was "*loving it for its entirety*", perhaps more so than anyone. As a rabid young punk hunter myself, I remember being astonished at hearing his laughter echo off the frozen hillside.

His courage making death seem small..., laughing in its face.

Over the years I have remembered that guy from time to time.

No, I didn't "get one" that year.

End of the trail.

The total package of all my advice actually involves just a few basic things. I've asked you to sharpen your skills with the use of your eyes and ears in a way that you might not have thought about before. Careful selection of your gear is mostly related with staying comfortable which allows you to be still and silent longer. I've also asked you to think more strategically and in advance about the location of your stand, and to run the scenarios in considering when you might make your move and to make a good shot. I've stressed the importance of doing all of this at the same time and of getting the "*big rocks*" in the box first. If you obey the seven rules your odds improve dramatically. But if you mess-up and tilt the odds against yourself, it might mean no success for many years. This tilt of the odds from one side to the other makes a huge difference. A truckload of the finest gear in the world will not improve your success rate until you do this. The rest of this writing was about the five-thousand details that help you obey the seven rules, or explaining theory and debugging myths. Beyond that, it's mostly just a matter of showing up and letting the hunting gods bless you as they see fit.

More than just increased success, it's also my hope that this writing brings you increased enjoyment from hunting. So, I have one final piece of personal / spiritual / attitudinal advice aimed mostly at "rabid" hunters. Even though you may have the company of brothers or good friends in hunting camp, you actually end up hunting alone. Your trails part somewhere along the way as you head out to your stand. You wish each other good luck. After that, everything that happens is known only between you and the hunting gods. You'll return to camp and sit by the fire knowing what happened that day. Good or bad, you learned something from it. You may know that you goofed up, or that you hunted well even if you didn't "get one". The experience from a dozen, and then a hundred, and then a thousand such outings, add up in total, to the spirit and guts and soul of a hunter. It's a thing that is quiet, and strong, and very deeply personal. Hold onto this thing. Keep it within yourself and in clear view in you own mind. Stand inside your own boots. Don't allow it to become corrupted. Don't let your hunting turn into some kind of competition. Don't let it turn into a thing where you're trying to prove something to anyone. You aint.

It's not a fashion show, and it's not about who has the coolest stuff, and it's not about killing the most deer or getting the biggest rack either. Don't miss out on the best part of hunting because you've been driven insanely rabid about *"getting one"*. Hunt because you love hunting and screw all that other stuff.

Years ago my Dad sat with me at my stand one morning, our backs to a huge rotted-out tree on the side of a ridge overlooking a valley. It was rare for us to sit together after I was an adult. Dad had worked all his life in the foundry breathing bad air and also had smoked two packs a-day. During my rabid years, I didn't like sitting near Dad because he had to cough or clear his throat every few minutes from the smoking and from the foundry dust. This must have reduced his chances of getting a deer by some huge factor. But still, he just loved being out there. After his first heart attack he stopped smoking and then stopped coughing. Also, I was a little older and maybe a little less rabid. So I asked him to sit with me at my stand that morning. Nothing at all memorable happened. We saw one deer, a doe. It rained and we shared the cover of a poncho. That morning seems like it should have been forgotten like a hundred other mornings where not much happened. But now, whenever I hike near the side of that ridge and look at that huge rotted-out tree, I stop for a minute in silence. I remember the sound of rain on the poncho and the warmth that was under it from twenty-some years ago. Somehow, that rainy cold morning in the woods has become my single favorite memory of all my years hunting. It's kind of odd that you don't usually recognize a moment like this at the time when it's happening. It might be with your father or brother, or a nephew, or your son, or a good friend. The point is, don't miss a shot like that if you get one.

Good hunting.

Special Acknowledgments and Thanks.

Dad & Mom: Thanks for taking the time and for giving all of us boys the gift of so many great memories. Mom, I know that dad wouldn't have gone if you really wanted to stop him. But thanks for always being so sweet about it. Thanks for not stopping him. Thanks for realizing how special this was to us. I hope you and Mary have good memories of these times spent together while we were away. Dad, there's a lot of you in this book. Don't worry too much about Jimmy, he's just scouting ahead.

Larry & Dale: It was you who got Dad back into the woods after many years away. Thanks for dragging me along with you when I was just a punk. Thanks for putting up with my decade in the Rabid stage. Thanks for letting Mark and Adam tag along with me. Adam has turned into a fine woodsman. I have a great memory of a day with Mark out at the end of the earth.

John: I'm sorry you got stuck with me when I was such a fanatic Rabid pain in the ass to hunt with. You've always been good company in deer camp. Some of my best days in the woods were with you. It's great to see how you are with Jacob and Ethan. They'll be straight shooters, and already have a few good stories to tell. You've tempted destiny by naming the little guy James Roy. Might as well plan on just dropping him off in the woods each fall.

Thanks to a few other great hunting companions:
For many years and from long ago, their experiences have contributed to this in some way: *Jim Wilber, Paul Buckner, John Nestel, Mark Schlicker, Steve Ciolek, Elmer Lietz,* and also thanks to the dogs; *Max, Brook and Scooter.*

Stories about me? Lies. All lies!
Thank you all.

Dedication
In memory of our brother, Jim Rivett

Jimmy died at the end of June 2001 from a rare neuromuscular disorder, Lou Gehrig's disease (A.L.S.) He was an avid hunter and fisherman. A lot of Jimmy is in this book.

Jim with Jeffery and Steven

It kind-a bothered me after the funeral, that I had trouble picturing your face among all the memories of hunting with you. But then I noticed something that maybe explains it. It's a funny thing about the way hunters walk the trails together as we did so many times. We move side by side always scanning with our eyes but rarely looking directly at each other. We look at the ground for the placement of the next footstep. We look at the wood line or the view to the horizon. We look into a campfire as we tell a story. But we don't look much at each other. In the predawn, I could always feel you there. You were perceived mostly as a dark silent shadowy figure with no face moving by my side. Maybe that's why I have trouble picturing you in my mind.

You did a great job with Steven and Jeffery. They're going to be O.K. I think. Steven is already outgrowing his bow. He carried your deer rifle this year and handles it just fine.

This Spring I got Jeffery started with the .22. I could feel you there watching him shoot. He wants to come up to deer-camp this year, but I think he's still a little too young. He'll have his time when he's ready like we all did. Both the boys are a pleasure to be with. I know you would be proud. Kim will be O.K. too I think in a couple years. The people at Thompson in Saginaw have been great, especially Roy Banks, Patti Ott, Connie Lingle, and Sue Korth. They even named the annual charity golf tournament after you. It's a big deal and it takes a lot of work from some very nice people. Imagine that Jimmy. Hundreds of golfers come out and generate thousands of dollars to fight disease and to help families. And you didn't even golf! The folks from your church in Freeland were great too. Especially the ladies of the congregation. They treated us all with real warmth, like part of their family. And my God Jimmy, where did you ever meet such outstanding people as Mike Proux and his family? What a great example they set for their kids. We will never forget what they did for you.

Steven was the dark shadowy figure on my left this past archery season. Only three months after your funeral, I didn't have much in my heart for going hunting. But a little voice told me to go anyway. So on the second day, in the pre-dawn, Steven and I walked out of camp together toward our stands. Our movements somehow became naturally synchronized just like with you. But then something happened on the trail. I noticed it out of the corner of my eye. We were walking stealth-mode down the hill, near where that tree branch sticks out, past the bend just before the clearing. Anyway, Steven was about to move forward when he must have felt a stick under the front of his right boot. He stalled the step, rocked back just a little, transferred weight back to the rear leg, angled his forward foot just enough to miss the stick and then moved forward. He barely missed half-a-beat. He did it so naturally that I don't think he even noticed what he was doing.

At first I didn't understand why my mind was suddenly racing through a thousand memories back twenty years. It was as if my brain was searching through hundreds and hundreds of dusty old file folders at some extraordinary speed. In a moment I found the file that contained the memory. It was from another trail and another dark morning. Instantly I knew. Nobody taught him that step. It was yours.

For the time of about four careful paces, I felt your presence with as much certainty as any provable fact I have ever known. Your spirit emanated with total joy from the space between us and within us, your arms around both our shoulders. I could see your face in my mind, grinning with pure joy. That big stupid grin.

I almost said something to Steven about it. But, what would I have said? Maybe he felt it too, maybe not. If he didn't, maybe he would think that he should've. If he did, maybe it would freak him out a little. Anyway, the kid doesn't need Uncle Roy to start acting all supernatural in the middle of a hunting trip. So, I kept quiet and kept walking. "Thank you God" is all I said under my breath "for not letting me miss this moment."

We stopped near some cover by the edge of the clearing. A white tail bounded away in the dark. Later that day, I again passed the tree branch hanging over the trail. You weren't there. But, the joy remained in the woods. "Thank you, God" I said again, to the air.

Just for the record Jimmy, I know you wouldn't want anybody to dive in after you. But, this pack of wild dogs that took you down needs to be hunted. So, if there ever are any profits from this book, maybe it'll buy some gear for a researcher to help get a shot at one of the bastards. It may never add up to much, but who knows. Just one shot. It could happen. Anyway, it makes me feel good and I got nothing better to do. Besides, I don't want us hunters to be outdone by a-bunch-a golfers.

We all miss you Jimmy. We think of you especially at deer season. I wonder if the others have trouble picturing your face too. But that's not really important. Because what we all remember most in our hearts is more the spirit of being with you. Good company in all weather. Pre-dawn, walk'n-in, I still feel you there.

Good hunting Jimmy.